The Victorian Actress in the Novel and on the Stage

Edinburgh Critical Studies in Victorian Culture
Series Editor: Julian Wolfreys

Recent books in the series:

Rudyard Kipling's Fiction: Mapping Psychic Spaces
Lizzy Welby

The Decadent Image: The Poetry of Wilde, Symons and Dowson
Kostas Boyiopoulos

British India and Victorian Literary Culture
Máire ní Fhlathúin

Anthony Trollope's Late Style: Victorian Liberalism and Literary Form
Frederik Van Dam

Dark Paradise: Pacific Islands in the Nineteenth-Century British Imagination
Jenn Fuller

Twentieth-Century Victorian: Arthur Conan Doyle and the Strand Magazine, *1891–1930*
Jonathan Cranfield

The Lyric Poem and Aestheticism: Forms of Modernity
Marion Thain

Gender, Technology and the New Woman
Lena Wånggren

Self-Harm in New Woman Writing
Alexandra Gray

Suffragist Artists in Partnership: Gender, Word and Image
Lucy Ella Rose

Victorian Liberalism and Material Culture: Synergies of Thought and Place
Kevin A. Morrison

The Victorian Male Body
Joanne-Ella Parsons and Ruth Heholt

Nineteenth-Century Settler Emigration in British Literature and Art
Fariha Shaikh

The Pre-Raphaelites and Orientalism
Eleonora Sasso

The Late-Victorian Little Magazine
Koenraad Claes

Coastal Cultures of the Long Nineteenth Century
Matthew Ingleby and Matt P. M. Kerr

Dickens and Demolition: Literary Allusion and Urban Change in the Mid-Nineteenth Century
Joanna Robinson

Artful Experiments: Ways of Knowing in Victorian Literature and Science
Philipp Erchinger

Victorian Poetry and the Poetics of the Literary Periodical
Caley Ehnes

The Victorian Actress in the Novel and on the Stage
Renata Kobetts Miller

Forthcoming volumes:

Her Father's Name: Gender, Theatricality and Spiritualism in Florence Marryat's Fiction
Tatiana Kontou

The Sculptural Body in Victorian Literature: Encrypted Sexualities
Patricia Pulham

Olive Schreiner and the Politics of Print Culture, 1883–1920
Clare Gill

Dickens's Clowns: Charles Dickens, Joseph Grimaldi and the Pantomime of Life
Johnathan Buckmaster

Victorian Auto/Biography: Problems in Genre and Subject
Amber Regis

Culture and Identity in Fin-de-Siècle Scotland: Romance, Decadence and the Celtic Revival
Michael Shaw

Gissing, Shakespeare and the Life of Writing
Thomas Ue

The Arabian Nights and Nineteenth Century British Culture
Melissa Dickson

The Aesthetics of Space in Nineteenth Century British Literature, 1851–1908
Giles Whiteley

For a complete list of titles published visit the Edinburgh Critical Studies in Victorian Culture web page at www.edinburghuniversitypress.com/series/ECVC

Also available:
Victoriographies – A Journal of Nineteenth-Century Writing, 1790–1914, edited by Diane Piccitto and Patricia Pulham
ISSN: 2044–2416
www.eupjournals.com/vic

The Victorian Actress in the Novel and on the Stage

Renata Kobetts Miller

EDINBURGH
University Press

Edinburgh University Press is one of the leading university presses in the UK. We publish academic books and journals in our selected subject areas across the humanities and social sciences, combining cutting-edge scholarship with high editorial and production values to produce academic works of lasting importance. For more information visit our website: edinburghuniversitypress.com

© Renata Kobetts Miller, 2019

Edinburgh University Press Ltd
The Tun – Holyrood Road
12(2f) Jackson's Entry
Edinburgh EH8 8PJ

Typeset in 11/13 Adobe Sabon by
IDSUK (DataConnection) Ltd, and
printed and bound in Great Britain.

A CIP record for this book is available from the British Library

ISBN 978 1 4744 3949 7 (hardback)
ISBN 978 1 4744 3951 0 (webready PDF)
ISBN 978 1 4744 3952 7 (epub)

The right of Renata Kobetts Miller to be identified as the author of this work has been asserted in accordance with the Copyright, Designs and Patents Act 1988, and the Copyright and Related Rights Regulations 2003 (SI No. 2498).

Contents

List of Figures	vi
Series Editor's Preface	vii
Acknowledgements	ix
A Note on the Cover	xii
Introduction: Setting the Stage – Views of Victorian Theatre	1
1. An Actress's Tears: Authenticity and the Reassertion of Social Class	36
2. The Actress at Home: Domesticity, Respectability and the Disruption of Class Hierarchies	72
3. The Actress and Her Audience: Performance, Authorship and the Exceptional Woman in George Eliot	106
4. Novelistic Naturalism: 'The Ideal Mother Cannot Be the Great Artist'	146
5. From Playing Parts to Rewriting Roles: Actresses and the Political Stage	173
Epilogue	226
Bibliography	229
Index	242

Figures

0.1	'The Great Bespeak for Miss Snevellicci', Hablot Knight Brown	4
1.1	Peg makes herself up	55
1.2	Peg in a painted miniature on the title page	56
1.3	Peg framed within theatrical architecture	57
1.4	Portrait of Fanny Stirling as Peg Woffington, used in the original productions of *Masks and Faces*	58
2.1	Act 2 of *Caste*. 'Scene from *Caste* by T. W. Robertson, Prince of Wales Theatre, probably 1867'	99
5.1	*Salomé*, Tailpiece, Aubrey Beardsley	181
5.2	'Coronation Procession, 17 June 1911, the Actresses' Franchise League'	199
5.3	'Coronation Procession, 17 June 1911, Actresses' Franchise League Banner'	199
5.4	'Coronation Procession, 17 June 1911'	201
5.5	Elizabeth Robins on the cover of *Sketch*, 17 April 1907	203
5.6	Diagram of the box set for act 1 of *Votes for Women*	211
5.7	Act 2 of *Votes for Women*, *Sketch*, 17 April 1907	213
5.8	'Mrs. Pankhurst at NWSPU [National Women's Social and Political Union] meeting, Trafalgar Square'	213

Series Editor's Preface

'Victorian' is a term, at once indicative of a strongly determined concept and an often notoriously vague notion, emptied of all meaningful content by the many journalistic misconceptions that persist about the inhabitants and cultures of the British Isles and Victoria's Empire in the nineteenth century. As such, it has become a byword for the assumption of various, often contradictory habits of thought, belief, behaviour and perceptions. Victorian studies and studies in nineteenth-century literature and culture have, from their institutional inception, questioned narrowness of presumption, pushed at the limits of the nominal definition, and have sought to question the very grounds on which the unreflective perception of the so-called Victorian has been built; and so they continue to do. Victorian and nineteenth-century studies of literature and culture maintain a breadth and diversity of interest, of focus and inquiry, in an interrogative and intellectually open-minded and challenging manner, which are equal to the exploration and inquisitiveness of its subjects. Many of the questions asked by scholars and researchers of the innumerable productions of nineteenth-century society actively put into suspension the clichés and stereotypes of 'Victorianism', whether the approach has been sustained by historical, scientific, philosophical, empirical, ideological or theoretical concerns; indeed, it would be incorrect to assume that each of these approaches to the idea of the Victorian has been, or has remained, in the main exclusive, sealed off from the interests and engagements of other approaches. A vital interdisciplinarity has been pursued and embraced, for the most part, even as there has been contest and debate amongst Victorianists, pursued with as much fervour as the affirmative exploration between different disciplines and differing epistemologies put to work in the service of reading the nineteenth century.

Edinburgh Critical Studies in Victorian Culture aims to take up both the debates and the inventive approaches and departures from convention that studies in the nineteenth century have witnessed for the last half century at least. Aiming to maintain a 'Victorian' (in the most positive sense of that motif) spirit of inquiry, the series' purpose is to continue and augment the cross-fertilisation of interdisciplinary approaches, and to offer, in addition, a number of timely and untimely revisions of Victorian literature, culture, history and identity. At the same time, the series will ask questions concerning what has been missed or improperly received, misread, or not read at all, in order to present a multi-faceted and heterogeneous kaleidoscope of representations. Drawing on the most provocative, thoughtful and original research, the series will seek to prod at the notion of the 'Victorian', and in so doing, principally through theoretically and epistemologically sophisticated close readings of the historicity of literature and culture in the nineteenth century, to offer the reader provocative insights into a world that is at once overly familiar and irreducibly different, other and strange. Working from original sources, primary documents and recent interdisciplinary theoretical models, Edinburgh Critical Studies in Victorian Culture seeks not simply to push at the boundaries of research in the nineteenth century, but also to inaugurate the persistent erasure and provisional, strategic redrawing of those borders.

Julian Wolfreys

Acknowledgements

This book has benefited from connecting with the textual and theatrical past through rich archival resources, and I am grateful to the staffs of the Theatre Collection of the Victoria and Albert Museum; London Guildhall Library; the Fawcett Library which is now The Women's Library, London School of Economics (LSE), London; the Manuscripts Department of the British Library; the Mander and Mitchenson Theatre Collection; the John Pierpont Morgan Library; the Fales Collection at New York University; and the Lilly Library at Indiana University for their assistance. Closer to home, I am grateful to the staff of the City College Library, and especially Special Collections Librarian Sydney Van Nort. This work was supported in part by grants from the City University of New York PSC/CUNY Research Award Program.

I am warmly grateful to Patrick Brantlinger, Susan Gubar, Joss Marsh, Andrew Miller – mentors without whom this work would not have come into being – and to Johanna Frank for her encouraging friendship. Elaine Showalter, my first academic mentor, remains an inspiration and a support. The Adaptation and the Stage Colloquium at the University of Warwick in Spring 2015 and discussions that occurred at conferences of the North American Victorian Studies Association (NAVSA) have contributed to my thoughts in this manuscript. Sharon Aronofsky Weltman has changed the field of Victorian Studies by building new communities of theatre researchers, and I am particularly appreciative of the NAVSA Theater Caucus that she founded.

An earlier version of part of Chapter 3 appeared in 'The Exceptional Woman and Her Audience: *Armgart*, Performance, and Authorship' in *The George Eliot Review* (2004), 38–45, and I thank the George Eliot Fellowship for permission to republish it here. Early versions of other portions of this book appeared in 'Child Killers and the Competition between the Late Victorian Theater and the Novel' in *MLQ* 66.2 (June 2005), and I thank its editorial staff and anonymous readers for their suggestions. Anonymous readers for Edinburgh University Press helped me to see this project in new ways. Michelle Houston, Ersev Ersoy, James Dale, Eliza Wright, Camilla Rockwood and their colleagues at Edinburgh University Press, as well as series editor Julian Wolfreys, made the final preparation of this book a pleasure.

While working on this book I served as chair of the City College English Department, and I was deeply appreciative of the cooperation and good will of its faculty. I would like to thank department programme directors and staff, in particular: Barbara Gleason, Yana Joseph, András Kiséry, Harold Veeser, Elizabeth Mazzola, Keith Gandal, Salar Abdoh, Emily Raboteau, Linsey Abrams and Rosaymi Santos. As current chair of English, Elizabeth Mazzola provided advice and support for the completion of this work. City College colleagues from within my department and across the college provided support, advice or inspiration, most particularly: Felicia Bonaparte, Bruce Cronin, Kevin Foster, Ellen Handy, David Jeruzalmi, the late Norman Kelvin, Christine Li, Rajan Menon, Glen Milstein, Mark Mirsky, Paul Oppenheimer and Josh Wilner. I would like to thank my undergraduate and MA students at City College for their thoughts and enthusiasm in discussing Victorian literature, especially Clara Boothby, Tyleen Kelly, John Kofron, Megan O'Donnell and Laura Wallace.

I am grateful for the support that I have received from deans in the City College Division of Humanities and the Arts over the years. J. Fred Reynolds provided opportunities and support that were critical to my professional growth. Geraldine Murphy has been a mentor, supporter and friend. Eric Weitz motivated me by example and precept to think ambitiously. Doris Cintrón is a model of feminist leadership and mentorship. Erec Koch has provided me with an opportunity to do useful, challenging work, and I am grateful for his support of my research and teaching.

In my own balancing of the worlds of work and home, I am fortunate to have family that have supported and nurtured me. Much reading, writing and revision for this project was undertaken while spending time with a warm family circle that gathers at the home of my father-in-law, Joel Miller. My mother, Patricia Kobetts, and my mother-in-law, Nan Miller, have given of their time and energy, enabling me to pursue my career knowing that my children were in the care of loving grandmothers. Both my mother and my father, Joseph Kobetts, devoted their lives to service in the New York City public schools. My father's love of history lives on in this book (and I wish he were here to read it), while my mother provided me my earliest view of women's work in the public world. My husband, Jethro Miller, and I met as undergraduates, and he has been a partner throughout the intellectual journey that lies behind this volume. His constant support as we have developed, pursued our respective careers and raised a family has made the worlds of work and home manageable and joyful. Finally, Sophie and Noah are my greatest passions and sources of pride. This book is dedicated, with much love, to them.

A Note on the Cover

The cover photo of *The Victorian Actress* is of Ellen Terry reading a book over her mother's shoulder. The Terrys were a theatrical family, both women pursued stage careers, and Ellen became one of the Victorian era's most iconic actresses. She enjoyed both popular celebrity and cultural prestige as the leading lady of Henry Irving's management at the Lyceum Theatre even as she belonged to a profession that had not entirely moved beyond its questionable standing with regard to respectability. (In 1895, Irving became the first actor to be elevated to knighthood, emblematising the shifting position of the theatrical profession in the nineteenth century.) The curtain-like photographer's drape behind the women reveals this photo to be a staged representation. In light of that, the fact that they are reading from a text that may or may not be a script evokes one of the central concepts of this book: that the figure of the actress was manipulated and controlled by how she was written in novels and plays of the Victorian period. Moreover, that this photo was taken by the writer Lewis Carroll speaks to the fascination that novelists had with actresses.

On the one hand, this is an intimate scene, domestic in nature as it depicts a mother and daughter intimately connected in the private act of reading. But these are actresses, striking a pose before a curtain. Whether intentionally or not, the full frame of the image reveals the edge of the curtain, playing up the performed nature of the image for consumption by an audience's gaze: there is a world outside of this photo, beyond the curtain's edge. This invites questions about authenticity and ascribes potential agency to the figures in the image. To play a part does not enforce passivity. Ellen Terry was a woman who mediated between the nineteenth and twentieth centuries. Her daughter, Edith Craig, was a suffragette in the early twentieth century, and Terry appeared in suffragette theatre.

A Note on the Cover xiii

Like this photo, this book is about generational connections, bonds between women, performance, authenticity and relationships between the private and public spheres. *The Victorian Actress* examines how the figure of the actress played a critical part in the development of the novel and the theatre and how, in turn, these literary forms shaped the actress as a cultural figure for women in the public sphere. From the mid-Victorian period through to the use of the theatre for the suffragette movement in the early twentieth century, it traces how the novel and the drama variously constructed the actress's authenticity and her ability to foster sympathetic bonds through affective and narrative strategies.

For Sophie and Noah, with love

Introduction: Setting the Stage – Views of Victorian Theatre

The Victorian actress was magnetic. For Victorian writers, she was a critical figure in defining their own work. Her engagement with popular audiences made her emblematic of women participating in the public sphere, investing her with a significance markedly different from the actor, whose masculinity granted him rights of citizenship and public participation without being on stage. For this reason she encapsulated what Victorian writers saw, variously, as the theatre's allure and its weakness: its intimate but dependent relationship with its audience. As a result, cultural understandings of actresses both shaped and were shaped by the competition that existed between the Victorian theatre and the novel – a competition that has remained neglected because of the consequent and enduring disregard that Victorian theatre suffers in the study of literature. *The Victorian Actress in the Novel and on the Stage* is a literary and cultural history about the actress as a figure in social and literary struggles, and it examines the interrelations between these fields as they informed each other. Using novels, plays, a short story, a closet drama, poetry, non-fiction prose, dramatic criticism, visual images and archival materials of suffrage organisations, it examines how writers, drawing on cultural understandings of the theatre and the actress in order to define their own formal, cultural and political positions, in turn shaped beliefs about the theatre and the actress. Crossing the disciplinary divide between criticism that focuses on novels and criticism that focuses on the theatre, it traces a genealogy of Victorian cultural attitudes towards female performers that culminated in the centrality of the theatre and actresses in the early twentieth-century women's suffrage movement. In doing so, it identifies important shifts in the novel and the theatre, and ways in which these two forms were responsive to each other. Thus, while the cultural significance of the actress cannot be fully understood without examining the cultural history that defined her, the figure of the actress also helps to shed light on the ways in which the novel and the theatre developed – and developed in relation to each other – during the second half of the nineteenth century.

Redressing theatre's neglect in literary study, this book treats the theatre not only as a figure in the Victorian imagination, but also as an active participant in the literary culture of its time. In the context of contemporary studies of Victorian theatre that can usually be classed either as the work of theatre historians interested primarily in the stage or the work of literary scholars focused on Victorian theatricality and the idea of theatre, Sharon Aronofsky Weltman has argued for 'the importance of researching theater in order to grasp more fully the culture that helped create the era's flowering of fiction, poetry, and art', David Kurnick has sought to redress how scholarship 'has hypostatized the novel and the theater as independent traditions', and Richard Pearson has explored 'what the mid-nineteenth century drama can tell us about the writers of the period and what they can tell us about the drama', seeking to 'open up new ideas about the integration of literature and drama, and a more symbiotic relationship between them'.[1] Gail Marshall's *Actresses on the Victorian Stage: Feminine Performance and the Galatea Myth* is another notable exception to which this study is indebted. Marshall's analysis of various kinds of cultural texts, from drama to novels to theatre criticism to autobiography, demonstrates that the actress was a hot spot of sorts in the Victorian period: a figure at which different cultural forms or influences converged. Jacky Bratton has pointed out that the current neglect that Victorian drama suffers has its roots in the Victorian period itself, when cultural critics largely believed that the British stage had reached its nadir. While many of the participants in the debate about the theatre's problems were novelists who arguably had a vested financial interest in attacking the theatre, the public conversation that appeared in print delineates some of the central concerns with which playwrights, as well as novelists, grappled, and these views of the theatre provide a critical backdrop to the give-and-take across cultural forms on the subject of the actress.

Although Charles Dickens dedicated his *Nicholas Nickleby* (1838–9) to the actor W. C. Macready, 'as a slight token of admiration and regard', the novel shows neither admiration nor regard for playwrights, and it lays out many of the most prominent complaints about the theatre that others would amplify and expound upon throughout the century.[2] En route to Portsmouth to become a sailor, the title character encounters the theatrical manager Vincent Crummles, who recruits him for a variety of miscellaneous duties. The fact that these include playwriting, and the fact that he is instructed to 'introduce a real pump and two washing-tubs' because Crummles had 'bought 'em cheap', parodies both the low esteem in which the theatre held writing and the secondary position of the dramatic text to concrete matters of stage production.[3] Dickens satirises trends in stage 'realism' in the person of Crummles, who says, 'That's the London plan. They look up some dresses, and properties, and have a piece written to fit them. Most of the theatres keep an author on purpose.'[4] Nicholas must also write the play to accommodate the demands of various members of the company and meet a deadline of a few days. Writing, however, turns out to be translating a play from French, as Dickens participates in propagating another commonly held belief about the nineteenth-century English stage: the dependence on Parisian drama for plots. George Henry Lewes noted the prevalence of French adaptations in Spain, England and Germany in 1867: 'French pieces, more or less adapted, hold possession of all stages.'[5] The French play that Nicholas translates is both absurdly sentimental and contrived. Yet Dickens is also satirical about critics who are nostalgic for earlier drama. Mr Curdle, for example, says, 'As an exquisite embodiment of the poet's visions, and a realisation of human intellectuality, gilding with refulgent light our dreamy moments, and laying upon a new and magic world before the mental eye, the drama is gone, perfectly gone.'[6]

Moreover, in addition to depicting actors, playwrights and critics, *Nicholas Nickleby* suggests that the drama is determined by the audience's taste. Nicholas and the actress Miss Snevellicci secure audience members for her benefit performance by agreeing to their requests. In fact, Hablot K. Browne's illustration of 'the great bespeak for Miss Snevellicci' depicts the audience as seen from the stage, rather than the action on the stage, suggesting the central importance of the audience to theatrical production.[7] The illustration's perspective echoes the effect of the mirrored curtain at the Royal Coburg Theatre, a transpontine house that, arguably, performed melodrama steadily to meet audience demand.[8] Similarly, in *Great Expectations*, Pip's description of Wopsle's *Hamlet* is devoted to recounting the running commentary provided by the audience, most notably its responses to questions that Hamlet asks in his soliloquys. The physical presence of the audience that is realised in each of these novels was absolutely at the heart of the debate about Victorian theatre.

Figure 0.1 'The Great Bespeak for Miss Snevellicci', Hablot Knight Brown (Mary Evans Picture Library)

An 1858 *Household Words* article by Wilkie Collins, for example, suggested that theatre managers, in contrast to publishers of novels, cater to the lowest tastes in the audience:

> I read at home *David Copperfield*, *The Newcomes*, *Jane Eyre*, and many more original authors, that delight me. I go to the theatre, and naturally want original stories by original authors, which will also delight me there. Do I get what I ask for? Yes, if I want to see an old

play over again. But, if I want a new play? Why, *then* I must have the French adaptation, or the Burlesque. The publisher can understand that there are people among his customers who possess cultivated tastes, and can cater for them accordingly, when they ask for something new. The manager, in the same case, recognises no difference between me and my servant.[9]

Collins's argument that theatre managers make no attempt to bring those with 'cultivated tastes' back into the theatre because 'the increase of wealth and population, and the railway connection between London and the country, more than supply in quantity what audiences have lost in quality' has become a chestnut of how Victorian theatre was shaped by rapid demographic and technological change.[10] Collins goes on to execrate the lack of discrimination in this broad-based, working-class audience. According to Collins, theatre managers cater to a

> vast nightly majority . . . whose ignorant sensibility nothing can shock. Let him cast what garbage he pleases before them, the unquestioning mouths of his audience open, and snap at it. . . . If you want to find out who the people are who know nothing whatever, even by hearsay, of the progress of the literature of their own time – who have caught no vestige of any one of the ideas which are floating about before their very eyes – who are, to all social intents and purposes, as far behind the age they live in, as any people out of a lunatic asylum can be – go to a theatre, and be very careful, in doing so, to pick out the most popular performance of the day.[11]

Such scathing criticisms of the theatre and its audience were not limited to mid-Victorian novelists. Writing as one of the foremost theatre critics of the *fin de siècle*, William Archer praised J. T. Grein's private theatre society as a British version of Paris's Théâtre Libre, but deplored the state of British theatre in terms that echoed those of Dickens and Collins:

> If such an institution was needed in Paris, how much more in London! Here we have not a single theatre that is even nominally exempt from the dictation of the crowd. Here the actor-manager reigns supreme. Here the upholsterer runs rampant, and it takes a hundred performances to pay his bill. Here the Censor swoops down on unconventional ethics, while he turns his blind eye to conventional ribaldry. Here the average intelligence of 'the drama's patrons' is much lower than in France, and there are far fewer loop-holes of escape from its dominion.[12]

While Archer and other theatre critics may have been influenced by the criticism that novelists had levelled against the stage, novelists were also explicitly invited to help shape the public image and the future of theatre. This essay and another by Archer that addressed England's lack of a 'literary drama' led the *Pall Mall Gazette* in 1892 to pose the question: 'In France and in Germany almost all the great novelists have been playwrights as well. . . . Why is it that in modern England, on the other hand, scarcely any of the popular novelists are known as writers for the stage?'[13] The series of responses that followed, in which novelists enumerated their concerns, dramatises how the cultural position of the drama was shaped by a give-and-take between the institutions of the theatre and the novel, with novelists playing a prominent role. In turn, it also reveals how the definition of the genre of the novel by novelists depended upon the abjection of the drama and how theatre, thus, could speak back, as it were, and shape the novel. Kurnick challenges the use of 'contest' and 'competition' as ways of understanding the relationship between fiction and theatre, and observes 'that writers do not always know what is good for "their" genre, or even which genre is theirs', yet such relationships between the drama and the novel emerge with some force in the Victorian periodical press.[14]

In various ways, the novel was defined in contrast to the materiality of the theatre.[15] Some of the responding novelists, like Thomas Hardy, described the apparatus involved in the staging of a play as inimical to artistic control and to the messages that they sought to convey. Echoing *Nicholas Nickleby*, Hardy cited the materiality of 'the play as nowadays conditioned', as a source of its weaknesses:

> parts have to be moulded to actors, not actors to parts. . . . The presentation of human passions is subordinated to the presentation of mountains, cities, clothes, furniture, plate, jewels, and other real and sham-real appurtenances, to the neglect of the principle that the material stage should be a conventional or figurative arena, in which accessories are kept down to the plane of mere suggestions of place and time, so as not to interfere with the required high-relief of the action and emotions.[16]

A recurrent theme in the novelists' responses was the qualitative difference between a reading audience and a theatre audience – a difference that is consistently linked to the audience's physical presence. While Ouida isolated 'the quality of the acting and the unintelligence of the audiences' as the reasons that 'writers of eminence [have stayed] off the English stage', Lucas Malet (Mary St Leger Kingsley) hit on the physical presence of the audience as a key difference between fiction writing and playwriting. In contrast to 'the Stage', which demands compliance with 'difficult and circumscribing' conventions,

> our Reading Public is so trustful, so divinely patient and amiable. It bears with us when we are lengthy and reflective; it cheerfully permits us to deal with any and everything except the matter in hand; it swallows down our rudimentary science, our crude art, our revivals of extinct heresies, our fatuous spiritual speculation, without gulping; it honours us alike where we are profane and puzzle-headed; it worships us when we are brutal, and reverently adores us when we are dull. Above all, it is unseen.
>
> How can we leave it? Is it not too much to ask that we shall present ourselves before dreadful rows of a completely visible concrete public, which has a right to clap its hands, audibly and materially right in front of us, and produce other and less engaging sounds at will?[17]

While Malet's description of sympathetic novel readers who willingly accept anything sounds like an ironic suggestion that the theatre audience might be more discriminating, most novelists were more clearly in agreement with Collins and with Margaret L. Woods, who argued that 'the novelist in England has the advantage of appealing to an audience not only larger than the dramatist's but somewhat more discriminating'.[18] In asserting the size of the novel's readership, Woods highlighted the dominance that novelists possessed in Victorian culture – a dominance that was both the cause and the effect of the novel's successful campaign against the theatre. She also avoided the elision, typical in Victorian characterisations of theatrical audiences, of a large audience with an audience that is indiscriminate and unsophisticated.

The notion of the novel having a larger audience than the theatre is counterintuitive to a reader in the twenty-first century, when 'a best-selling book may reach a million readers; a successful Broadway play will be seen by 1 to 8 million people; [and] a movie or television adaptation will find an audience of many million more'.[19] A best-selling nineteenth-century novel certainly reached much more than a million readers. Dickens's *Pickwick Papers* (1836–7) had sold 800,000 copies by 1879, and Harriet Beecher Stowe's blockbuster import *Uncle Tom's Cabin* (1852) sold 1,500,000 copies in England and the colonies in its first year alone. Neither of these statistics accounts for the prominence of the circulating libraries in the distribution of novels: each copy purchased by a circulating library would have had numerous users.[20]

In contrast, William Archer suggested by his 'Law of the Hundred Thousand' that the mark of a play's success was a run of at least one hundred nights. At a theatre seating 1,000 this means a minimum of 100,000 needed to see a play, yet 'it is absurd to imagine that there are in London, at any one time, 100,000 playgoers of keen intelligence and delicate perception – capable, in short, of appreciating the highest order of drama'.[21] While Woods imagined an intelligent, far-reaching, novel-reading public, even a drama critic suggested that any large theatre audience – even one several times smaller than the readership of a best-selling novel – must be an inferior one.

George Gissing described the unintellectual taste of theatre audiences in much more extreme terms, and his rhetoric provides a good example of the vitriol that motivated novelists' attacks on the stage:

> The acted drama is essentially a popular entertainment; author and player live alike upon the applause of crowds. When the drama flourished in England, it was by virtue of popular interests, for in those days the paying public was the intellectual public. . . .
>
> Nowadays, the paying public are the unintelligent multitude. The people who make a manager's fortune represent a class intellectually beneath the groundlings of Shakespeare's time. . . . When Johnson, or when Lamb, sat in the pit, they had no such fellow playgoers about them as now crush together at the unopened doors, but a majority of men who with us would merit the style of gentle. Our democratic populace, rich and poor, did not exist. What class of readers made the vogue of the Waverley Novels? Those books were never *popular*, as the word is now understood; price alone proves that. Nor was Sheridan popular in this sense. The spiritual mates of those who now pay for a stall at Drury Lane or the Adelphi sat then in stalls of another kind – cobbler's or huckster's – and recked not of dramatic literature.
>
> Our throwing multitude, with leisure and money undreamt of by their predecessors, must somehow find amusement after a daytime of more or less exhausting labour; to supply this amusement is naturally a profitable business; and so it comes about that the literary ideal of the stage-play is supplanted on the stage itself by the very practical notions of a popular impresario. Hence the sundering of theatre and literature.[22]

In contrast to Wood's practical view that the novel attracted more readers, Gissing's rhetoric exaggerates the numbers of theatre-goers as he evokes the notion of 'popularity' to mean an appeal to a crowd that is large, working-class and uneducated. Patrick Brantlinger has provided an astute analysis of nineteenth-century novelists' anxiety about mob-like reading audiences.[23] Novelists employed the drama as a convenient scapegoat on which to project anxieties about their own relationships to an audience, and this projection accounts for their magnified notion of the masses that attended London theatres. Indeed, just as Gissing resented the 'democratic' theatrical audience, Harold Frederic's central thrust against the drama was that it was subject to majority rule. In Frederic's view, for a play, 'nobody cares about its merit *qua* merit. The only question is whether a theatre-going public will like it.'[24] The novelist, on the other hand,

> writes for just the audience that he feels in touch with, and need not think of the others. If, on a given day, of 500 people reading his book there are 50 who like it and are glad it was written, the fact that the other 450 yawn affects nothing. The book was not written for them, that is all; and it will go on finding its way to those for whom it was written. . . .
>
> The work of the novelists is never wasted or lost. The hostile majority I have assumed above cannot prevent the appreciative minority from enjoying the work written for them. In the playhouse absolutely the reverse is true. There the hostile majority can, and does, decree that the play it does not like shall be seen no more of men.[25]

Yet even as he bristled against the control that the theatrical audience exercises, Frederic paradoxically believed that an advantage of the novel is that it is less distanced from its audience. Describing how the publisher of one of his novels suggested that he cut a scene but ultimately indulged the author's desire to leave it in, Frederic concludes: 'Nobody stands between the novelist and his audience.'[26] In contrast, Frederic offers an anecdote about a theatre manager who refused to produce a play of Frederic's unless his unreasonable requests for revision were met. Frederic's view of the theatre manager standing between writer and audience once again represents the theatre as fully embodied materiality.

Amid the panoply of feelings about why the theatre falls short of fiction – the audience is more demanding, the audience is less discriminating, the audience is more immediate, the audience is distanced from the writer by the manager – most novelists writing in the *Pall Mall Gazette* agreed that the theatre's 'democratic' audience was less exclusive than the novel-reading public. Mary Elizabeth Braddon specifically described the heterogeneous audience of the theatre in contrasting 'the kindly public of the circulating library' with 'that triple-headed monster of the stalls, pit, and gallery whom the playwright has to please'.[27]

Just as Braddon used the theatre's ticket levels to stand metonymically for the economic strata that comprised the audience, J. Henry Shorthouse elided the physical properties of the theatre with the social class of its audience. He believed that *'vast theatres, and mechanical apparatus'* were responsible for 'the decadence of the English stage', and argued that if

> there [were] maintained in London a *very small* theatre in which all the 'pit seats were stalls', and there was no gallery, or a very small, high-priced one, and in which no mechanical apparatus was allowed excepting scene-shifting – and that very seldom and occasional – ... such a theatre might become a school for a class of English actors who would recall the past, and might perchance attract the highest genius to write for the stage.[28]

Shorthouse's desire for assigned, individual seats rather than communal benches in the pit reveals a classism, because stalls would have been higher-priced seats like the small gallery that Shorthouse envisions. Because the stall seat physically recognises and delineates an individualised subjectivity, Shorthouse's preference for the stall in contrast to communal benches also belies Victorian writers' fears of mob-like popular audiences.

In addition to stage technology and the class of the audience, Shorthouse views the quality of performers as a precondition for attracting high-calibre writers. There is no logical foundation for why the actor or actress should be the single impetus that would improve the stage: one could just as easily argue that higher-quality playwrights and plays would attract a better class of performers. Perhaps writers were more inclined to blame actors, rather than other writers, for the stage's shortcomings. More importantly, the fact that the actor or actress was viewed as the narrow end of the wedge for improving the theatre reveals how the performer metonymically served as a personification of the stage and all of its shortcomings.

Although Jonas Barish identifies the theatre's reliance on actors as central to the nineteenth century's 'antitheatrical prejudice', the belief that dramatic writing would improve if theatrical performers were not only more proficient but also more respectable precedes the Victorian period.[29] Denis Diderot's *The Paradox of Acting* was written in 1773 and published in 1830, but the influence that it exerted over the Victorian era is most apparent in the fact that it was reprinted, with an intensely defensive preface by the eminent actor-manager

Henry Irving, in 1883. In Diderot's dialogue, the first speaker characterises those who pursue a career on stage:

> What makes them slip on the sock or the buskin? Want of education, poverty, a libertine spirit. The stage is a resource, never a choice. Never did actor become so from love of virtue, from desire to be useful in the world, or to serve his country or family; never from one of the honourable motives which might incline a right mind, a feeling heart, a sensitive soul, to so find a profession.[30]

From this position, the speaker develops his theory that, 'if players were people of position and their profession an honoured one', then the lines that playwrights would pen for them 'would soon attain to a purity, a delicacy, a grace'.[31] Following Diderot, Victorian writers, seeking either to improve the respectability of the stage or to challenge it, focused their energy on the social position of actors. More particularly, because the actress's public performance and professionalism was positioned against the Victorian equation of respectable femininity with domesticity, the actress became the central figure in a battle between the novel and the drama.

Very little attention has been paid to such interactions between the Victorian theatre and the novel. Despite the recuperative work of theatre historians, which this book draws on throughout, and despite outstanding works of recent literary criticism that have drawn attention to the centrality of theatre in the Victorian imagination and in the minds of novelists in particular, Victorian theatre continues to receive short shrift in literary studies, where the novel continues to control the image of the stage.[32] This explains why Victorian literature survey courses seldom venture beyond the drama of Ibsen, Wilde and Shaw – examples of the 'literary drama' that Archer hailed in the 1890s – and why students do not read Dion Boucicault, T. W. Robertson or Henry Arthur Jones alongside Tennyson, Dickens and Ruskin. Two studies in particular, however, have established how the novel and the theatre developed in relation to each other, and *The Victorian Actress* is indebted to and develops out of them.

First, J. Jeffrey Franklin's *Serious Play: The Cultural Form of the Nineteenth-Century Realist Novel* (1999) considers books in the context of a marketplace that, he argues, was shaped by competition between the novel and the theatre. To Franklin, 'The pervasiveness of the figure of the theater in the 1840s to 1860s . . . expresses an historical contest that reaches culmination in the first half of the nineteenth century between two, major, competing cultural forms:

the realist novel and the popular theater', and 'the so-called rise of the novel was materially related to the decline of the drama, and the decline of the theater was in part a result of the cultural and commercial success of the form of novelistic realism'.[33] This accounts for 'the repeated juxtaposition of non-theatrical and theatrical figures' in Victorian novels, because such figures stand for the contrast between the novel and the theater and allow the novel to consider its own 'formal assumptions'.[34] Franklin's study concludes with 1860, ending before the significant break in theatre history that Katherine Newey identifies in the early 1860s with the emergence of sensation drama, the long run of a theatrical production, increasingly middle-class audiences, and the greater mobility of audiences. It was also in the 1860s that the theatre became both more respectable and more realistic. Following Franklin's logic that the rise of the novel depended on the fall of the theatre, an alteration in the status of one form surely would elicit a response from the other form. *The Victorian Actress* traces not only the rise of the novel against the theatre, as Franklin does, but also the theatre's response as it regains respectability and cultural capital, the novel's response to that in turn, and the emergence of an early twentieth-century political theatre that was shaped by the give-and-take between these literary forms. Franklin points out that the nineteenth-century novel defined itself as 'a model for the ideal spectator and the ideal citizen', identifying how novels reflected changes in the theatre's audience during the first half of the nineteenth century – from the 1900 Old Price riots 'toward an audience form that is more discrete, civil, and ideally distanced, not only from the action on the stage but from social and political action as well'.[35] *The Victorian Actress* demonstrates how the political theatre of the early twentieth century developed a model for 'the ideal spectator and the ideal citizen' that was imagined as fluid, potentially disruptive, and both elided with the action on the stage and directly involved in political action. In keeping with the view of novelists in the *Pall Mall Gazette* series, this theatre was also conceived as democratic and less exclusive than novel-reading audiences.

Second, Emily Allen's *Theater Figures: The Production of the Nineteenth-Century British Novel* (2003) provides further attention to the literary marketplace that Franklin explored and examines 'how novelistic representation of theater and theatricality helped manage relations among novels, readers, and the market'.[36] Allen provides a view into the nineteenth-century novel as a hotly contested field of sub-genres by analysing how the figure of theatre was used to claim 'cultural capital and literary value' for individual novels that were competing with and distinguishing themselves from other types of novels.[37] According to Allen, the centrality of theatre to the novel has much to do with the female reader, 'whose figure must negotiate the conflict between women's multiple ties to the voracious appetites of the market and the consuming fiction of women's private, readerly, removal from the public sphere'.[38] Allen's historical analysis reveals that 'the nineteenth-century ideal of domesticated, privatized, female subjectivity' displaces 'a model that held particular sway in the eighteenth century, an account of woman as sexually voracious, highly changeable, and inherently theatrical'.[39] This leads Allen to articulate a relationship between genre and gender that forms one of the foundations of *The Victorian Actress*: 'in the nineteenth-century novel, generic competition between the theater and the novel (and among novels) works to focus and manage competing representations of woman. This is also true the other way around – conflict between competing models of female gender works to focus and manage underlying generic conflicts.'[40]

Realism and melodrama, formal terms that are commonly aligned with the Victorian novel and the drama respectively, are also of foundational importance to my study of how Victorian cultural works define themselves and draw on these modes, often using them in complicated and overlapping ways. Melodrama has so successfully been restored to literary and cultural study that its prominence in these fields has all but obliterated other threads in Victorian theatre, including what theatre historians know and challenge as the familiar, traditional narrative of development from melodrama towards realism.[41] I build on recent and established critical work on these concepts, including that of Peter Brooks, Matthew Buckley, Rae Greiner, Elaine Hadley, George Levine, Teresa Mangum and Carolyn Williams. Among studies of novelistic realism, Rae Greiner's *Sympathetic Realism in Nineteenth-Century British Fiction* offers a definition of realism that eschews melodrama's emotional affect through visual display. The sympathy that 'produces' realism, according to Greiner, is based on Adam Smith's view, in *The Theory of Moral Sentiments*, that sympathy 'facilitated special modes of thinking about feeling even when feeling itself did not develop', and 'is grounded in the pursuit of narrative effects rather than epistemological certainty'.[42] Greiner contrasts Smith's view of sympathy with David Hume's: 'Smith's sympathizer abstracts feeling, routing it through cognition, while Hume allows for sensation to be transmitted both directly and unconsciously from one person to the next.'[43] Key to Greiner's distinction between Smith and Hume is 'that sympathy and feeling are not the same'.[44] If, as Greiner argues, Smith's view of sympathy is a realistic mode, then I would argue that we may associate Hume's direct transfer of feeling as melodramatic or sensational. While melodrama, as theorists such as Peter Brooks have argued, depends on visual display, Greiner holds that for Smith, 'The mere sight of violent feelings, happy or sad, is inimical to sympathy as Smith understands it; time and again, he calls on the abstracting powers of figuration to mitigate the deleterious effects brought on by strong visual and emotional display.'[45] Yet, as we shall see in the chapter that follows this introduction, the notion of genuine feeling and affect was itself an area of concern for Victorian theorists of acting.

Jacky Bratton has discussed how the binaries of text versus context, high versus popular culture, and literature versus theatre have their roots in the Victorian period and maintain their force in criticism today, even when the privileged term in the binary is reversed as it is in studies of melodrama as popular culture. In tracing influences between the novel and the stage, this book uncovers and interrogates the classifications that Victorian writers and the critics that followed them have drawn between the Victorian novel and drama, as well as those that have been made among the novel's various authors and sub-genres. Novelists used the figure of theatre to define and distinguish their work, but the theatre itself can be used to trouble these distinctions. As George Levine has pointed out, 'Realism exists as a process.'[46] Realistic novels, according to Levine, are driven by 'an attempt to use language to get beyond language, to discover some non-verbal truth out there', but they are also responsible 'to an audience that requires to be weaned or freed from the misnaming literatures past and present'.[47] A critical aspect of realism's process, however, is that it was at work in print literature and the theatre simultaneously. In fact, while the theatre often functioned as the novel's abjected other, as Allen has shown, this relationship is complicated by the fact that the novel served a similar role for the theatre, and that the novel and theatre influenced each other in more concrete ways. As the novel and the drama each strived for greater realism and defined its relation to the other, the actress's relationship to the domestic world came to serve not only as a way of representing the actress's – and the theatre's – respectability or lack thereof, but also served as a figure for the play or novel's realistic representation.

The Victorian Actress traces the ways in which the novel employed melodramatic conventions of signification as well as realistic methods of fostering sympathy, the ways in which the theatre's increasing claims to realism and naturalism in the nineteenth century competed with the novel, and the ways in which developments in the novel influenced changes in the theatre. It argues that the increased respectability and realism of the stage in the 1860s was a contributing factor to the rise of novels that attempted to attract an avant-garde, rather than popular, audience. Suffrage theatre, in turn, developed out of the theatre's emerging avant-garde movements and attempted to balance formal and political innovation with appeal to a large audience through the familiar conventions of melodrama. This study also provides a finer-grained view of the trajectory of the actress's increased respectability over the course of the nineteenth century.

In a rough chronology by decade, the chapters of this book focus on particular movements or motivations in the novel's and/or the drama's representations of actresses: seeking to establish the actress's authenticity through melodramatic conventions of expression and doing so by maintaining her status as an outsider to respectable class hierarchies in the 1850s; using domesticity as a source of authenticity that challenges class hierarchies in the 1860s and, in so doing, establishing both a new realism and respectability for the stage; exploring the particular ways in which talented women who performed for public audiences, in George Eliot's novels of the 1870s, could command tenuous power outside of the domestic sphere; and seeking a more select, intellectual audience in novelistic sub-genres in the 1880s and 1890s. The fifth chapter turns to how this history was appropriated and confronted by flesh-and-blood actresses in the early twentieth-century women's suffrage movement, as they became playwrights who used drama to appeal to a mass audience, writing new dramatic and social parts for women.

While some of the reactions and responses between fiction and theatre occur within chapters, many of them occur across chapters and over time. Although this book does hold that there are critical moments of response and large-scale trends that can be traced over time, it does not argue for a strict linear chronology or clear lines of demarcation between different phases, as attitudes and beliefs linger and remain in the cultural consciousness, particularly since novels remained in circulation and plays lived on in repertoires and revivals.

Chapter 1 begins with critical discussions of the extent to which actors and actresses must feel in order to perform effectively, including Denis Diderot, George Henry Lewes, William Archer and Henry Irving. These provide a context for how Victorian novelists and playwrights asserted the actress's authentic identity as they grappled with the mutable class identity that she enjoyed, both as a working woman and as a woman who could convincingly perform various class roles. The acting theories and the plays in this chapter qualify the concept of 'imaginative sympathy' that Rae Greiner argues is not the transmission of feeling but, rather, an intellectual bridging of the distance between individuals that is at the core of Victorian novelistic realism. Even as the Victorians theorised that acting could not be the direct expression of felt emotion, but rather required a double consciousness or, as Archer put it, 'imaginative sympathy', the theatre employed the melodramatic conventions of strong feeling, sentimentalism and the reliability with which physical symptoms express inner feelings, in order to assert authenticity. Although this book will trace the degree to which later works employ such melodramatic conventions in their representations of actresses, this chapter examines those conventions in their strongest instantiations in dramas that cluster around the 1850s.

It first uses Edward Lancaster's brief interlude 'The Manager's Daughter', produced at the Haymarket in 1837 and later adapted by Dion Boucicault into 'The Young Actress' (1860), which thematises the actress as a protean mimic at a time when the theatre increasingly focused its attention on the Victorian mass audience of various and changeable classes, rather than on the patronage of the gentility. The chapter then focuses on a cluster of plays – and one novel adapted from a play – from the 1840s and 1850s that curb the actress's ability to undermine class structures. Boucicault's *Peg Woffington* (1845) depicts an actress who can make or break men's stations, while she herself, having risen from poverty, remains a social outsider despite her wealth, as she trades on her perceived sexual availability and tenuous social standing. Boucicault's *The Prima Donna* (1852) takes up the orphan actress whose lack of family origins, as in *Peg Woffington*, is both a concrete and symbolic instantiation of the actress's lack of fixed social position. This melodrama, about an actress whose adopted sister is coincidentally pining away after the nobleman whom the actress loves, thematises authenticity: the nobleman falls in love with the actress's sister in actuality only after he has been compelled to feign love for her. The play balances this suggestion that performance can create a new reality by using the actress's love for her adopted sister – the only family she has known – to serve as a source of authentic feeling and, in turn, to maintain the actress as an outsider by preventing her marriage into a respectable social standing as she sacrifices her own happiness for that of her sister.

Tom Taylor and Charles Reade revisited Boucicault's *Peg Woffington* in their co-authored play *Masks and Faces* (1852) and in Reade's subsequent novelisation of the same story, *Peg Woffington* (1853), working more aggressively with the themes of her class status in order to explore the actress's authenticity. In both the play and the novel, Taylor and Reade employ the melodramatic convention of the legibility of physical emotions to establish the actress's genuine feelings, which are grounded in her working-class origins, in order to reclaim Peg from her changeability and prevent her from disrupting class hierarchies. A comparison of the play and its novelisation reveals challenges that the stage poses to establishing authenticity for the actress.

Although Chapter 2 continues to examine how Victorian writers sought to establish the actress's authenticity, it focuses on works of the 1860s, which do not curb the actress's challenge to traditional class distinctions but rather embrace such challenges. Actresses, whose public performances transgressed gender expectations by taking them out of the domestic sphere, were far more socially problematic than actors. Attempting to improve the prestige of the theatre, therefore, included refiguring the actress as compatible with domesticity. In order to establish the actress's authenticity and, by extension, respectability, the novel and plays that this chapter examines employ family and the domestic – even when they are not part of the actress's origins. Thus, even as the actress, historically, became more respectable, she was used as a figure for class disruption. The works examined in this chapter range from melodrama and the sensation novel to a play that, although it is widely recognised as a breakthrough in theatrical realism, paradoxically depends on melodramatic conventions in order to claim its own realistic status.

The famous melodramatist Boucicault's *The Life of an Actress*, which was first performed in London in 1862, thematises authenticity as the much maligned bit-part actor Grimaldi criticises the star Julia for being mechanical, rather than achieving the 'double consciousness' that Lewes theorised. Grimaldi vocalises the position of the play: that authenticity is located in emotions, and the great actress must be sentient. In contrast, lacking any standing in the social world, the orphaned street beggar Violet performs with real feeling that stems from her own griefs, and she is consequently adopted by Grimaldi. The vulnerable social status of the actress is instantiated by the melodramatic plot, in which Violet is abducted by a villainous seducer. Further, the problem of her class status is embodied in her secret marriage to Lord Arthur. In the end, it is through the creation of family ties and her authentic acting that Violet's status is elevated, and the play both valorises the nobility of acting as an artistic profession and celebrates the power of popular audiences.

Wilkie Collins's sensation novel *No Name* (1862–3) explicitly criticises traditional landed wealth and emphasises the acted nature of class, stressing family relationships and domestic life as the basis for individual identity. The novel's heroine, Magdalen, prostitutes herself both as an actress and by marrying, under a false identity, for mercenary reasons. Her fall is precipitated by a loss of family and inheritance; her redemption is effected by a symbolic return to her family. Contrary to criticism of the novel that holds that it focuses on plot rather than character, I argue that the central mission of *No Name* is to establish the basis of Magdalen's internalised subjectivity. *No Name* traces an elaborate plot of its heroine's identity loss – Magdalen loses herself as she constantly mimics identities that are not her own – only to restore her to her true character through her re-domestication. Just as Charles Reade and Tom Taylor found it difficult to assert Peg Woffington's authenticity on stage, Collins struggled to adapt Magdalen's story to the stage. In addition to examining Collins's novel, this chapter traces its stage adaptations, including one by Collins himself. The conditions of the theatre caused Collins, in adapting his novel for the stage, to make drastic changes to his narrative – changes that represent Magdalen as more genuine on stage than she is in the novel.

Finally, this chapter turns to a pivotal moment in the theatre – a moment whose influence on the novel's development has gone unremarked. T. W. Robertson's play *Caste* (1867) occupies a prominent position in the development of formal realism on stage, and the figure of the actress and her relationship to the domestic is crucial for this development, as the plot grappled with whether the actress truly belonged in the home, which was realised on stage in the 'box set' that Robertson helped to popularise. Like Boucicault's Violet, Robertson's Esther marries a member of the nobility and faces the censure of his mother, and her respectability is founded in her authentic feelings which, in this play, are inextricably linked to her identity as a mother. Retrospectively, the thematic and representational similarities between *The Life of an Actress* and *Caste* reveal the importance of melodrama in the development of realism, as a play that has been considered a landmark in the development of stage realism remained indebted to and grounded in melodramatic strategies.

Turning from the domesticated actress to women who choose careers as performers instead of marriage or motherhood, Chapter 3 takes as its subject performing women created by the landmark novelist George Eliot in the 1870s: the title character of Eliot's poetic closet drama *Armgart* (1871) and the diva Alcharisi in her novel *Daniel Deronda* (1876). These works emphasise the importance of performance not for self-expression but for the influence and independence that performing for a public audience provides. Elizabeth Barrett Browning's *Aurora Leigh* (1856), which Eliot reviewed and which invoked antitheatricality as it portrays a female poet's scorn for theatrical performance and being controlled by any audience, throws Eliot's interest in women's public performance into greater relief. In *Armgart*, Eliot demonstrates how the female artist can gain control over her audience – albeit control that is negotiated and tenuous – in order to attain a greatness unavailable to women confined to the domestic sphere. In *Daniel Deronda*, she explores how Gwendolen Harleth, in contrast to the Alcharisi, lacks the talent to perform in public and is relegated to performing in a domestic world in which she lacks self-determination and is controlled by her husband. Ultimately, Eliot presages the women's suffragette movement not only in her exploration of how an exceptionally talented woman can wield power in the public sphere but also in her insistence on a bond of sympathy between the public, performing woman and women who lack such power. Eliot emphasises that this bond requires a sympathetic connection greater than can be achieved through melodramatic spectacularity.

Chapter 4 examines an unremarked way in which the development of stage realism influenced the development of the novel. It argues that the figure of the actress is crucial for the novelistic naturalism that George Moore propounded in his novel *A Mummer's Wife* (1885), and that she reveals how the theatre's movement away from melodrama and towards domestic realism, exemplified by Robertson's *Caste* in Chapter 2, contributed to a historical shift in the novel. Moore's own theatre criticism helps to reveal how the naturalism of *A Mummer's Wife*, its form as a one-volume novel intended to dodge the bourgeois taste of the censorial circulating libraries, and its plot that focuses on the theatre's incompatibility with respectable domestic life all respond to the theatre's increased claims to respectability and realism in the 1860s. Rather than competing with the theatre for market share, Moore rejected the theatre's appeal to popular middle-class audiences in favour of attracting a more avant-garde readership. In both Robertson's play and Moore's novel, the actress's artifice is juxtaposed with a domesticity that each author uses to signify reality. While Robertson's play shows how the actress can be at home in the domestic sphere, and Eliot's performers avoided motherhood, Moore's novel uses the extreme case of maternal infanticide to demonstrate the actress's incompatibility with domestic life. Moore, reacting not only against Robertson but also against Eliot, whom he satirises in the figure of a female writer, mobilises the home to repudiate the public woman and claim realistic representation, and a new audience, for himself. While the next chapter will examine drama by the actress-turned-writer Elizabeth Robins, this chapter concludes by analysing Robins's satirical novel *George Mandeville's Husband* (1894) as a pointed response to Moore's attack on the theatre. Robins knew Moore, and she vehemently opposed his views on the theatre. *George Mandeville's Husband* defends both the theatre and the public woman by exposing the commercialism of the market for novels and by satirising criticism of women who participate in the public sphere. It also engages explicitly with the legacy of George Eliot's exceptionalism for feminism.

This book concludes, in Chapter 5, with Henry James and Elizabeth Robins, two American expatriates whose lives and, I argue, writing became intertwined through Robins's career as an actress and as a pioneering figure in the production of Ibsen on the London stage. Henry James's short story 'Nona Vincent' (1892), about the pressure on an actress to play her role, frames the chapter, which then proceeds to examine Miriam Rooth, the main character in James's *The Tragic Muse* (1890), in the context of James's theatre criticism from 1871 to 1901 that was collected in *The Scenic Art* (1948). The chapter argues that in these two works James recapitulates many of the themes about the actress and the state of the theatre in Victorian England that this book explores in its earlier chapters; and that Miriam embodies that cultural history of the figure of the actress. It is notable, therefore, that James places Miriam's importance to an English national theatre in juxtaposition and as a threat to Julia Dallow's importance on the national political stage. This distinction between the actress and the political woman is challenged by actresses who themselves became involved in politics as they became key participants in the women's suffrage movement. The long-term friendship between James and Robins that is documented in Robins's *Theatre and Friendship* (1932) traces a transition from Robins as an actress struggling to play roles – both literally as an actress playing a part on stage and figuratively as an actress with a rich cultural legacy scripting her place in society – to Robins as a playwright who reworks both theatrical conventions and the ways in which actresses and women participated in the public sphere. The remainder of this chapter traces that transition from James and Robins's shared enthusiasm for Ibsen as a cornerstone of a new English drama, to Robins's first play *Alan's Wife* (1893), to her novel *The Convert* (1907) and her play *Votes for Women* (1907). The works in this chapter, from James's fiction to Robins's suffrage drama, also chart a course from the scepticism about popular audiences that we saw in George Eliot and George Moore, towards the use of theatre to function as propaganda for a broad audience. The chapter examines *Votes for Women* within the context of archival materials about the Actresses' Franchise League, for which the play was written, and its relationship to other suffrage organisations in order to demonstrate that the theatricality of the suffragettes, both on stage and in their spectacular political tactics, resulted from and challenged the Victorian cultural tradition surrounding the theatre and the actress. It demonstrates that the issues that had accrued around the actress – the blurring of class distinctions, the social and aesthetic significance of domesticity, the challenges to gender politics, the power of public opinion and the use of both melodramatic and realistic methods for developing connections through either feeling or sympathy – were issues of central concern to the women's suffrage movement. These issues provide additional explanations, beyond that of the actress's significance as a public woman, for why the theatre and theatricality were important to the suffragettes. A brief epilogue describes the activities of the Actresses' Franchise League in the years between the beginning of World War I and the enfranchisement of women in 1918.

Prologue: Thackeray's Uneasy Dependence on the Actress

Although this history will end with actresses who became playwrights, it begins with William Makepeace Thackeray's *Vanity Fair* (1847–8), which defined the role of the novelist, the realism of the novel, and the novel's relationship to its audience by using the figure of theatre and, more specifically, the actress, and *The History of Pendennis* (1848–50), in which the actress is both essential to and abjected by the novel. Extraordinarily vexed in their relationships to the theatre, *Vanity Fair* and *Pendennis* provide outstanding examples of how the novel both asserted and contributed to the decline of the theatre. They provide a starting point from which we can better understand the struggle that the theatre would mount in order to re-establish its and the actress's respectability among middle-class audiences, and the competition in which the theatre and the novel would be embroiled for the second half of the nineteenth century.

Becky Sharp is an actress. More than an actress, she is a star. She is a star in the sense that Thackeray's *Vanity Fair* is one of a series of English novels – the following chapters will explore others – that are driven by the energies of a theatrical heroine. In many of these cases, the actress is problematic enough that, as in Thackeray's 'novel without a hero', she does not fit neatly into the category of 'heroine', although she is the very centre of the novel. Becky reveals that, as Victorian novelists were troubled by their relationship to the literary marketplace, they often defined their work in relation to the theatre for commercial, as well as ideological, reasons. Becky, the daughter of a French 'opera-girl', is consistently associated with theatricality, performs throughout the novel and, reputedly, tries her hand on the professional stage.[48] The narrator's uneasy relationship to her is symptomatic of the author's uneasy relationship to the theatre more generally – an ambivalence that is evident in Thackeray's narrative techniques. Thackeray seeks to emulate the theatre's close relationship with its audience.[49] At the same time, however, he emphasises that the theatre has lost its cultural prominence and that the novel has not only supplanted it but has improved upon it. Accordingly, he draws distinctions between his own mode of representation and that of the theatre.

Vanity Fair's 'Before the Curtain' preface evinces what Janice Carlisle calls Thackeray's 'preoccupation with his audience that might be termed obsessive'.[50] When the narrator enacts the 'conscription' of a reading audience, he begins with a theatrical model, creating the illusion of a physically present audience.[51] Casting himself as 'Manager of the Performance', the narrator concludes his preface with: 'And with this, and a profound bow to his patrons, the Manager retires, and the curtain rises.'[52] Later the narrator continues to elide the novel and theatre when he states, 'Every reader of a sentimental turn (and we desire no other) must have been pleased with the tableau with which the last act of our little drama concluded.'[53] The preface, however, is not without ambivalence towards the audience, for it begins: 'As the Manager of the Performance sits before the curtain on the boards, and looks into the Fair, a feeling of profound melancholy comes over him in his survey of the bustling place', a place which is 'not a moral place certainly; nor a merry one, though very noisy'. The narrator proceeds to suggest,

> A man with a reflective turn of mind, walking through an exhibition of this sort, will not be oppressed, I take it, by his own or other people's hilarity. . . . An episode of humour or kindness touches and amuses him here and there; . . . but the general impression is one more melancholy than mirthful. When you come home, you sit down, in a sober, contemplative, not uncharitable frame of mind, and apply yourself to your books or your business.[54]

This audience that provokes such mixed feelings is not only the reader of Thackeray's novel but its subject as well.

Reminding readers of the theatre's lost heyday as a middle-class attraction, *Vanity Fair* uses its historical retrospective to signal that in emulating the theatre it has supplanted it. Joseph Sedley, as well as Mrs Sedley, Amelia and Becky, 'frequented the theatres, as the mode was in those days', meaning in 1813.[55] Several references to dramatic stars of that time, including Mrs Siddons and John Philip Kemble, invited readers of 1847 to reflect nostalgically on the theatre's past greatness.[56] References to the scandalous affairs of the actress Mrs Rougement and the association of the married actress Mary Robinson and the Prince of Wales suggest, however, that the theatre enjoyed only tenuous respectability.[57] Meanwhile, Mrs Sedley's 'curtain lecture' to Mr Sedley reflects a historical movement away from the stage.[58] Douglas Jerrold's 'Mrs Caudle's Curtain Lectures', a series that appeared in *Punch* in 1845, were a turn towards fiction by Jerrold, the son of an actor and a playwright in his own right.[59]

Yet even as Thackeray tries to emulate and supplant the drama, he also differentiates his novel from it. Sutherland argues that

> Gordon Ray is surely right in his insistence that Thackeray labours in *Vanity Fair* to raise the tone of mid-nineteenth-century fiction and with it the status of the novelist. . . . Thackeray, one might paraphrase, found the English novel sloppy romance, he left it solid realism.[60]

Thackeray emphasises his novel's realism by contrasting it to other, purportedly less realistic forms, as Levine argues is a characteristic of realism.[61] Thackeray simultaneously contrasts *Vanity Fair* to other novels and the theatre as he elides the two. The narrator states, 'As his hero and heroine pass the matrimonial barrier, the novelist generally drops the curtain', and proceeds to explain how he will treat the story of Amelia differently.[62] Similarly, immediately after addressing the audience at the beginning of Chapter 6, referring to his own novel as the performance of 'piping', the narrator proceeds to discuss how he might have 'treated this subject', and famously outlines various novelistic sub-genres less realistic than his own.[63]

Thackeray highlights his own narrative technique as one that is at odds with theatrical representation. In the same chapter in which the narrator states that Joseph Sedley 'frequented the theatres, as the mode was in those days', playing up the theatre's lost, respectable past, the narrator provides a view of Joseph's internal thoughts, noting parenthetically, 'for novelists have the privilege of knowing everything', before Joseph departs for the theatre in order to flee Becky Sharp, who is singing in the drawing room.[64] Sutherland points out that Joseph's determination 'to go and see the *Forty Thieves* . . . and Miss Decamp's dance' signals 'that Joe can admire fast, fashionable women on stage (the demi-mondaine De Camp background was, incidentally, not unlike Becky's) but is terrified of them in the flesh'.[65] The significant difference here is that the performances of actresses on stage do not have the interiority of Becky Sharp, who is an actress off stage, both in the sense that she is a social performer and in the sense that she is a character in a novel with a fully developed interiority. Thackeray's reference to the theatre, therefore, highlights the contrast between the surface appearances of theatrical performance, and the novelist's privilege of knowing everything. At the same time, the reference to Sheridan's *The Forty Thieves* carefully uses theatre history to emphasise the theatre's fallen state. Joseph would have seen it in 1813 at the transpontine Surrey theatre, where it opened in 1812. Jim Davis and Victor Emeljanow point out that by 1842 'the Surrey was reputedly the leading minor theater in London', and that it drew 'a broad range of spectators' despite its reputation for nautical melodrama.[66] Nevertheless, to Thackeray's readership as well as to Joseph, it was a significantly less highbrow venue than the Drury Lane patent house where *The Forty Thieves* first opened in 1806 under Sheridan's own management. Drury Lane itself had suffered financial problems before it burned to the ground in 1809, and the Prince Regent stopped supporting Sheridan's political career in 1811. The play itself, a musical, spectacular, violent melodrama, represents a generic fall from Sheridan's earlier works such as *The School for Scandal* (1777). Thackeray's readers of 1848 would also have been familiar with the fact that Marie-Thérèse Kemble, formerly DeCamp, had returned to the stage in 1829 as Lady Capulet in a production in which her daughter Fanny Kemble played Juliet in order to save the family business, Covent Garden, from bankruptcy. Thus, the reference to 'Decamp' brought to reader's minds the fact that even the patent houses, the most respectable and venerable theatres, were no longer commercially competitive.[67]

But in its attempt to supplant the theatre's cultural and commercial position, *Vanity Fair* is not a simple matter of a narrator claiming both theatrical intimacy with a reading audience and, at the same time, an omniscience about characters that the theatre does not achieve. As the narrative progresses, the narrator does not consistently know everything and instead presents the external performances of characters without penetrating their façades. As Becky performs increasingly effectively, she becomes increasingly opaque. *Vanity Fair* initially supports Mary Ann O'Farrell's argument that the nineteenth-century English novel 'finds in the blush an implicit promise to render body and character legible. The blush's efficacy in fulfilling its pledge for the novel depends upon its seeming, by means of its involuntarity, to evade the constructive capacities of gesture, disguise, and will.'[68] Early in the novel, we learn that, upon a mention of her beau George Osborne, Amelia 'blushed as only young ladies of seventeen know how to blush, and as Miss Rebecca Sharp never blushed in her life – at least not since she was eight years old, and when she was caught stealing jam . . . by her godmother.'[69] The ironic statement that one can 'know how' to blush, however, suggests the potentially performative nature of a supposedly natural act. Shortly thereafter, when Becky blushes during her pursuit of Joseph, her blush remains an impenetrable part of her performance.[70] On the basis of earlier information regarding her motives we can infer that Becky is quickly learning to feign the signs that are taken as genuine. As the narrator says of Becky's departure from the Sedley household:

> Finally came the parting with Miss Amelia, over which picture I intend to throw a veil. But after a scene in which one person was in earnest and the other a perfect performer – after the tenderest caresses, the most pathetic tears, the smelling-bottle, and some of the very best feelings of the heart, had been called into requisition – Rebecca and Amelia parted, the former vowing to love her friend for ever and ever and ever.[71]

Andrew H. Miller points out that, when 'Thackeray gestures toward the spheres of existence – moral conscience, prayer, private desires – to which he has no access', he 'shift[s] the ground of his claims: the reader and author, he now implies, share a set of circumstances and a set of attitudes toward those circumstances. . . . [T]he significant identification is with readers in the drawing room'.[72] Theatrical representation, in other words, allows Thackeray the close relationship to audience that he has used the theatre to signify.

Thackeray's dual-mode narrative trains the reader to read his representation of Becky, in particular, suspiciously and ironically: 'So, in a word, Briggs told all her history, and Becky gave a narrative of her own life, with her usual artlessness and candour.'[73] The narrator's dual point of view is clearest when he describes 'the manners of the very polite world':

> To us, from outside gazing over the policemen's shoulders at the bewildering beauties as they pass into Court or ball, they may seem beings of unearthly splendour, and in the enjoyment of an exquisite happiness by us unattainable. It is to console some of these dissatisfied beings, that we are narrating our dear Becky's struggles, and triumphs, and disappointments.[74]

The narrator assumes the point of view of an outsider, viewing, as it were, the superficial pomp and ceremony of a theatrical performance, but also evinces a determination to penetrate superficial appearances. This appears to be the 'blurring of the boundary between narration's extradiegetic distance, on the one hand, and on the other a level of affective engagement (and historical embeddedness) ordinarily the province of characters only', that Greiner, citing Harry E. Shaw, sees as a sympathetic impulse for the novel.[75] Consistent with Greiner's argument that sympathy is a thought process that emerges from the failure to fully access a character's experience, the narrator ultimately declares Becky opaque to him, because it is impossible to ascertain truth amidst all of her dissembling:

> What *had* happened? Was she guilty or not? She said not; but who could tell what was truth which came from those lips; or if that corrupt heart was in this case pure? All her lies and her schemes, all her selfishness and her wiles, all her wit and genius had come to this bankruptcy.[76]

In a radical denial of the ways in which the novel shapes and creates the figure of the actress, Thackeray writes as if the actress possesses a power that baffles the novelist. Indeed, in this sense Thackeray the novelist and Becky the character parallel each other, to the extent that the actress-character serves as a figure for the author.

Thackeray's oscillation between the theatrical representation in which the narrative point of view shares his audience's limitations and, in that way, establishes a close relationship with his audience, and an omniscient narrator who nevertheless attempts to maintain the illusion of a physically present, theatrical audience by 'conscripting' it even as he claims a novelist's privileged ability to penetrate superficial appearances, reveals the novel's determination to compete with, supplant and exceed the theatre as a form of popular entertainment. In this sense, however, Becky is not merely an actress whose performance can be treated either omnisciently or non-omnisciently. Rather, as a performer who drives the narrative forward, Becky is another figure, along with the 'Manager of the Performance', for the novelist's work. As Jonas Barish has noted: 'If Thackeray is the puppet master of the show, Becky is the puppet master's puppet mistress, for whom others serve mainly as under-puppets.'[77] Further, that Becky represents the novel itself is evident in the narrator's comment immediately after Rebecca's letter to Amelia describing Queen's Crawley:

> Everything considered, I think it is quite as well for our dear Amelia Sedley, in Russell Square, that Miss Sharp and she are parted. Rebecca

is a droll funny creature, to be sure; and those descriptions of the poor lady weeping for the loss of her beauty, and the gentleman 'with hay-coloured whiskers and straw-coloured hair', are very smart, doubtless, and show a great knowledge of the world. That she might, when on her knees, have been thinking of something better than Miss Horrocks's ribbons, has possibly struck both of us. But my kind reader will please to remember that this history has 'Vanity Fair' for a title, and that Vanity Fair is a very vain, wicked, foolish place, full of all sorts of humbugs and falsenesses and pretensions. And while the moralist, who is holding forth on the cover (an accurate portrait of your humble servant), professes to wear neither gown nor bands, but only the very same long-eared livery in which his congregation is arrayed: yet, look you, one is bound to speak the truth as far as one knows it, whether one mounts a cap and bells or a shovel-hat; and a deal of disagreeable matter must come out in the course of such an undertaking.[78]

Combining direct address to the reader with the metaphor of a speaker who has an immediately present audience and with a reminder of the novel's verisimilitude, this paragraph also draws a direct link between the narrator and Becky, as the narrator begins by acknowledging the unease that readers have with Becky but ends by making a plea on her behalf. Both narrator and Becky view the world from a satirical point of view, and, as Becky's letter takes the place of the narrator in opening the chapter, both serve as narrative points of view. Moreover, just as Becky is a performer, the narrator explicitly reemphasises his role as performer. He proceeds to describe 'a brother of the story-telling trade' whose representation of villainy prompted the audience's fervent donations, and 'the little Paris theatres' where French actors refused higher salaries because they would not appear as the villains who aroused the audience's passion, explaining, 'I set the two stories one against the other, so that you may see that it is not from mere mercenary motives that the present performer is desirous to show up and trounce his villains; but because he has a sincere hatred of them, which he cannot keep down.'[79] He asks to be able to have even more intimate contact with the audience than a performer can, 'And, as we bring our characters forward, I will ask leave, as a man and brother, not only to introduce them, but occasionally to step down from the platform, and talk about them', specifically because

> [o]therwise you might fancy it was I who was sneering at the practice of devotion, which Miss Sharp finds so ridiculous; that it was I who laughed good-humouredly at the reeling old Silenus of a baronet – whereas the laughter comes from one who has no reverence except for prosperity, and no eye for anything beyond success. Such people there are living and

flourishing in the world – Faithless, Hopeless, Charityless: let us have at them, dear friends, with might and main. Some there are, and very successful too, mere quacks and fools: and it was to combat and expose such as those, no doubt, that Laughter was made.[80]

Indeed, this conclusion of the chapter, like other passages that handle Becky, must be read ironically, for the narrator has already demonstrated his affinity with Becky. Thackeray is signalling not that his performer-narrator is different from Becky but that he shares Becky's mercenary motives, and that the character of Becky, the narrator's treatment of her, and the figure of theatre all serve the commercial purpose of the success of the novel.[81] Just as Becky casts a satiric eye on everything, the satire that Thackeray employs ultimately takes its own narrative as its subject as he associates himself with a character within the narrative. While Kurnick also traces 'the convergence between Becky and her narrator' and points out that in *Vanity Fair* 'the theater becomes an emblem for what stubbornly resists accommodation in the domestic sphere', part of this resistance stems from the actress as public woman, for it is as a result of her violation of the gendered separation of spheres that the actress comes to stand for the theatre and its commercialism.[82]

Ultimately, Thackeray ascribes his narrative technique, which teaches the audience not to trust appearances even though the novel ceases to expose what lies behind deceptive performances, to the audience's demands that his novel has met, ostensibly for commercial success:

> We must pass over a part of Mrs Rebecca Crawley's biography with that lightness and delicacy which the world demands – the moral world, that has, perhaps, no particular objection to vice, but an insuperable repugnance to hearing vice called by its proper name. . . . [I]t has been the wish of the present writer, all through this story, deferentially to submit to the fashion at present prevailing, and only to hint at the existence of wickedness in a light, easy, and agreeable manner, so that nobody's fine feelings may be offended. I defy any one to say that our Becky, who has certainly some vices, has not been presented to the public in a perfectly genteel and inoffensive manner. In describing this siren, singing and smiling, coaxing and cajoling, the author, with modest pride, asks his readers all round, has he once forgotten the laws of politeness, and showed the monster's hideous tail above water? No! Those who like may peep down under waves that are pretty transparent, and see it writhing and twirling, diabolically hideous and slimy, flapping amongst bones, or curling round corpses; but above the water line, I ask, has not everything been proper, agreeable, and decorous, and has any the most squeamish immoralist in Vanity Fair a right to cry fie?[83]

In the sense that Victorian writers often criticised the theatre for pandering to its audience, the narrator describes a theatrical relationship to his readership. Just as Becky shrewdly performs for financial gain, so, too, does the novel itself. In fact, the narrator connects duplicity and commerce when he describes how Becky must lie to Amelia when they are reunited: 'When one fib becomes due as it were, you must forge another to take up the old acceptance; and so the stock of your lies in circulation inevitably multiplies, and the danger of detection increases every day.'[84] It is at this very point that the novel shifts away from its omniscience towards a re-told tale, the mode in which the narrator avoids telling us the sordid details of Becky's life. Given the commercial awareness of the novel, this statement, by implication, likens fiction to lying and, thus, through association with Becky, to theatrical performance. Like Becky, *Vanity Fair* is also 'eminent and successful as a practitioner in the art of giving pleasure'.[85]

The centrality of the actress to the novel, and the degree to which she both attracted and repulsed Thackeray, is evident in the novel that immediately followed *Vanity Fair*: *The History of Pendennis* (1848–50). Pearson argues that Thackeray 'brings into the domestic sphere of his readers that very threat to family morality represented by the public theatre, but demonstrates that the divide is only a social construction'.[86] While in *Vanity Fair* the actress Becky constantly crosses the line between the theatre and the home, the plot of *Pendennis* is driven by society's desire to enforce that line. The defining moment in the life of this Bildungsroman's protagonist, Arthur Pendennis, is his 'infatuation' and entanglement with his first love: a provincial actress known as The Fotheringay.[87] This is posed as a problem at the opening of the novel, and it is not until Pen is happily married to his adopted sister at the end of the novel, a match for which his mother had hoped from the start, that the theatrical energies of the novel are controlled. *The History of Pendennis* is, thus, essentially a history of attempting to move beyond the theatre.

Nicholas Dames has written about how in Thackeray 'celebrity is at once exalted and punctured', and the narrator's treatment of the Fotheringay both reveals how star-struck Arthur is and how baseless his admiration is.[88] No matter what the Fotheringay performs on stage – and she is described as performing with consistency of expression – her own existence remains prosaic:

> And after she had come out trembling with emotion before the audience, and looking so exhausted and tearful that you fancied she would faint with sensibility, she would gather her hair the instant she was behind the

curtain, and go home to a mutton chop and glass of brown stout; and the harrowing labours of the day over, she went to bed and snored as resolutely and as regularly as a porter.[89]

Nevertheless, in Arthur's eyes she becomes more than she is:

> Now the reader, who has had the benefit of overhearing the entire conversation which Pen had with Miss Fotheringay, can judge for himself about the powers of her mind, and may perhaps be disposed to think that she has not said anything astonishingly humorous or intellectual in the course of the above interview.
>
> But what did our Pen care? He saw a pair of bright eyes, and he believed in them – a beautiful image, and he fell down and worshipped it. He supplied the meaning which her words wanted; and created the divinity which he loved.[90]

The novel traces Arthur's heartache and gradual disillusionment with his first love, as he continues to cross paths with her. While the actress is not a suitable match for someone of Arthur's social station, even though his own origins have their roots in his father's success as an apothecary, she marries into the aristocracy and becomes Lady Mirabel. She thus emblematises a variety of challenges to class pretensions that the novel explores, most particularly in the Clavering family and in Major Pendennis being outclassed by his own valet.

Notably, Arthur's journey away from the theatre occurs in parallel with his establishing himself professionally and financially through becoming a writer. The theatre, in addition to related worldly corrupt influences that threaten Arthur's relationships with his family, remains a constant presence throughout the novel, which is full of theatrical metaphors, visits to the theatre, and references to dramas. In fact, a challenge to Arthur's progress from a theatrical infatuation to familial stability erupts roughly halfway through the novel. After revising the 'wet proof-sheet' of an article he had completed, he crosses the river for an evening of amusement at Vauxhall Gardens, where he meets the theatrical aspirant Fanny Bolton on the arm of the Fotheringay's father.[91] That this is a relapse for Arthur is realised metaphorically by the fact that his mother discovers his involvement with Fanny when she discovers Fanny nursing him during a critical illness.

In contrast, as Pen later attempts to settle into a relationship without illusions with Blanche Amory, he mockingly describes her as Morgiana from *The Forty Thieves*, but he proceeds to suggest that their relationship should be untheatrical:

To the necessary deceits and hypocrisies of our life, why add any that are useless and unnecessary? If I offer myself to you because I think we have a fair chance of being happy together, and because by your help I may get for both of us a good place and a not undistinguished name, why ask me to feign raptures and counterfeit romance, in which neither of us believe? Do you want me to come wooing in a Prince Prettyman's dress from the masquerade warehouse, and to pay you compliments like Sir Charles Grandison?'[92]

Among the characters that Arthur demurs to play, Prince Prettyman was a character from the Duke of Buckingham's comedy *The Rehearsal* (1672).[93] Blanche, however, also displays theatrical tendencies, and the novel and Arthur accordingly reject her en route to their final conclusion.

That the theatre remained in the background for Pen while he worked as a writer speaks to the position that the actress occupied in the lives, as well as imaginations, of many Victorian writers. In addition to playwrights such as Boucicault and Robertson, whose own work in the theatre either as actors or playwrights put them in the company of actresses who would become their wives, novelists such as Dickens and Reade had irresistible and troubling relationships with actresses. Dickens's relationship with Ellen Ternan was not only a secret extramarital affair that threatened the Dickens brand in the Victorian marketplace but was also deliberately long-suppressed in the scholarly world that perpetuated the Dickens legacy before becoming the subject of Claire Tomalin's aptly named dual biography, *The Invisible Woman*, which in turn became the basis for a 2013 feature film.[94] Reade, while obligated to remain celibate as a condition of his fellowship at Oxford, fell in love with the married actress Mrs Stirling, who would originate the role of Peg Woffington in his play of that name, and enjoyed a long-term and supportive relationship with the actress Laura Seymour, but he discontinued his relationship with his adopted daughter Katie, an actress, when she married an actor against his wishes.[95]

Vanity Fair and *The History of Pendennis* weave various threads regarding theatre and the actress that later plays and novels would rework, most notably: the relative abilities of plays and novels to establish authenticity, the actress's respectability and relationship to the domestic sphere and to social classes, and the ways in which women can command power. These are the subjects of the following chapters. Thackeray also depicted the actress as a challenge to the writer even as his novels played the powerful cultural role of helping to shape the actress. The following chapters trace how novelists and playwrights, responding to each other, continued to shape the actress and how the actress, both as a figure in plays and novels and as a playwright and novelist herself who spoke back to that cultural tradition, shaped these cultural forms.

Notes

1. Weltman, 'Theater, Exhibition, and Spectacle in the Nineteenth Century', p. 69; Kurnick, *Empty Houses*, p. 6; Pearson, *Victorian Writers and the Stage*, p. 20.
2. Dickens, *The Life and Adventures of Nicholas Nickleby*, p. 44.
3. Ibid. p. 360.
4. Ibid. p. 360.
5. Lewes, *On Actors and the Art of Acting*, p. 254.
6. Dickens, *The Life and Adventures of Nicholas Nickleby*, p. 385.
7. Ibid. p. 390.
8. For both an illustration of the Coburg's curtain and an account of melodrama's popularity, see Weltman, 'Theater, Exhibition, and Spectacle in the Nineteenth Century', pp. 75–8. The illustration of the curtain also appears on the cover of Jim Davis and Victor Emeljanow, *Reflecting the Audience*.
9. [Collins], 'Dramatic Grub Street: Explained in Two Letters', p. 266.
10. Ibid. p. 269. See, for example, George Rowell's classic chronicle, *The Victorian Theater 1792–1914* (1978).
11. [Collins], 'Dramatic Grub Street: Explained in Two Letters', p. 269.
12. Archer, 'The Free Stage and the New Drama', p. 666.
13. Archer, 'The Stage and Literature', p. 219; 'Why I Don't Write Plays', *Pall Mall Gazette*, 31 August 1892, p. 1.
14. Kurnick, *Empty Houses*, p. 8.
15. Victorian writers' disdain for the physicality of the theatre is consistent with Leah Price's claim that 'the Victorians cathected the text in proportion as they disowned the book' (*How to Do Things with Books in Victorian Britain*, p. 4).
16. Hardy, 'Why I Don't Write Plays', *Pall Mall Gazette*, 31 August 1892, p. 1.
17. Ouida, 'Why I Don't Write Plays', *Pall Mall Gazette*, 20 September 1892, p. 1; 'Lucas Malet' [Mary St Leger Kingsley], 'Why I Don't Write Plays', *Pall Mall Gazette*, 1 September 1892, p. 2.
18. Woods, 'Why I Don't Write Plays', *Pall Mall Gazette*, 2 September 1892, p. 2.
19. Hutcheon, *A Theory of Adaptation*, p. 5.
20. Altick, *The English Common Reader*, pp. 383–4.

21. William Archer and H. Granville Barker, *A National Theatre: Scheme and Estimates* (1904) (rev. edn, New York: Duffield, 1908), quoted in Tracy C. Davis, 'The Show Business Economy, and Its Discontents', pp. 39–40.
22. Gissing, 'Why I Don't Write Plays', *Pall Mall Gazette*, 10 September 1892, p. 3.
23. Brantlinger, *The Reading Lesson*.
24. Frederic, 'Why I Don't Write Plays', *Pall Mall Gazette*, 12 September 1892, p. 3.
25. Ibid. p. 3.
26. Ibid. p. 3.
27. Braddon, 'Why I Don't Write Plays', *Pall Mall Gazette*, 5 September 1892, p. 3.
28. Shorthouse, 'Why I Don't Write Plays', *Pall Mall Gazette*, 1 September 1892, p. 2.
29. Barish, *The Antitheatrical Prejudice*.
30. Diderot, *The Paradox of Acting*, p. 64.
31. Ibid. p. 68.
32. Important book-length works about the novel and theatricality include David Marshall, *The Figure of Theater: Shaftesbury, Defoe, Adam Smith, and George Eliot* (1986); Joseph Litvak, *Caught in the Act: Theatricality in the Nineteenth-Century English Novel* (1992); J. Jeffrey Franklin, *Serious Play: The Cultural Form of the Nineteenth-Century Realist Novel* (1999); and Emily Allen, *Theater Figures: The Production of the Nineteenth-Century British Novel* (2003). For an exploration of how the stage played an important role in novelists' self-definitions of their missions as writers see Renata Kobetts Miller, 'Imagined Audiences: The Victorian Novelist and the Stage'.
33. Franklin, *Serious Play*, pp. 81, 92.
34. Ibid. p. 108.
35. Ibid. p. 127.
36. Allen, *Theater Figures*, p. 12.
37. Ibid. p. 3.
38. Ibid. p. 19.
39. Ibid. p. 16.
40. Ibid. p. 17.
41. Newey, for example, argues that nineteenth-century women's theatre writing 'has the potential to disrupt the historiographical model of a smooth evolutionary development towards psychological realism and representational naturalism at the end of the nineteenth-century – that male-centred account of the British theater' (*Women's Theatre Writing in Victorian Britain*, p. 9).
42. Greiner, *Sympathetic Realism*, p. 21.
43. Ibid. p. 5.
44. Ibid. p. 16.

45. Brooks, *The Melodramatic Imagination*; Greiner, *Sympathetic Realism*, p. 8.
46. Levine, *The Realistic Imagination*, p. 22.
47. Ibid. pp. 6, 12.
48. Thackeray, *Vanity Fair*, p. 16.
49. According to Kurnick, 'Thackeray's work is shot through with an attachment to the publicity and social promiscuity for which the theater stands' (*Empty Houses*, p. 30).
50. Carlisle, *The Sense of an Audience*, p. 4.
51. Stewart, *Dear Reader: The Conscripted Audience in Nineteenth-Century British Fiction*.
52. Thackeray, *Vanity Fair*, p. 2.
53. Ibid. p. 179.
54. Ibid. p. 1.
55. Ibid. p. 27.
56. Ibid. pp. 516, 49.
57. Ibid. p. 128. See Sutherland's notes to *Vanity Fair*, p. 934.
58. Thackeray, *Vanity Fair*, p. 36.
59. See Sutherland's notes to *Vanity Fair*, p. 888.
60. Sutherland, Introduction to *Vanity Fair*, p. ix.
61. Levine describes 'the struggle inherent in any "realist" effort – the struggle to avoid the inevitable conventionality of language in pursuit of the unattainable unmediated reality. Realism, as a literary method, can in these terms be defined as a self-conscious effort, usually in the name of some moral enterprise of truth telling and extending the limits of human sympathy, to make literature appear to be describing not some other language but reality itself (whatever that may be taken to be); in this effort, the writer must self-contradictorily dismiss previous conventions of representation while, in effect, establishing new ones' (p. 8). The history of troubled stage adaptations of *Vanity Fair* that Robert A. Colby ('"Scenes of all Sorts": *Vanity Fair* on Stage and Screen') traces suggests that the novel's realism was distinctly different than stage representation, despite the novel's association of itself with drama.
62. Thackeray, *Vanity Fair*, p. 319.
63. Ibid. p. 16.
64. Ibid. pp. 27, 31.
65. Ibid. p. 31. See Sutherland's notes to *Vanity Fair*, p. 888.
66. Davis and Emeljanow, *Reflecting the Audience*, pp. 5–6.
67. Newey, *Women's Theatre Writing in Victorian Britain*, pp. 20–4. While Kurnick's analysis of how 'two key features of [Thackeray's] narrative technique' – 'the markedly melancholy attitude of the Thackerayan narrator, [and] his interest in the representation of interior experience' – 'emerge as records of a traumatized reaction to the felt contraction of the public sphere', I believe that reading *Vanity Fair* within the context of cultural arguments about the stage's commercialism calls attention to

Thackeray's own preoccupation with the commercial popularity of the stage as both appealing and problematic (*Empty Houses*, p. 31).
68. O'Farrell, *Telling Complexions*, p. 4.
69. Thackeray, *Vanity Fair*, p. 35.
70. Ibid. p. 43.
71. Ibid. p. 76.
72. Andrew H. Miller, '*Vanity Fair* through Plate Glass', p. 1050.
73. Thackeray, *Vanity Fair*, p. 521.
74. Ibid. p. 643.
75. Greiner, *Sympathetic Realism*, p. 27.
76. Thackeray, *Vanity Fair*, p. 677.
77. Barish, *The Antitheatrical Prejudice*, p. 310.
78. Thackeray, *Vanity Fair*, pp. 94–5.
79. Ibid. p. 95.
80. Ibid. p. 96.
81. See Andrew H. Miller, '*Vanity Fair* through Plate Glass', for Thackeray and Becky's shared mercenary interests.
82. Kurnick, *Empty Houses*, pp. 51, 42.
83. Thackeray, *Vanity Fair*, pp. 812–13.
84. Ibid. pp. 839–40.
85. Ibid. p. 856.
86. Pearson, *Victorian Writers and the Stage*, p. 106.
87. Thackeray, *The History of Pendennis*, p. 39.
88. Dames, 'Brushes with Fame', p. 42.
89. Thackeray, *The History of Pendennis*, p. 93.
90. Ibid. pp. 87–8.
91. Ibid. p. 489.
92. Ibid. p. 678.
93. Donald Hawes's notes to *The History of Pendennis*, p. 805.
94. Nisbet, *Dickens and Ellen Ternan*, and Tomalin, *The Invisible Woman*.
95. Burns, *Charles Reade*, p. 41; 'Reade's Niece a Pauper', *The New York Times*, 18 January 1914, p. 2.

Chapter 1

An Actress's Tears: Authenticity and the Reassertion of Social Class

[The actor's] talent depends not, as you think, upon feeling, but upon rendering so exactly the outward signs of feeling, that you fall into the trap. He has rehearsed to himself every note of his passion. He has learnt before a mirror every particle of his despair. He knows exactly when he must produce his handkerchief and shed tears; and you will see him weep at the word, at the syllable, he has chosen, not a second sooner or later. The broken voice, the half-uttered words, the stifled or prolonged notes of agony, the trembling limbs, the faintings, the bursts of fury – all this is pure mimicry, lessons carefully learned, the grimacing of sorrow, the magnificent aping which the actor remembers long after his first study of it, of which he was perfectly conscious when he first put it before the public, and which leaves him, luckily for the poet, the spectator, and himself, a full freedom of mind. Like other gymnastics, it taxes only his bodily strength. He puts off the sock or the buskin; his voice is gone; he is tired; he changes his dress, or he goes to bed; and he feels neither trouble, nor sorrow, nor depression, nor weariness of soul. All these emotions he has given to you. The actor is tired, you are unhappy; he has had exertion without feeling, you feeling without exertion. Were it otherwise the player's lot would be the most wretched on earth: but he is not the person he represents; he plays it, and plays it so well that you think he is the person; the deception is all on your side; he knows well enough that he is not the person.[1]

Diderot's characterisation, in *The Paradox of Acting*, of the actor's emotional detachment from his representations is notably different from modern method acting but is essential to Victorian concepts of acting and, more specifically, what the Victorians called 'mimicry'. Like Diderot's dialogue, which represents the anti-emotionalist stance about acting in conversation with an interlocutor who challenges that position, nineteenth-century writers were concerned about the simulation or dissimulation involved in acting, and theatre critics

George Henry Lewes, in his *On Actors and the Art of Acting* (1875) and William Archer, in *Masks or Faces? A Study in the Psychology of Acting* (1888), both explored questions of the 'sources of theatrical emotion', modifying and moderating the position of Diderot's speaker.[2] These non-fictional explorations of acting and feeling provide a context for how Victorian novelists and playwrights asserted the actress's authentic identity as they grappled with the mutable class identity that she enjoyed, both as a working woman and as a woman who could convincingly perform various class roles, thereby revealing class identities as performances.

In his collection of essays, Lewes's emphasis on training defines acting as both an art and a profession. Echoing Diderot's speaker, Lewes answers the question, 'how far does the actor feel the emotion he expresses?' by arguing that an actor must 'feign' because he 'would be unable to withstand the wear and tear of such emotion repeated night after night', and that 'the mere presence of genuine emotion would be such a disturbance of the intellectual equilibrium as entirely to frustrate artistic expression'.[3] According to Lewes, feeling in and of itself is not effective on the stage, rather: 'Passion in its *real*' must be transmuted into 'symbolical expression'.[4] To the extent that an actor feels, it must be controlled feeling:

> If the actor were really in a passion, his voice would be a scream, his gestures wild and disorderly; he would present a painful, not an aesthetic spectacle. . . . The rarity of fine acting depends on the difficulty there is in being at one and the same moment so deeply moved that the emotion shall spontaneously express itself in symbols universally intelligible, and yet so calm as the perfect master of effects, capable of modulating voice and moderating gesture when they tend to excess or ugliness.[5]

For Lewes, however, the best acting does require feeling, in that the actor sympathetically identifies with the character and manifests the feelings of that character in universally recognisable symbols.[6] In the best acting, the performance is not a direct expression of the actor's feelings, but rather a fusing of the actor with the part, as the actor in a sense becomes the part:

> When an actor feels a vivid sympathy with the passion or humour, he is representing, he *personates, i.e.* speaks through the *persona* or character; and for the moment *is* what he *represents*. He can do this only in proportion to the vividness of his sympathy, and the plasticity of his organisation, which enables him to give *expression* to what he feels; . . . But within the

limits which are assigned by nature to every artist, the success of the personation will depend upon the vividness of the actor's sympathy, and his honest reliance on the truth of his own individual expression in preference to the conventional expressions which may be accepted on the stage. This is the great actor, the creative artist. The conventional artist is one who either, because he does not feel the vivid sympathy, or cannot express what he feels, or has not sufficient energy of self-reliance to trust frankly to his own expressions, cannot *be* the part, but tries to *act* it, and is thus necessarily driven to adopt those conventional means for expression with which the traditions of the stage abound. Instead of allowing a strong feeling to express itself through its natural signs, he seizes upon the conventional signs, either because in truth there is no strong feeling moving him, or because he is not artist enough to give it genuine expression.[7]

The great actor does not express his own emotions, but sympathetically experiences the emotions of the character that he plays. As a result, rather than communicating feeling through formulaic symbols, he naturally expresses the feelings of the character in a widely cognisable performance.

Following on Lewes's argument about actors balancing emotion and control, thirteen years later Archer explicitly criticised both the evidence and experience of Diderot, and sought to explore further the extent to which actors feel. Archer states that, in contrast to Diderot, he has faith in the 'sincerity' and 'intelligence' of actors.[8] According to Archer, 'The real paradox of acting... resolves itself into the paradox of dual consciousness': being able to experience emotion while simultaneously remaining master of effects.[9] Archer's methodology includes both interviews with actors and observations, in which he takes 'tear, blush, or tremor' as signs of true feeling, emphasising that because actors are unable to produce such effects of emotion 'in cold blood', they must use recollected feeling. He points out that this and the replicatability that Diderot sees as essential to successful performance are not mutually exclusive: 'absolute preregulation of even the minutest gestures is quite consistent with genuine feeling – that is, with the presence in the actor's own organism of the physical symptoms of the emotion he is trying to express'.[10] Archer suggests that 'mimetic emotion', the reproducing of one's own personal 'external manifestations of... feeling', differs only in degree from experiencing personal feeling on stage, and that recollected feeling cannot be employed 'in cold blood'.[11] Like Lewes, Archer believes in the importance of external signs: 'the use of inward emotion is to reinforce, not to supplant, outward expressions. No one has ever doubted that the actor must be able to express what he feels, or feeling will avail him nothing.'[12] Archer aligns himself with the 'emotionalists', rather than the 'anti-emotionalists', writing: 'the more we look into the matter, the less are we inclined to believe that even the greatest virtuoso of mechanical mimicry can attain to the subtle and absolute truth of imitation which is possible to the actor who combines artistically controlled sensibility with perfect physical means of expression'.[13] It is 'imaginative sympathy' that allows the actor to accomplish the 'muscular and vascular' changes required to muster 'blushing and pallor' on stage.[14] Rae Greiner uses the same term, 'imaginative sympathy', as theorised by Adam Smith, to denote not the transmission of feeling but, rather, an intellectual effort of bridging the distance between individuals that is at the core of Victorian realism. In harmony with Lewes and Archer, Greiner explains that for Smith, an excess of emotion interferes with sympathy.[15] The idea of dual consciousness on the stage further reveals that for the Victorians feeling and thinking were not easily disambiguated.[16] Even as Archer's view of acting echoes the sympathetic imagination associated with realism, he and other Victorians who worked in the theatre relied on what Carolyn Williams characterises as the conventions of melodrama's 'semiotic convention of physiognomic legibility', and its 'sentimentalism . . . , with its strong association of feeling and virtue' in order to assert authenticity.[17]

Henry Irving's preface to the 1883 English translation of Diderot's *The Paradox of Acting* further evinces a desire to reclaim the actor from the accusation of being a mimic who did not experience authentic feeling. Irving, who would become the first actor to be knighted, uses Diderot's ideas as the basis for a definition of craft:

> Perhaps it will always be an open question how far sensibility and art can be fused in the same mind. Every actor has his secret. . . . It is often said that actors should not shed tears, that real tears are bad art. This is not so. If tears be produced at the actor's will and under his control, they are true art; and happy is the actor who numbers them amongst his gifts. The exaltation of sensibility in art may be difficult to define, but it is none the less real to all who have felt its power.[18]

Irving's view of craft incorporates 'sensibility'. This definition functions to defend actors as respectable professionals, as Irving particularly parries Diderot's representation of how the actor's lack of authentic feeling leads to a lack of social connection and, by extension, a lack of clearly delineated social class rank:

> Diderot had the highest opinion of acting as an art. The great actor, he said, was even a more remarkable being than the great poet. Yet the great actor was in some respects a worthless creature, without character or even individuality, and wholly lacking in moral sense. The actors of Diderot's day were not only devoid of sensibility on the stage; they had

not a particle of sentiment in private life. They were often seen to laugh, never to weep. They were 'isolated, vagabonds, at the command of the great', and had 'little conduct, no friends, scarce any of those holy and tender ties which associate us in the pains and pleasures of another, who in turn shares our own'.[19]

Irving suggests that, while this characterisation might have been true 'in Diderot's time', 'nobody will pretend that it is true now. The stage in Diderot's time did not enjoy that social esteem which makes public spirit and private independence. Actors were the hangers-on of the Court; actresses were, in too many cases, worse than hangers-on.'[20] In his argument for the theatre's improved stature, which he presents as a *fait accompli* rather than something for which he was actively fighting, Irving's association of feeling, private life, and social connectedness illuminates the importance that writers placed on locating the actress's authentic identity and on the significance of the actress's tears – which he and Archer saw as indices of emotional experience – in order to establish her authenticity and, in turn, her social position. But while Irving, writing late in the century, sought to anchor the shiftless actor to a stable and respectable class identity, earlier Victorian novelists and playwrights used the actress as the focus of nuanced views of class mobility and, in representing the actress's social adaptability, writers sought to establish a source of authentic identity. As Lynn M. Voskuil has argued, for the Victorians 'theatricality and authenticity often functioned dynamically together to construct the dynamic typologies by which the English knew themselves'.[21] Although later works would employ the actress in order to challenge class hierarchies, this chapter examines how a series of works that cluster around the 1850s evince anxiety about shifting structures of social class and the actress's challenge to class identities. Accordingly, they use expressions of emotional authenticity to ground the actress in a social position, establishing her identity in ways that neutralise her threat to the established social order.

Responding to Diderot's argument that the 'great actor ... must have ... penetration and no sensibility; the art of mimicking everything, or, which comes to the same thing, the same aptitude for every sort of character and part', Irving stated, 'The obvious answer to this is, that an actor's aptitude, however great may be his versatility, must have limits. He cannot, any more than another man, be born without a temperament.'[22] Melodramatic conventions of strong feeling, sentimentalism and the reliability with which physical symptoms express inner feelings were critical to the assertion of the actress's authentic temperament, and the works of the prolific Victorian melodramatist Dion Boucicault are foundational texts in this regard. While Edward Lancaster's brief interlude 'The Manager's Daughter', produced at the Haymarket in 1837 and later adapted by Boucicault in the 1850s into 'The Young Actress', thematises the actress as a protean mimic at the same time that it emphasises the increasing fluidity of social classes, plays from the 1840s and 1850s by Boucicault – *Peg Woffington* (1845) and *The Prima Donna* (1852) – curb the actress's ability to undermine class structures as they anchor her to an authentic identity. Tom Taylor and Charles Reade revisited Boucicault's *Peg Woffington* in their co-authored play *Masks and Faces* (1852) and in Reade's subsequent novelisation of the same story *Peg Woffington* (1853), working more aggressively with the themes of her class status and with the melodramatic convention of the legibility of physical symptoms in order to reclaim Peg from her changeability and prevent her from disrupting class hierarchies. A comparison of the play and its novelisation reveals challenges that the stage poses to establishing authenticity for the actress, and the ways in which the novel, even while differentiating itself from the drama, nevertheless also relied on melodramatic conventions for reclaiming the actress from mimicry by claiming her authenticity.

Mimicry and Social Class in Lancaster's 'The Manager's Daughter' and Boucicault's 'The Young Actress'

With a protean mimic as its eponymous heroine, Edward Lancaster's 'The Manager's Daughter' was first performed in Richmond in 1836 and licensed for performance at the Theatre Royal Haymarket in 1837.[23] Margaret is driven to perform because she hopes that her theatre-manager parents can avoid financial ruin when their company, holding out for higher salaries, refuses to perform. The play is thus premised on a labour action, a hallmark of industrial society, that suggests the transitional moment with regard to social class structures in which the action of the play is set. While Elaine Hadley characterises how melodrama often evinced nostalgia for 'status hierarchies and their patronage economies', Carolyn Williams provides a somewhat different perspective on melodrama's handling of social organisation:

> Melodrama is devoted to the expansion of democracy, as well as to the exploration and construction of modern forms of social organization like class, gender, nationality, ethnicity, and race. Like the novel, melodrama helps to mediate the transition from a society based on inherited status to one based on social class.[24]

Such mediation includes 'highlight[ing] the suffering attendant upon an emerging new social order'.[25] Although Lancaster's interlude does not have the plot structure of a melodrama, it nevertheless thematises a particular historical moment of shifting societal structures, providing a useful backdrop against which we can understand other melodramas of the time.

The actors in the plot of this play seek higher salaries because they are performing in Lord Loftus's 'bespeak', a benefit performance that will raise funds for the manager himself, who has sustained great losses. The manager worries that if they 'disappoint Lord Loftus [they] shall forfeit his patronage for ever'.[26] Nevertheless, the manager is also concerned about his obligations to a broader audience – one that undoubtedly reflects greater diversity in social class and the greater class fluidity, at least in theory, of industrial society. Unlike the anxiety and contempt for audience taste that we saw among novelists explored in the introduction of this book, the theatre manager is respectful towards his audience. He rejects his daughter's offer to recruit her schoolfellows as amateur replacements by saying, 'I should not dare to bring anything but genuine and well tried talent before the Public. It is a manager's duty when he is paid by his audience to let them have full face value for their money.'[27] His distress at the prospect of 'disappoint[ing] half the town' speaks more to the modern urban theatre manager's concerns about his audience than to a manager's desire to please a landed patron.[28] And indeed, at the play's end, Margaret's use of a traditional, poetic appeal in a pair of couplets that asks for the audience's applause serves to reflexively emphasise that the play has thematised its own concerns about the need to appeal to a popular audience.[29] In fact, while the manager valorises this need as an obligation and duty, his striking players are represented as misguided and mean-spirited in their focus not on the townspeople but instead on their elitist demand to be 'paid double salaries' in order to perform 'before Noblemen'.[30]

Within this context, Margaret role-plays various different identities, as she pretends to be an array of her school friends with talents at the ready to replace the striking actors in order to dupe and intimidate them into relinquishing their demands. This draws a connection between the class structures of the industrial nineteenth century that are so central to understanding the Victorian theatre in the context of its detractors' complaints that it was driven by its need to appeal to mass, heterogeneous, urban audiences, and the idea that identities can be convincingly performed. Disguising herself as an American boy actor from Connecticut, a northern English actress, an Irishman, and a French orphan who melodramatically describes a blood-drenched experience of the Revolution that claimed the lives of his parents, she claims and demonstrates various talents, including dancing and singing in the character of each of her impersonations. In her final role as an upper-class young woman who herself mimics other classmates' performances, she asserts that she can play 'anything from a girl of 15 to an old woman of Fifty', and then proceeds to don a costume to demonstrate how she can play an older woman in a way that passes for nature.[31] The danger that this gestures towards is that in a world of less rigid social classes, one's identity can be founded on, or lost among, performances.

The play responds to this danger by providing Margaret with a grounding in genuine feeling. Her acting is motivated by her genuine feelings for – actually her desire to feel along with – her parents. Seeing her parents' sadness is not enough to elicit a similar sensation in Margaret; Margaret appeals to her parents to give her the information that will allow her to feel with them, evincing Greiner's intellectually based concept of sympathy. When Margaret asks her mother, 'Do tell me what's the matter if only that I may cry with you', she explains: 'You and Papa are always so happy that I am joyful that when I see you grieved I almost think it a duty to be sad too.'[32] That she achieves this through a process of intellectual understanding does not make it the less authentic. Rather, it asserts her authentic identity through her connection to her family even as she plays different roles. This point was underscored by the fact that the play was performed by ten-year-old child prodigy Jean Margaret Davenport, for whom the play was written, and her parents.[33]

That the play itself is designed to underscore the virtuosity and versatility of actresses to play a wide range of roles is evinced by the fact that it was adapted by Dion Boucicault into a new play, 'The Young Actress', for his wife, Agnes Robertson. Robertson appeared in 'The Young Actress' in Montreal in 1853 and in New York, before it was staged at London's Adelphi Theatre in 1860.[34] This version made large-scale changes to diction, such as the inclusion of the terminology: 'they have struck'.[35] The freshness of this word in labour politics is underscored by his wife's misapprehension that he means he has been physically assaulted. Significantly, while the performance remains a benefit for the actor, and the house is sold out, there is no mention of an aristocratic patron. Thus, the text of the play licensed for London performance twenty-three years after Lancaster's version underscores the shifting class structures of the mid-nineteenth century.

As the main character, now called Maria, mimics a different array of characters and nationalities, the play also reflects a pointed argument for training, rather than simply performing one's own identity. The professional actors challenge the manager, who would hire the alternative company of actors – from Yorkshire, Germany, and Ireland – who play their own nationalities, dancing and singing national songs. They challenge the 'ability' of their replacements, and ask: 'You call that art? Why, anybody could do that!'[36] In fact, however, Maria is playing them all. As she mimics a Yorkshire actress with a strong accent who complains about being typecast in lower-class roles only, she herself demonstrates that acting allows one to pass for other identities.[37] 'The Young Actress' thus continues to define the problem of the instability of identity in a society in which class identity can be performed.

Anchoring the Actress: Boucicault's *Peg Woffington* and *The Prima Donna*

Boucicault's *Peg Woffington: Or The State Secret*, a two-act comedy first produced at the Adelphi Theatre on 24 June 1845, is a play that counteracts the actress's performative powers.[38] Although she can make or break men's stations and although she herself has risen from poverty, Peg remains a social outsider despite her wealth, as she trades on her perceived sexual availability and tenuous social standing. A review of the play in the *Illustrated London News* emphasises the biographical Peg, who lived from 1720 to 1760, as being a consummate performer. She 'never permitted her love of pleasure to occasion the least defect in her duty to the public as a performer; and she was famous for playing any part, however humble, that best suited the interest of her manager'.[39] Yet her ability to perform successfully, even regardless of her own physical condition, was motivated by a good heart: 'She was often on the stage when she ought to have been in bed from real illness; and she never refused playing [benefits] for the lowest performer in the theatre.'[40] Thus, the review suggests that she remains psychologically connected to her humble origins, maintaining her own authentic identity despite moving in prestigious social circles: 'Courted and caressed by all ranks and degrees, she always remained the same gay, affable, obliging, good-tempered "Woffington" to every one around her.'[41] The review remains further grounded in the authentic identity of the actress, in contrast to her performances or how she is depicted in works of art, when it concludes by directing readers to read more about the biographical Peg Woffington. In fact, *The Era* panned the play precisely because it was based on a fictional incident rather than on one drawn from the life of Peg Woffington.[42]

Peg's stratospheric rise from poverty precedes her own appearance on stage in Boucicault's play when her fellow actor Merestick explains the narrative of her career: 'Five years ago, a poor, ragged little girl offered herself to this theatre to do everything for fifteen shillings a week. Her misery won my good nature, and I got her an engagement. That little girl, as the celebrated Miss Woffington, now gets fifty pounds a week!'[43] Not only does Peg embody the actress's ability to rise in socio-economic status, but she is also able to effect such change for others, as Merestick indicates: 'When she first came here, I was only a back figurant at eighteen shillings a week, and found my own pumps, calves, and tights. However, as she went up she pulled me along with her, and I now get a solo every night.'[44] Merestick is the most humble of her handful of male admirers: she is desired by a banker's heir, a Dutch ambassador and a French marquis. While Merestick credits her for elevating her station, the banker's son, George Tarleton, attributes his ruin to his obsession with her. Yet Peg herself, as she is being made up with cosmetics, a conceit for artifice that would be exploited more fully in Reade and Taylor's depiction of Peg Woffington, notes how despite her 'prudence' and 'virtue', as an actress her respectability is at the mercy of the world's gossip, and as she is pursued by her various suitors she is preoccupied with maintaining her 'reputation'.[45]

Peg is recruited by the premier's wife to play the role of international diplomat, 'empowered to ratify a treaty of commerce between France and England'.[46] She undertakes to do so with a speech about the premier's goodness:

> For he is as good as he is great. On a bleak winter's day, some nine years hence, a poor girl without a home or a hearth to shelter her, fatherless and motherless crying for very want of food – her heart too proud to beg – was observed by your husband, lady. 'This is real want', said he, and, giving me a purse, bade me be of better cheer and use it honestly. The child could not speak, but falling on her knees held up a grateful prayer for her benefactor's weal. That timely aid saved her from endless misery.[47]

That the premier's wife asks Peg how she knows the story and Peg explains that she was the young girl, simultaneously emphasises both Peg's distant social remove from her class origins and her rootlessness in orphanhood, and her emotional connection to those humble origins. Rise as meteorically as she has, and perform her new status as effectively as she does, she does not escape her past.

At the same time, Peg begins to discover that she has a heart, saying about George Tarleton, the banker's son: 'And he has sacrificed his fortune, prospects, hopes – all – all for me, and I can restore him nothing. For me, I never felt I was loved before. Loved! I wonder what loving is like. Is it what I begin to feel here – *(touches her heart)* – for him?'[48] Peg resolves that she is able to influence men's stations in life: 'Stay! Yes, I see how I can restore to him his forfeited position. I can make him the State creditor – '.[49] Notably, while her suitor Stulph, the Dutch ambassador, sees Peg only as a sexual object, she is actually his diplomatic rival, charged with seeing the Marquis de Mousseux in Paris before he does. She conducts state business under the guise of sexual assignations, and Sheila Stowell describes the 'continual assumption of different roles during Act 2'.[50] Yet even as she succeeds in elevating George to British Chargé d'Affaires and a baronet, she herself remains an outsider, telling George: 'Forgive me, George, if I have deceived you; but, you see, my intention was to serve you. You have regained the station you lost for my sake, forget me in its grandeur.'[51] Still sexually propositioned by the various men, she evades them in the end, ultimately concluding the play by turning to the audience and telling them, for the author's 'sake', that they 'are at liberty to make an assignation at seven every evening with Peg Woffington'.[52]

Boucicault further developed the figure of the orphan actress whose lack of family origins is both a concrete and symbolic instantiation of the actress's lack of fixed social position in *The Prima Donna*, which was first performed at the Royal Princess's Theatre on 18 September 1852. The background to the casting of its title role, which Boucicault himself describes briefly in his prefatory note to the published text of the play, but which is more fully described in other accounts, is itself the stuff of dramatic legend. Walking with a colleague through Soho, Boucicault happened upon an amateur performance of stolid mediocrity with the exception of the performance of a very talented fifteen-year-old, Caroline Heath. The next day he brought her to see Charles Kean, the manager at the Princess's Theatre, and six months later she debuted there in the lead role in *The Prima Donna*, and despite her youth she succeeded in personating the role of '"a matured woman, proud of her position."'[53] Biographer Richard Fawkes describes how Boucicault wrote the play, with its plot about two sisters, expressly for his secret lover and eventual wife, Agnes Robertson, the ward of Kean until Kean's discovery of her affair with Boucicault led to her departure from Kean's theatre and home and to her moving in with Boucicault.[54] In 1853, the play served as a vehicle for Robertson's North American fame. After being tremendously successful in 'The Young Actress' in Montreal on 19 September 1853, she played *The Prima Donna* the following night to critical acclaim and commercial success.[55] 'New York fell at her feet' when she played in it on 22 October, and Fawkes's description of Agnes's great success in America and Boucicault's work to write for her and manage her tour suggests that she was an important contributor to her husband's success as a playwright. In fact, Boucicault did not announce Agnes as his wife until four months after they had become married by common-law conventions in the state of New York, because he believed that she would be 'a much bigger draw at the box office if she appeared as a Miss rather than a Mrs'.[56]

That mature woman played by Heath was Stella, the prima donna of the title, who at the play's opening has been pursued by Rouble, a court jeweler and banker, from Milan to her father's home in Switzerland. Stella greets him with a reflection on the actress's position outside of respectable society, claiming her family home as a refuge: 'I can guess your errand. I am an actress – as such, I know I am defenceless, and the offer you would blush to make to another woman you deem an honour to me; but I appeal to your generosity – this is my father's house – my home.'[57] Nevertheless, Stella turns down Rouble's proposal because of her own lack of class standing: she is 'an orphan – a foundling, without name'.[58] Rouble's response that she will obtain a family and a class identity ready-made upon marrying him – 'When you marry my fortune, you will find your relations forthwith' – emphasises the malleability of Stella's class identity, and how class identity goes hand in hand with family relations.[59] Rouble's view, however, that family will accompany his fortune is a reversal of the financial structures of the landed aristocracy, whereby fortune is derived from family inheritances. It thus situates the action of the play in social class structures that are more changeable, even as family remains a touchstone of stability.

Stella herself was taken in and adopted as a child by Holbein and raised with his biological daughter, Margaret. She describes how she became a performer in order to support and preserve her adopted family: 'My benefactor was a physician; but the income he derived from his patients he spent in medicines for the poor – he was verging on ruin – my voice; hitherto valued only as a solace to my father, I reflected that it might save us.'[60] Stella remains emotionally connected to her adopted family: she has returned to ask her only relatives for permission to marry the man she loves, Count Eric Mansfeldt. Moreover, she is visibly moved to see how Holbein has aged, and she is terrified to learn that her sister Margaret is gravely ill. A month after her return from a trip to Como with a rich English patient, Margaret was healthy 'but changed', 'yielding slowly to some fearful invisible malady – without pain, with a smile always on her livid lip'.[61] Stella is so staunchly loyal to her adopted family that when Eric arrives, she tells him they cannot speak of their engagement because of her sister's illness, even though Eric declares that 'delay is ruin' because he is a fugitive, having escaped from being imprisoned by his father, an Austrian minister who sought to prevent his son's marriage to a woman of the stage.[62] Regardless of her success and fame, Stella's profession renders her unacceptable to the aristocracy. Stella's background, meanwhile, grounds her emotionally, providing the actress with a source of authentic feeling. Eric tells her he won't interfere in her 'sorrows' because he 'prize[s] every gentle impulse of that heart too much'.[63] Her connection to her past is also a source of goodness. Later in the play she gives a benefit concert for foundlings, because, 'a foundling myself, I feel as if such unfortunates are my only relatives'.[64]

The plot hinges on melodramatic extremes and coincidence. Margaret reveals to Stella that she was saved from a burning hotel in Como by an Austrian officer: 'I was roused from sleep by a dreadful sensation of oppression, the room was filled with a dense smoke – confused cries, mingled with the roar of flame, bewildered my senses. I flew to the window and shrieked for help.'[65] Her 'senses fled', and she woke in the arms of the Austrian officer who rescued her.[66] That the fire functions as a symbolic sexual encounter is apparent in her description: 'My first sensation was one of shame – so burning, so bitter, that I almost hated him.'[67] Over time, even though she had not seen him since the day after the fire, her hate turned to obsessive love. Just as she utters that she irrationally expects to see him again, Eric enters the room and Margaret identifies him as her Austrian officer.

Holbein advises Stella to 'Nurse her delusion', and Stella uses her acting in order to do so.[68] When Margaret has snatched the letter that Eric was writing to his father seeking forgiveness for himself and Stella, Stella says, 'Heaven inspire me' and improvises a false text that she pretends to read to Margaret.[69] The stage direction emphasises that the actress playing Stella must perform in such a way that reveals Stella's behaviour as performance. She '*appears to peruse the letter, but by her manner intimating that she is inventing what she pretends to read*'.[70] After we learn that Eric did indeed save Margaret,

Stella, thinking that she is bringing joy to her sister's 'last hours' of life, compels Eric to declare that he is there to ask for Margaret's hand in marriage.[71]

Just as the power of Rouble's wealth suggests that performance of social status can make social position rather than social position being based on family background, the plot of the play underscores that performance can become reality, as Lewes suggested when he described the actor becoming fused with the part he is playing. As Eric and Margaret's wedding date nears, Eric rejects Stella's language for a letter of revelation to Margaret, and he sets about to write his own. When Margaret reads his letter aloud, which begins by attesting to the 'sincerity of [his] passion' and when Stella walks in on Eric kissing Margaret passionately, Stella begins to realise that Eric's feigned passion has become sincere.[72] When a letter arrives from Eric's father granting Eric permission to marry Margaret, because the request was tendered by Rouble, whose assistance with a loan is required by Austria's royalty, Eric's father reiterates his view of the actress's disreputable social status, explaining that he accepts the marriage to Margaret because he is only 'too thankful to have escaped the alliance with an actress that lately threatened our family'.[73] Although Eric asserts that 'The insult contained in that letter makes [his] former vows [to Stella] more sacred – more inviolate', Stella, indignant about the insult, tells him to marry Margaret.[74] She says that she hopes Eric's performance will become actual love, that 'this feeling which is now but a pretense – might become a – a – reality', her stammer revealing that as she speaks, she perceives that this has already occurred.[75]

The play reflects a fear that performance can overtake reality, but it balances that possibility by asserting that the actress possesses genuine feeling. The actress is connected to her roots, which serve as a source of authentic feeling for her. Stella gives up Eric because of her love for Margaret: 'And do you think I would owe my happiness to her death, to your pity, and so deserve your father's curse, and – worse than all – my own contempt? You know me better, Eric! No, no!'[76] Given that Stella was an orphan, the threat posed by the actress's theatricality is neutralised through a paradox. Stella has authentic feelings of gratitude paradoxically rooted in her own rootless past, and those feelings prevent her from assuming a social rank among respectable classes. Stella concludes by marrying Rouble and recommitting herself to her profession: 'I will devote to it my whole time and passion', thereby remaining an outsider to respectable society.[77]

Peg Woffington and the Iconography of Authenticity

Charles Reade revisited the character of Peg Woffington in his play *Masks and Faces* (1852), written with Tom Taylor, and then again in his novel *Peg Woffington* (1853). In performance, there was an inter-theatrical relationship between Taylor and Reade's *Masks and Faces* and Boucicault's *Peg Woffington*, because the Dick's Standard Plays edition of the latter suggests that costumes may be used from *Masks and Faces*, which Dick's also published. But Reade and Taylor's play overlaps with other elements of the Boucicault dramas that this chapter has examined, as it more fully and coherently represents the actress's performance and ability to mimic as a threat to social class identities while at the same time countering this threat by establishing the actress's authenticity and position as an outsider. In fact, it is precisely because Peg, in Taylor and Reade's play, cannot convincingly display a genuine, unperformed self, that Reade felt compelled to revisit her story in his novel. In a letter to the *Athenaeum*, responding to a review that questioned the degree of collaboration between Reade and Taylor in writing the play, Reade explains:

> 'Peg Woffington' [the novel] was written for three reasons: – First, I was unwilling to lose altogether some matter which we had condemned as unfit for our dramatic purpose; secondly, the exigencies of the stage had, in my opinion, somewhat disturbed the natural current of our story; thirdly, it is my fate to love this dead heroine, and I wished to make her known in literature, and to persons who do not frequent the theatres.[78]

Many sources credit the actress Laura Seymour, who would later become Reade's life partner, with having directed Reade to adapt his play into a novel and to ask Tom Taylor to lend his name to the endeavour. Reade's letter, however, suggests that Peg's story, as he relates it in his novel, could not be told in a play, and also notes that the novel and the theatre attracted different audiences.

Charles Reade and Tom Taylor's pair of accounts of Peg Woffington struggle to position her outside the genteel social classes that she mimics and to dispel the threat of her ability to pass for a lady. They ultimately make her perform a drama that neutralises her own subversive influence in a genteel marriage and establishes an authentic, class-based identity for her. In both the novel and the play, Peg is pursued by the rival suitors Sir Charles Pomander and Ernest Vane. While enjoying the attentions of Vane, who thinks she is better than the theatrical world in which she lives, Peg financially aids the poet, painter and actor James

Triplet, whom she knew when she was a child selling oranges in the streets of Dublin. When Vane's wife Mabel, who has remained in the country while her husband transacts business in London and of whom Peg is ignorant, surprises her husband by arriving in London, it is the comic character Triplet who brings the plot to a crisis by revealing Peg's affair with Vane to Mabel. The slighted Sir Charles Pomander, meanwhile, seeks to revenge himself against Ernest Vane by seducing Mabel. In the end, Peg, driven by the same generosity that impels her charity to the Triplet family, disguises herself as Mabel Vane in order to mend the marital rift that she herself has unwittingly caused.

In both the novel and the play, Peg's protean ability to alter her identity is thematised by Triplet's painting of her. In a pivotal scene, Peg inserts her own face into the painting in place of Triplet's depiction, which she has cut out of the canvas. Several observers are unable to perceive the 'real' Peg because, as she says in the play, 'I am painted as well as my picture'.[79] Archer cites the actress Helen Faucit's criticism of the overuse of cosmetics on the stage for creating 'a painted mask' that conceals natural blushes: '"Whence proceeds the deadness of a too much made-up face, if not from the suppression of the natural play of colour?"'[80] Faucit's comment participates in a Victorian system of iconography that aligns, on the one hand, make-up with artifice and death and, on the other hand, the blush or the tear with genuineness and life.[81] Archer identifies tears in performance as likely to be produced by genuine feeling, but sets the blush apart as a '[symptom] of emotion which [is] utterly beyond the control of the will, and cannot possibly be simulated'.[82] As Archer's interrogation into the degree to which actors experience emotion on stage indicates, acting stands in the centre of this network of concepts. The cultural significance and interrelations of these concepts in the Victorian era, therefore, helped to shape the representation of the actress and are critical to understanding how Reade's novel, in particular, reclaims Peg.

'Making up the face for the stage' was an 'essential part of a performer's duty', and 'to ladies it [was] of the utmost importance', according to 1868 additions made to an 1827 guide to pursuing a stage career.[83] This was particularly a development of the nineteenth century, because the technology of gas lighting had made 'more powerful coloring than that formerly used, decidedly necessary'.[84] To a Victorian audience make-up would not only have been emblematic of the actress's profession but suggestive of prostitution as well. Cosmetics, the actress and prostitution had been connected with each other more than one hundred years earlier in Jonathan Swift's poem 'A Beautiful Young Nymph Going to Bed' (1731), in which the prostitute disassembling the elaborate mechanisms that make her artificially beautiful is associated with the Drury Lane and Covent Garden theatres and, while she sleeps, leaves her false eyebrows in 'a play-book'.[85] Michael Baker explains that although Victorian actresses, in contrast to their Restoration counterparts, did not wear cosmetics outside of the theatre in order to avoid being considered prostitutes, women who used cosmetics were nevertheless 'readily categorised as actresses in tones of disparagement which reflected the traditional association made with prostitutes'.[86]

Mary Elizabeth Braddon used make-up in order to emphasise that the title character in her novel *Lady Audley's Secret* (1861–2), although not a professional actress, is a deceptive woman acting a part. Moreover, the ambiguity in her description of Lady Audley's appearance underscores the observer's (and the reader's) inability to determine what is real and what is artificial. Lady Audley's 'pencilled eyebrows' could mean either that her eyebrows are pencilled or that they are naturally so precise that they are like pencilled eyebrows.[87] Similarly, Lady Audley's comment to her maid Phoebe, 'with a bottle of hair dye, such as we see advertised in the papers, and a pot of rouge, you'd be as good-looking as I any day', hints that the difference in colour between the two women may be induced by Lady Audley's own use of cosmetics.[88] Although the artificial effect of cosmetics may not always be distinguishable from 'nature', cosmetics nevertheless stand for mimicry as opposed to authenticity and in this way function as the opposite of the blush. Robert Audley muses on the differences between actresses of the past and the present by describing the blushes of the early nineteenth-century actress Eliza O'Neill. In addition to her fame for blushing, O'Neill appears in Archer's essays as 'that living embodiment of womanly pathos' who had a talent for shedding tears without distorting the aesthetic effect of her facial expressions.[89] Robert suggests that the ability to perform a blush lends the actress a degree of authenticity, as the blush suggests the actress feels her role: 'I think our modern O'Neils [sic] scarcely feel their stage wrongs so keenly; or, perhaps, those brightly indignant blushes of to-day struggle ineffectually against the new art of Madame Rachel, and are lost to the public beneath the lily purity of priceless enamel.'[90] 'Madame Rachel' refers to Mrs Rachel Levison, a New Bond Street purveyor of beauty products who is referred to by name elsewhere in the novel.[91] Along these lines, the actress Eleonora Duse was known for her naturalness in acting, her lack of cosmetics, and her famous ability to blush on stage.[92] Conversely, Max Beerbohm, in his 1896 'The Pervasion of Rouge', points out that although actresses do not require cosmetics in order to achieve artifice, Miss Cissie Loftus, who was famed for cosmetic-free stage appearances, is nevertheless artificial because she does not blush.[93]

Cosmetics were not only associated with artifice, but also with sculpture. In her analysis of actresses and sculpture, Gail Marshall argues that

> for the Victorians, sculpture is a way of achieving, rather than simply commemorating, the association of timeless ideals with women. The timelessness, the material persistence of sculpture ... absorbs the contradictions between eternal ideals and temporal female forms, whilst absorbing also the life and autonomy of the female model or celebrated woman.[94]

The stasis of sculpture, in Marshall's analysis, has a deadening effect on women. It was precisely this statue-like nature that often attracted admiration for the actress and her cosmetics. Charles Baudelaire argued in his 1863 essay 'In Praise of Make-Up' that cosmetics 'create an abstract unity of texture and colour in the skin, which unity, like the one produced by tights, immediately approximates the human being to a statue, in other words to a divine or superior being'.[95] Unlike the blush, which is assumed to be the external expression of internal feeling, the actress as a statue leads to the complete disassociation of superficial appearance and internal emotional life. Echoing Swift, Beerbohm points out that, because there is little relation between the made-up face and the natural face beneath, the widespread use of cosmetics will destroy the ability to read appearances. While Beerbohm's ideal art would be like made-up women, about whom he says: 'beautiful and without meaning are their faces', the lack of meaning in an actress's appearance also made her a central figure for authors of realism who, according to George Levine, 'recognizing the difference between truth and the appearance of truth, did try to embrace the reality that stretched beyond the reach of language'.[96] As a corollary to his aesthetic perspective, Beerbohm argues that drama, as 'the presentiment of the soul in action', should not rely on spectacle but on the voice: visual beauty should be reserved for pure aesthetic value and not used as a mode of signifying.[97] One strategy of realism was to separate voice from spectacle. As I demonstrate in Chapter 4, George Eliot, who sought to claim performing as a source of power for women despite their objectification as things to be looked at, located power – and authenticity – in the female performer's vocal talent. Thus, for both realists and aesthetes, visual appearance is treated with scepticism, while sound is taken as a reliable signifier.

Discourse about cosmetics themselves emphasises the importance of realising the difference between art and living organisms. Chemist John Scoffern, in a series of articles written for *Belgravia*, argued that the skin 'is not a mere expansion of painter's panel, whereon experiments may be remorselessly daubed', while Rede pointed out: 'There can be little doubt that all paint is injurious to the skin, and the object should be, therefore, to neutralize its pernicious qualities as much as possible.'[98] Scoffern finds harm not only in the creation of an artificial skin that does not allow real skin to breath, but also in the influence of artifice on the real functions of a human organism because cosmetics can be absorbed through the skin. Archer, by extension, speculates that the capacity for natural expression on stage may suffer permanent damage from a dependence on cosmetics: 'blushing . . . depends on a certain delicacy of the skin which is probably not fostered by the habitual use of cosmetics'.[99] Scoffern uses the harmful impact of cosmetics on the body to argue for a more 'genuine' form of beauty, not only free from 'things laid on bodily' but actually generated from within:

> to develop the skin's own latent beauty, no other than the beauty of health, is better than to produce, or aim at producing, an artificial semblance of it. There cannot be a greater mistake than that founded on the assumption that a soft, clear, well-conditioned skin is wholly the result of external treatment. Of course this counts for something, in fact a good deal; but still more nearly affecting the condition of the skin is the state of general health as determined by constitution, or by what we eat, drink, and avoid.[100]

Although Scoffern claims to set aside the 'moral' question of cosmetics, his prescription for naturally healthy and clear skin incorporates a regime of modest behaviour in the same breath as instructions about the best type of soap to use:

> My advice to ladies . . . would be to keep their complexions good by observance of certain points of discipline. Early hours, not too much dancing, distilled water for the toilet, and low alkalised soap; if soap for the face, an alkali will do much. If asked to specify the greatest enemy to the duration of a lady's complexion, I would state the London season, recurring again and again, with all its hard work, its mental anxieties and general rigour.[101]

Scoffern thus suggests that women who avoid cosmetics do so because they live authentic, moral lives.

Taylor and Reade asserted, and sought to recover, an authentic, wholesome Peg despite paint and performance. While both the play and the novel participate in the iconography of artifice and genuineness developed in Victorian texts about make-up in order to explore the extent to which the drama or the novel can access authenticity, Reade's novel relies heavily on such iconography to trace Peg's conversion as it reclaims her from a theatrical life. This reclaiming contrasts markedly with the fin-de-siècle celebration of self-fashioning that we have seen in Beerbohm – an interest that is evident in the 1899 edition of the novel, which displays a preoccupation with the surface of Peg's performance rather than with the novel's attempts to penetrate that surface. Hugh Thompson's illustrations include an image of Peg applying her makeup (Fig. 1.1), while Austin Dobson's introduction emphasises the unknowability of Peg Woffington beyond her acting.[102] Dobson catalogues a variety of portraits of Peg, some of which depict her playing theatrical roles, but he makes no claims about what they represent. On the title page, the illustrator represents Peg's image within a painted miniature (Fig. 1.2), suggesting that we know the actress through representations of her. Similarly, Chapter 1 begins with Peg within an ornamental piece of theatre architecture (Fig. 1.3).

Figure 1.1 Peg makes herself up (*Peg Woffington*, 31)

Figure 1.2 Peg in a painted miniature on the title page

Figure 1.3 Peg framed within theatrical architecture (*Peg Woffington*, 1)

These late-century views of Peg are not alone in noting the central significance of Peg's portrait in the play and novel. Painted by Henry Windham Phillips after a portrait of Peg Woffington by Hogarth, the painting that was used in the play is itself a portrait of Fanny Stirling, the actress who originated the role of Reade and Taylor's Peg Woffington, and has a history of being confused with a portrait for which Stirling sat, in costume as Peg, late at night after her performances (Fig. 1.4).[103] Accordingly, the *Athenaeum*'s 1853 review of the novel directs the reader to a variety of portraits of Peg but makes no distinction between representations of her in theatrical roles and representations of her as herself.[104] This omission suggests that such a distinction is irrelevant because the actress may always be playing a role: she is always an artistic representation.

Indeed, in an exchange between Peg's rival admirers, the urbane Sir Charles Pomander tells the naïve Ernest Vane that 'Peg is a decent actress on the boards, and a great actress off them', pointing out that the fact that Peg's performances off stage in the social world go undetected is evidence of her dramatic ability.[105] Pomander contradicts

Figure 1.4 Portrait of Fanny Stirling as Peg Woffington, used in the original productions of *Masks and Faces* (Courtesy of the Garrick Club)

Vane's claim that Peg's 'voice is truth, told by music: theirs are jingling instruments of falsehood', by pointing out that she differs from other actors only in ability, 'No – they are all instruments; but hers is more skilfully tuned and played upon.' Pomander's response denies a facile designation of the voice for authenticity. When Vane says, 'She is a fountain of true feeling', Pomander replies, 'No – a pipe that conveys it, without spilling or retaining a drop.'[106] Pomander's view of the actress as a hollow conduit is repeated later in the century by *The Picture of Dorian Gray*'s Lord Henry Wotton, who shares Pomander's foppery and describes the actress Sybil Vane as 'a reed through which Shakespeare's music sounded richer and more full of joy'.[107] Both of these characterisations echo Diderot's analysis of acting, which Gail Marshall characterises: 'Far from suggesting that the actor is an immoral rogue whose performances are supremely self-conscious and deceitful representations of emotion, Diderot implies that off-stage the actor must be sufficiently sensitive either to his own or to others' emotions to garner material for his impersonations.'[108] These characterisations are also in keeping with Archer's citation of

John Hill's anonymously published 1755 *The Actor: Or, A Treatise on the Art of Playing*:

> Charles Reade, if we may believe [the author of *The Actor*], was justified in making the famous tear roll down Peg Woffington's cheek. 'Mrs Woffington,' he says, 'has great sensibility; and she had, more than most players of either sex, given a loose to nature in the expressing it; to this she owed the greatest part of her fame as an actress; and in this she always excelled, when her private passions did not interfere.'[109]

Hill viewed Peg Woffington's talent as the ability to sympathetically feel her role, rather than to channel her own feelings into a part. Taylor and Reade, however, in contrast to fin-de-siècle writers and illustrators, voice these views of the actress as an instrument without an authentic identity only to prove them wrong when they locate a source of authenticity in her class origins.

Peg is able to pass for a lady. The Irish brogue that she re-assumes when united with Triplet, who knew her as a girl selling oranges in the streets of Dublin, belies her own daily behaviour as a representation and imitation of classes above her lowly origin. Reade was criticised for not having 'made "Peg Woffington" sufficiently Irish', according to his relations Charles L. Reade and the Rev. Compton Reade, who defend Reade by noting Peg's ability to learn a new social identity: 'He introduced "Peg" as a leading lady on the London stage, not as a savage Irishwoman from Kerry; and he could hardly have been far wrong in his presumption that she had learned the English language.'[110] The threat to traditional class and ethnic divisions that Peg's talent of mimicry poses is represented concretely in the play and novel when, in a social setting, she uses her acting abilities off stage and assumes the identity of 'Lady Betty Modish' – a character in Colley Cibber's play *The Careless Husband* – in order to dupe Mabel and spite Vane after learning that he is married. The particularly theatrical nature of her social behaviour is emphasised by the critics who are present at the party, who speak of it as a play, and by Peg's comment: 'Yes; there are triumphs out of the Theatre.'[111] Peg's ability to mimic a class standing that she does not possess intrigued Taylor and Reade's audience: the *Athenaeum* cites this scene as being compelling in both novel and play, and contemporary and Victorian critics alike have distinguished between the authentic and the performing women in the play.[112] Michael Booth's argument that the play 'shows two women in sharp contrast: the gay, careless, immoral, generous Peg Woffington and the simple, timid, domestic Mabel Vane' echoes the review in the *Times*, which praised the ensemble of actors, stating that Mrs Stirling, as Peg Woffington, had 'all the benefit of a contrast in the girlish effusive manner' of Miss Rose Bennett, who played Mabel Vane.[113] The *Times*, however, underscored how good acting undermines clear distinctions between nature and artifice, praising not only Mrs Stirling for '[s]tepping gracefully from seriousness to gaiety, and [being] equally *natural* in both', and for being 'completely in her element as Peg Woffington' but also 'the girlish effusive manner which is very prettily *assumed* by Miss Rose Bennett in the character of Mrs Vane'.[114] This comment on the two lead actresses also suggests that an actress can be natural playing an actress but can only mimic the genuine emotions of a respectable woman. Yet it is precisely such easy distinctions that Taylor and Reade reject. Tricked by Peg and her colleagues, Mabel thinks that all of her husband's guests are 'persons of quality' when they are actually actors.[115] Later in the play and novel, Peg is able to mimic even Mabel, who represents feminine, genteel respectability, and to convince both Vane and Pomander that she really is Mabel.

When Peg mimics the genteel classes, she assumes the aristocratic title that the Vanes lack. There appears to be little class difference between Ernest Vane and his rival suitor, the titled Sir Charles Pomander: both enjoy the luxuries and leisure that accompany inherited wealth. In the novel, we learn that Mabel's mother disapproved of Ernest Vane until he inherited his uncle's estate.[116] Yet the two men are psychically different. While Vane could plausibly be viewed as a class upstart playing a role, his rustic, authentic naïveté contrasts with Sir Charles Pomander's urbanity. Pomander is a man of decadent pleasures who recognises and appreciates Peg's artifice even as he pursues Mabel Vane as a refreshing change of pace. Baker describes how only 'the aristocracy' were confident enough in their class standing to risk associating with actresses and, even then, became more skittish of such involvements in the Victorian period, when marriages between 'titled peers' and 'successful actresses . . . became a rare occurrence'.[117] The play and the novel express anxiety about the connection between Ernest Vane and Peg in Vane's infidelity to his genteel wife. After Peg and Pomander have each pursued one of the Vanes, and after Pomander has placed his ring on Peg's finger thinking she is Mabel, Peg keeps his ring and we are led to believe that Peg and Pomander may each have found his or her match in the other: Pomander is as capable of deceit as she and feels unthreatened by class fluidity.

Because Mabel participates in cultural views that treat actors and actresses as beneath respectable society, she is shocked to learn of

Lady Betty Modish's true identity. She is also horrified to discover that her husband frequents the green room, the room in the theatre used by actors and actresses when not on stage and where audience members can meet them – a site, therefore, that blurs the boundary between the seemingly fixed classes of the audience and the changeable identities of the actor or actress, the social world and the world of the stage. The green room is a place where upper-class men can form liaisons with women outside their own class, but Mabel finds it impossible to believe that her husband would mingle with such people for any reason other than charity, saying, 'Invite an actress to his house! . . . These poor actors and actresses! I have seen some of them down in Huntingdonshire, and I know what a kindness it is to give them a good meal.'[118] Although Mabel's fantasy of her husband's charitable impulse towards actors and actresses reinforces class distinctions, her understanding of the social stature of actors and actresses becomes difficult to maintain in London, where an actress like Peg sometimes enjoys wealth that elides financial distinctions between classes. Peg's response when Mabel, later in the play, refers to her as her sister reveals how the earnings of performers, nevertheless, do not buy respectability: 'You do not know what it is to me, whom the proud ones of the world pass with averted looks, to hear that sacred name from lips as pure as yours.'[119]

Ultimately, the play and novel suggest that Mabel is able to see beyond Peg's profession and mask to recognise the concealed, genuine feeling that shows Peg to be more than an actress. Mabel says to Triplet's portrait of Peg in which the actress has, for a second time, substituted her own face for the image of herself, 'I will cry to her for justice and mercy; – I never saw a kinder face than this lady's – she must be good and noble!'[120] Mabel's faith in Peg's appearance as an index of her character appears naïve, given Peg's artifice, but the fact that Mabel speaks to the painting as if it is alive suggests that she, as a virtuous woman, may unknowingly be a better reader of appearances than other characters in the story. Mabel's virtue speaks to the moral mission of the realistic literary or theatrical work: she alone recognises the goodness in Peg that becomes a central theme in the play and the novel. It is this reclaiming of the actress that the *Times* identified as the central idea of the play, stating that its 'purpose is the vindication of the histrionic profession in the eyes of general society'. Peg is vindicated because her generosity reveals that she has an untheatrical emotional core. According to the review, 'Mrs Woffington [is] rendered a new character by a happy combination of benevolence and mirth.'[121]

The sisterhood forged between Peg and Mabel at the end of both the play and the novel can be viewed as a radical threat to class identity. This threat, however, is diminished because it results not from Peg's ability to feign but from her working-class origin. Unable to abandon completely the class from which she has spectacularly risen, Peg recognises Triplet as a friend from her childhood in the streets. Peg is redeemed through helping Triplet's career and sacrificing her own happiness in order to resolve the marital rift that she caused between the Vanes. Significantly, Peg's redemption occurs in the poverty of Triplet's garret apartment, the sole set for the second act, which contrasts sharply with the more plush act 1 settings of the green room and Vane's London home. Peg's generosity towards the impoverished Triplet family reveals that she has an untheatrical emotional core and renders her less threatening by re-establishing her ties to the lower classes. Tracy C. Davis discusses the fascination that Victorians had for the 'rags-to-prosperity story of hard work, talent, and beauty' that contemporary periodicals repeated in biographies of various actresses.[122] *Masks and Faces* and *Peg Woffington* suggest that such stories served to assuage cultural anxieties by anchoring the actress to a specific class identity from which she ultimately cannot escape despite material gain.

Peg shows emotion when she describes her plight of being pursued by genteel men, yet not treated as a member of their own class. She is first angry, saying to Triplet: 'You forget, sir, that I am an actress! – a plaything for every profligate who can find the open sesame of the stage-door. Fool! to think there was an honest man in the world, and that he had shone on me!'[123] But her feeling then shifts to sadness, when she says, 'These men applaud us, cajole us, swear to us, lie to us, and yet, forsooth, we would have them respect us too', and concludes by suggesting that Vane might have enabled her to feel genuine, unperformed emotion: 'I thought this man truer than the rest. I did not feel his passion an insult. Oh! Triplet, I could have loved this man – really loved him.'[124] Yet such avowals and displays of emotion remain suspect in a play that not only defines great acting as that which is indistinguishable from nature but also underscores its own artificiality. Peg's outpouring of emotion is prompted by Triplet's comment: 'To see what these fine gentlemen are! to have a lawful wife at home, and then to come and fall in love with you! I do it for ever in my plays, it is all right there! – but in real life it is abominable!'[125] Triplet's observation about the difference between plots designed to fascinate an audience and acceptable real-life behaviour reminds the viewer that the events he or she is witnessing are not real, even as it superficially naturalises the on-stage events as real. Within the genre of the play, all of Peg's behaviour, and particularly her apparently genuine emotional outburst immediately following Triplet's comment, remains suspect. In the play, therefore, Peg remains a potentially threatening force. Sheila Stowell, echoing Reade's own preference for *Masks and Faces* over *Peg Woffington*, argues that the novel 'is not as successful as the play largely because the question of the theatre's relationship to life cannot be treated with the immediacy it receives in the playhouse where the production itself reflects upon the issues raised in the drama'.[126] It is this very difference that enables Reade's novel to establish more firmly the genuineness of Peg's supposedly unfeigned emotions.

While the novel's narrator emphasises the deceit of Peg's acting, the narrator also asserts the authenticity of Peg's emotional response to Mabel Vane. In the theatre Peg's misrepresentations that deceive her on-stage audience are visibly signified to the play's actual audience, who are not duped. In a scene unique to the novel, however, Peg poses as a famous, retired actress, Mme Bracegirdle, who visits the green room.[127] The narrator allows the reader to be surprised by Peg's mimicry – her performance is only revealed to us when it is revealed to her audience of colleagues within the novel. For the reader of the novel, who feels the full impact of Peg's deceit, her ability to mimic appears more threatening than it does to the playgoer. Yet, in response to this mistrust of theatricality, the novel strongly distinguishes between Peg's performances and her genuine feelings. When she brings joy into Triplet's home, the narrator intervenes to reveal her performed gaiety to readers and assert the genuine sadness in her that is concealed from the characters within the novel. The narrator describes her blithe behaviour in the midst of Triplet's poverty:

> and suppose this was more than half acting, but such acting as Triplet never dreamed of; and to tell the honest simple truth, I myself should not have suspected it; but children are sharper than one would think, and Alcibiades Triplet told, in after years, that when they were all dancing except the lady, he caught sight of her face – and it was quite, quite grave, and even sad: but as often as she saw him look at her, she smiled at him so gaily – he couldn't believe it was the same face.[128]

The narrator explains his or her own experience of being convinced by the performance, and employs an omniscient perspective with the benefit of commanding a range of time to shed light on Peg's concealment. Perceiving the truth that underlies theatrical performance is reserved for figures who are the least theatrical: children and honest women like Mabel Vane. Nina Auerbach has examined how the non-theatricality of children in Victorian literature deconstructed itself into theatricality, suggesting the conventional nature of the novel's use of the child and the honest woman as an index of authenticity.[129] Such reliance on conventions to assert authenticity dominates the novel, as it employed a form of realism distinct from the play from which it was adapted.

The novel relies on another such formula when it draws on Victorian understandings of how physical symptoms signal authenticity while cosmetics signify artifice and uses Peg's 'flush' as a sign of authentic feeling. When Peg decides to help Mabel, the narrator fathoms Peg's 'heart' and even her 'soul':

> At the bottom of Margaret Woffington's heart lay a soul, unknown to herself – a heavenly harp, on which ill airs of passion had been played – but still it was there, in tune with all that is true, pure, really great and good. And now the flush that a great heart sends to the brow, to herald great actions, came to her cheek and brow.[130]

While the play contains the same sentimental language of 'heart' to refer to Peg's non-theatrical self, it lacks the novel's omniscient narrator to provide such statements with credence. Although the narrator's ability to penetrate performances is undercut by this hackneyed sentimental language, which points out how narrator and author revert to a formulaic mode of asserting authenticity in a theatrical world, Levine has argued that '[t]he refusal of major realists to acknowledge the conventionality of [strategies of realistic representation] . . . was essential to the convention itself. It supported the special authenticity the realist novel claimed by emphasizing its primary allegiance to experience over art.'[131] Reade's narration, complete with personification of Peg's heart and of the blush as a herald, describes the impulse that caused Peg's flush before noting its outward manifestation. Positing that Peg's flushed face is an accurate index of internal emotion, Reade participates in the 'fantasy' of 'legibility' that Mary Ann O'Farrell argues marked nineteenth-century novelists' use of the blush or flush, without acknowledging it as a fantasy.[132] O'Farrell writes, 'in seeming involuntarily and reliably to betray a deep self – blushing assists at the conversion of legibility into a sense of identity and centrality'.[133] In Reade's novel, Peg's flush is a bodily event that bespeaks her unfeigned, authentic self.

A second outward physical event that Reade employs as evidence for Peg's authentic emotional self is the tear that she sheds, betraying her presence in the portrait in which she has for a second time substituted her own face for an image of herself. Peg's tear is provoked by Mabel's appeal to what she thinks is a portrait of her husband's mistress, and the narrator states that Peg's tear 'proved her something more than a picture or an actress'.[134] Echoing the scene in Shakespeare's *The Winter's Tale* in which Hermione, posing as a statue, is recalled to life from her supposed death, this involuntary expression of emotion signals Peg's awakening to natural, unacted life. Hermione aptly encapsulates the Victorian belief, expressed in discussions of cosmetics that link make-up to statues and death, that artifice yields lifeless, aesthetic objects. In George Eliot's *Daniel Deronda* (1876), Gwendolen interrupts her own performance of Hermione's awakening with a spontaneous scream of terror that emphasises, by contrast, the lifelessness of Gwendolen's own theatricality. Even though in Taylor and Reade's play the performed nature of the play's actions reminds us that all such emotive moments may be performance, the acting theories of Archer and Irving discussed at the beginning of this chapter held that blushes and tears could not be produced without feeling. Moreover, Taylor and Reade's use of 'heart' and tears recalls Diderot's comment, 'The player's tears come from his brain, the sensitive being's from his heart', and thus attempts to distinguish between authentic feeling and calculated performance.[135]

In addition to serving as evidence for her authentic self, Peg's flush signals an emotional connection between her and Mabel Vane. O'Farrell posits that 'the blush in the nineteenth-century English novel can also work the work of local resistance, embodying with a flush relations – not always fully articulable in the nineteenth-century novel – that cross or evade the strictures and compulsions of class and gender and the marriage plot'.[136] In this case, while the novel attempts to control the actress's subversion of class stratification, the flush signals the bond between women of different classes. Yet the novel employs this bond, and Peg's transgressive performance of class status, in order to reinstate marital and class order. Peg serves Mabel's interests, pretending to be Mabel in order to prompt Vane's declaration of love for his wife, and reconciles husband and wife. Peg's emotional connection to Mabel, in the novel, leads to her own redemption when she abandons acting and, with it, the power to mimic class identities. Relating her religious conversion and subsequent departure from the stage in favour of a life of charity and piety, the novel's epilogue makes a greater case for Peg's authentic emotional identity. The epilogue is notable not only for its contrast with the play, but also for its claim that it is distinct from the 'art' of the novel – a claim that places it squarely within Levine's point that 'if it were possible to locate a single consistent characteristic of realism among its various rejections of traditional forms and ideals, it would be that antiliterary thrust . . . and this thrust is also – inevitably – antigeneric in expression'.[137] In the play, Peg gives Ernest Vane back to his wife but is re-ensconced in the theatre, signified by her troupe of actor and critic colleagues. The troupe's call, at the conclusion of the play, to distinguish faces from masks is undercut by its stagy moralistic verse, unmediated by a narrator's credence.

Long before her conversion from the theatre, Peg, in the novel, points out that the illusions provided by the theatre are cheap substitutes for a genuine life. In the play, Peg's complaint that actresses are excluded from domestic pleasures suggests that the theatre offers a modicum of consolation: 'But what have we to do [*walks agitated*] with homes, and hearts, and firesides? Have we not the theatre, its triumphs, and full-handed thunders of applause? Who looks for hearts beneath the masks we wear?'[138] The novel, in contrast, places greater emphasis on the artificiality and vacuity of the theatre in contrast to the real pleasures of the home: 'And what have we to do with homes, or hearts, or firesides? Have we not the play-house, its paste diamonds, its paste feelings, and the loud applause of fops and sots – hearts? – beneath loads of tinsel and paint? Nonsense! The love that can go with souls to Heaven – such love for us? Nonsense!'[139] According to the heroine of the novel, the home can provide not only real pleasures but pleasures that transcend the material world.

Both the play and the novel exhibit anxieties about the impact of the actress on class and both displace these anxieties into the eighteenth century, where the actress functions within a society marked by a land-based, genteel class system rather than the Victorian social world increasingly dominated by entrepreneurs and professionals. Tracy Davis points out that, after the deregulation of theatres in 1843, the rise of a middle-class drama called for actresses from the middle class who would not merely mimic the lives experienced by audience members, but draw on their own experiences of middle-class life – a demand that was itself symptomatic of the cultural desire to locate an authentic, class-based identity for the actress.[140] Thus, Taylor and Reade explore an actress's life in an era in which classes were more clearly defined and more stable and in which acting represented both a greater transgression and greater possibilities for social advancement from one extreme of society to the other. For Taylor and Reade, as well as Boucicault, living in a society of increasing class fluidity, the eighteenth century provided a setting in which they could explore fears and possibilities about theatricality in exaggerated form. As the nineteenth century progresses, other writers embrace the class fluidity that the actress represented. The home world that Reade's Peg spoke about would play a central role in their works as they grappled with questions of identity and authenticity.

Notes

1. Diderot, *The Paradox of Acting*, pp. 16–17. Diderot wrote this work in the 1770s, but it was first published in 1830.
2. Lewes, *On Actors and the Art of Acting*, p. xi.
3. Ibid. p. 97.
4. Ibid. pp. 98–9.
5. Ibid. p. 95.
6. For an analysis of Lewes's emphasis on abstraction in acting and on an 'idealized collective subjectivity', see Voskuil, *Acting Naturally*, pp. 40–50.
7. Lewes, *On Actors and the Art of Acting*, pp. 167–8.
8. Archer, *Masks or Faces?*, p. 9. Much of Archer's book first appeared in *Longman's Magazine* in January, February and March 1888, under the title 'The Anatomy of Acting'.
9. Archer, *Masks or Faces?*, p. 150.
10. Ibid. p. 25.
11. Ibid. pp. 77, 104.
12. Ibid. p. 89.
13. Ibid. pp. 201, 208.
14. Ibid. p. 208.
15. Greiner, *Sympathetic Realism*, p. 18.
16. Voskuil describes how in Lewes 'the feeling and judging capacities are . . . closely intertwined' (*Acting Naturally*, p. 53).
17. Williams, 'Melodrama', pp. 204, 195.
18. Diderot, *The Paradox of Acting*, pp. xix–xx.
19. Ibid. p. xi.
20. Ibid. p. xi.
21. Voskuil, *Acting Naturally*, p. 3.
22. Diderot, *The Paradox of Acting*, p. xiii.
23. Varty, *Children and Theatre in Victorian Britain*, p. 118.
24. Hadley, *Melodramatic Tactics*, p. 5; Williams, 'Melodrama', p. 201.
25. Williams, 'Melodrama', p. 202.

26. Lancaster, 'The Manager's Daughter', p. 894 recto.
27. Ibid. p. 895 recto.
28. Ibid. p. 894 verso.
29. Ibid. p. 903 recto.
30. Ibid. p. 894 verso.
31. Ibid. p. 902 recto.
32. Ibid. p. 894 verso.
33. Varty, *Children and Theatre in Victorian Britain*, p. 110.
34. Hogan, *Dion Boucicault*, pp. 36–7; Orel, 'Reporting the Stage Irishman', p. 68.
35. Boucicault, 'The Young Actress', p. 2.
36. Ibid. p. 24.
37. Ibid. p. 9.
38. Although the published version of the play claims that it was 'First Produced at the Adelphi Theatre, 19 January 1845', Nicoll, *A History of Early Nineteenth Century Drama, 1800–1850* records its licensing date as 10 June 1845 and its first performance as 24 June 1845. Newspaper reviews in June 1845 suggest that this is correct (vol. 2, p. 508).
39. Review of Peg Woffington, *Illustrated London News*, 28 June 1845, p. 403.
40. Ibid. p. 403.
41. Ibid. p. 403.
42. 'The Theatres', *Era*, 29 June 1845, p. 5.
43. Boucicault, *Peg Woffington*, p. 4.
44. Ibid. p. 4.
45. Ibid. p. 6.
46. Ibid. p. 12.
47. Ibid. p. 7.
48. Ibid. p. 7.
49. Ibid. p. 7.
50. Stowell, 'Actors as Dramatic Personae', p. 125.
51. Boucicault, *Peg Woffington*, p. 17.
52. Ibid. p. 18.
53. 'Portraits: XXXI – Miss Heath', p. 189.
54. Fawkes, *Dion Boucicault*, p. 76.
55. Ibid. p. 79.
56. Ibid. pp. 79, 81–2, 84, 80.
57. Boucicault, *The Prima Donna*, p. 5.
58. Ibid. p. 6.
59. Ibid. p. 6.
60. Ibid. p. 6.
61. Ibid. p. 7.
62. Ibid. p. 8.
63. Ibid. p. 8.
64. Ibid. p. 14.

65. Ibid. p. 9.
66. Ibid. p. 9.
67. Ibid. p. 9.
68. Ibid. p. 9.
69. Ibid. p. 10.
70. Ibid. p. 10.
71. Ibid. p. 13.
72. Ibid. p. 19.
73. Ibid. p. 22.
74. Ibid. p. 22.
75. Ibid. p. 22.
76. Ibid. p. 23.
77. Ibid. p. 24.
78. Reade, letter, *Athenaeum*, 15 January 1853, p. 82.
79. Tom Taylor and Charles Reade, *Masks and Faces*, p. 157. When citing incidents that appear in the both the play and the novel, I have chosen to refer to the play since it is usually more concise.
80. Archer, *Masks or Faces?*, p. 122.
81. Ibid. p. 116.
82. Ibid. p. 116.
83. Rede, *The Guide to the Stage*, p. 54. Originally published in England, the 1868 edition included material on both the British and American stage, and the passages on cosmetics are additions by Francis C. Wemyss.
84. Ibid. p. 54.
85. Swift, 'A Beautiful Young Nymph Going to Bed', p. 109.
86. Baker, *The Rise of the Victorian Actor*, pp. 101–2.
87. Braddon, *Lady Audley's Secret*, p. 79.
88. Ibid. p. 58.
89. Archer, *Masks or Faces?*, pp. 46–7.
90. Braddon, *Lady Audley's Secret*, pp. 405–6.
91. Ibid. pp. 223, 336. David Skilton's explanatory notes to *Lady Audley's Secret*, p. 452.
92. For an analysis of Duse's blush, including George Bernard Shaw's description of it, see Gail Marshall, *Actresses on the Victorian Stage*, pp. 148–51.
93. In its original appearance in *The Yellow Book* in 1894, 'The Pervasion of Rouge' bore the title 'A Defense of Cosmetics'. Beerbohm, 'The Pervasion of Rouge', p. 117.
94. Marshall, *Actresses on the Victorian Stage*, p. 3.
95. Baudelaire, 'In Praise of Make-Up', p. 497.
96. Beerbohm, 'The Pervasion of Rouge', p. 107; Levine, *The Realistic Imagination*, p. 12.
97. Beerbohm, 'The Pervasion of Rouge', p. 109.
98. Scoffern, 'Cosmetics', p. 213; Rede, *The Guide to the Stage*, p. 54.
99. Archer, *Masks or Faces?*, p. 124.

100. Scoffern, 'Cosmetics', p. 213.
101. Scoffern, '"Beautiful for Ever"', pp. 227–8.
102. Reade, *Peg Woffington*.
103. The painting that was used in the original production of *Peg Woffington* is owned by the Garrick Club in London: <http://garrick.ssl.co.uk/object-g0778> (last accessed 23 May 2018).
104. Review of *Peg Woffington*, by Charles Reade, *The Athenaeum*, 1 January 1853, p. 15.
105. Taylor and Reade, *Masks and Faces*, p. 126.
106. Ibid. p. 126.
107. Wilde, *The Picture of Dorian Gray*, p. 255.
108. Marshall, *Actresses on the Victorian Stage*, p. 123.
109. Archer, *Masks or Faces?*, p. 45.
110. Charles L. Reade and Rev. Compton Reade, *Charles Reade*, vol. 2, pp. 3–4.
111. Taylor and Reade, *Masks and Faces*, pp. 143–4.
112. Review of *Peg Woffington*, *The Athenaeum*, 1 January 1853, p. 16.
113. Booth, *Prefaces to English Nineteenth-Century Theatre*, p. 81; Review of *Masks and Faces*, *The Times*, 22 November 1852, p. 8.
114. Review of *Masks and Faces*, *The Times*, 22 November 1852, p. 8; emphasis added.
115. Taylor and Reade, *Masks and Faces*, p. 147.
116. Reade, *Peg Woffington*, pp. 169–70.
117. Baker, *The Rise of the Victorian Actor*, p. 176.
118. Taylor and Reade, *Masks and Faces*, pp. 147–8.
119. Ibid. p. 164.
120. Ibid. p. 163.
121. Review of *Masks and Faces*, *The Times*, 22 November 1852, p. 8.
122. Tracy C. Davis, *Actresses as Working Women*, p. 72.
123. Taylor and Reade, *Masks and Faces*, p. 160.
124. Ibid. p. 161.
125. Ibid. p. 160.
126. Reade and Reade, *Charles Reade*, vol. 2, p. 3; Stowell, 'Actors as Dramatic Personae', p. 129.
127. Reade, *Peg Woffington*, p. 51.
128. Ibid. p. 157.
129. Auerbach, *Private Theatricals*.
130. Reade, *Peg Woffington*, p. 259.
131. Levine, *The Realistic Imagination*, p. 18.
132. O'Farrell, *Telling Complexions*, p. 4. See also the Introduction of this book for a discussion of O'Farrell and the blush.
133. O'Farrell, *Telling Complexions*, p. 5.
134. Reade, *Peg Woffington*, p. 254.
135. Diderot, *The Paradox of Acting*, p. 17.
136. O'Farrell, *Telling Complexions*, p. 7.

137. Reade, *Peg Woffington*, p. 279; Levine, *The Realistic Imagination*, pp. 11–12.
138. Taylor and Reade, *Masks and Faces*, p. 161.
139. Reade, *Peg Woffington*, p. 241.
140. Davis, *Actresses as Working Women*, p. 77.

Chapter 2

The Actress at Home: Domesticity, Respectability and the Disruption of Class Hierarchies

> But what have we to do ... with homes, and hearts, and firesides? Have we not the theatre, its triumphs, and full-handed thunders of applause? Who looks for hearts beneath the masks we wear?[1]

Peg Woffington continued to ask these questions as *Masks and Faces* played on the stage of the Theatre Royal, Haymarket, into the 1880s. We have seen how Reade, Taylor and Boucicault in the 1850s established the actress's authenticity through her connection to her origins and her social class. In contrast, this chapter examines works from the 1860s that employed the actress's class mobility and ability to reveal the performativity of class precisely to destabilise class structures. As they looked for the actress's heart, they located her authentic emotional life in the home. Using domesticity and family to ground the actress in the real, they also assert her respectability and, by extension, make claims for the respectability of the theatre, even as they use the actress as a figure for the disruption of social class hierarchies.

The significance of domesticity for asserting authenticity draws on Victorian melodramatic conventions regarding the sanctity of the home and motherhood, and this chapter begins with another play by the melodramatist Dion Boucicault: *The Life of an Actress* (1855, 1862). But this convention remains in use by Wilkie Collins's sensation novel *No Name* (1862–3) and its adaptations to the stage, and in T. W. Robertson's play *Caste* (1867), which, even as it employs the actress at home as an important touchstone for its own realism as it claims to penetrate performances in order to present the actual, nevertheless continues to depend on melodramatic conventions in order to do so. Moreover, the thematic as well as representational similarities between *The Life of an Actress* and *Caste* further underscore the importance of melodrama in the development of realism, as a play that has been considered a landmark in the development of stage realism remained indebted to and grounded in melodramatic strategies.

The Actress and the Aristocracy in Boucicault's *The Life of an Actress*

Grimaldi; or, Scenes in the Life of an Actress (also called *The Life of an Actress*, or *Violet* at times) was first performed in 1855 in Cincinnati and follows in the line of Boucicault's earlier 'The Young Actress' and *The Prima Donna*, examined in Chapter 1, as yet another vehicle for his wife Agnes, who played Violet. Boucicault himself played Grimaldi. The play's different emphasis with regard to an actress's social class may have been influenced by where it comes in the success that Agnes had enjoyed and the contributions that she had made to Boucicault's career in the United States – in part through playing in his earlier actress plays. The play also, however, represents a larger cultural body of actress plays. A review of its London premiere at the Adelphi on 1 March 1862, as *The Life of an Actress*, in *The Illustrated London News* reveals that it was derived from various source texts and histories: 'the events have been compounded of more than one French drama – namely, "Vie d'une Comédienne" and "Le Père de la Débutante", both of them previously known to English boards under the title of "The Reigning Favourite" and "The First Night". An anecdote of Rachel's early life has also been taken advantage of.'[2] Although Fawkes has called the play an 'adaptation', it would itself later become the first play to be the subject of an action brought by Boucicault based on the United States 1856 amendment to the 1831 Copyright Act, which gave dramatists rights to their work.[3] The *London Daily News* greeted it with a review that described how it participated in a cultural fascination with the stage that was so extreme that the 'behind-the-scenes business has been done to death'.[4] Such 'behind-the-scenes' depictions may refer to backstage, including the green room setting that we saw in Chapter 1, in which the theatrical profession and respectable society mingled. The *Era* review identifies Boucicault's depiction of backstage as 'the most perfect and illusive from first to last that was ever put on stage', delighting in how the subject of its own stage illusion is the unmasking of the reality behind stage illusions:

> It represents the Stage *behind* the curtain, with all the bustle of carpenters' setting Scenes, ballet girls practising, Actors slapping their heads and heroically striding about, part in hand, declaiming their speeches, the bellowing Prompter setting his Scene, the vociferous call-boy summoning 'all for the next piece', the terror of the *debutante*, and the anxiety of old Grimaldi, in his hopes and fears for the success of his adopted child; in fact, the manner in which the whole of this scene is managed, the applause heard from the suppositious audience, makes up an illusion admirably perfect.[5]

Thus, the play thematises the actual. 'Behind-the-scenes' depictions, however, also speak to realistically rendered domestic settings that revealed the unglamorous side of the acting profession, both of which figure prominently in this and other plays about the actress that this chapter examines. Acts 1 and 2 contrast what the *Era* characterised as 'the fashionable lodgings of Julia . . . a great tragic star', and 'the miserable attic of Grimaldi, . . . the poor utility man'.[6]

The play also foregrounds authenticity. In act 1 the much maligned bit-part actor Grimaldi criticises the star Julia when she refuses to act in his benefit, contrasting his own natural acting with her mechanical artifice:

> Mademoiselle, I act with you, I see your eyes fix on de private box – I see your stereotype smile on de parquete, your tear artificial, your laugh mechanique, while I – I wiz my little word to say – I say it badly, ze publique laugh – oui, hiss me, but de tear of feeling was in my eye, oui – I laugh wid my heart, I act wid my soul, eh bien – den – I – morbleu! I was de artiste, and you – oui – you was de Policinelle [puppet]!'[7]

Grimaldi accuses Julia of failing to achieve Archer's 'double consciousness' of being self-conscious about her performance while at the same time achieving authentic feeling. Just as 'The Young Actress' represented a theatre that was moving away from patronage and towards a theatre of the people, in contrast to Julia's artificiality and association with the upper classes, Grimaldi's genuine acting is associated with populism, as he refuses her offer of ten pounds, saying that he will only accept money from the public, rather than charity, an act that prompts Lord Shafton to say, 'That creature has the soul of a gentleman under his rags.'[8]

Grimaldi vocalises the position of the play that authenticity is located in emotions, and the great actress must be sentient. In contrast with Julia, the orphaned street beggar Violet, who lacks any standing in the social world, performs with real feeling that stems from her own griefs. She enters as a figure of melodramatic pathos and victimhood when Julia and her guests hear her singing in the street, and Lord Arthur Shafton recognises the song and recalls the singer as someone he aided when he found her in a ditch mourning her dead dog:

> As well as her grief would permit her to speak, she related to me that this animal was her sole friend in the world – her companion! – by exhibiting his tricks and by singing her ballads, she gained her livelihood.

The previous night, as they journeyed along to this town, a man had attacked her in the lane, with insult; she uttered a cry for help – her dog flew at the ruffian's throat – during their struggle she fled – all night she remained concealed in a corn-field – at daylight she ventured out to find her companion – only to find that the man had killed him.[9]

Julia insists that Violet sing 'My poor Dog Tray', noting that Violet's associations with her own dog 'will make [her] give expression to the words', and Grimaldi even urges Violet to 'suffer a little; it will please de kind lady'.[10] Violet accordingly *bursts into tears, and falls on Grimaldi's breast* in the second verse, whereupon Grimaldi identifies in her another true artist because she expresses true feeling: 'Oui, bravo! Sacrebleu, bravo! . . . oui, in dis child dere is truth, de germ of art; dere is feeling, de life of art. Listen to me, mon enfant; you are not alone in de world, for God has made de sincere hearts to be all of one famille.'[11]

Violet has a Moses-like story of abandonment that has left her rootless: 'I never had any parents. I was found upon the bank of the canal in a basket, with some bouquets of violets, which a flower girl had left there; they said she had drowned herself.'[12] Her story also touches on her disreputableness as the child of a fallen woman. But Grimaldi literalises his point that art makes them of the same family, and adopts her. One year later, in act 2, Violet is living happily with Grimaldi, who buys her clothing fit for a lady, has taught her to read and write, has her learning music from the orchestra leader and is schooling her in a theatrical repertoire of Shakespeare, Racine and Corneille. Grimaldi points out that because he has provided for her, loved her and not abandoned her as her birth parents did, he is an authentic father, thereby suggesting that domestic ties, regardless of how they are formed, constitute family relationships.[13] Meanwhile, he has known that Violet was in love with Lord Arthur because it is only through actually feeling that she has been able to perform so effectively: 'when I teach her to act, she know not what spirit inspire her, what give light to her eye, glow to her cheek, passion to her voice; but I know, it was her love for you!'[14] By following Lewes's notion that acting requires the sublimation of true feeling, the play ascribes authenticity to the actress through her ability to feel.

Central to the plot of the play, however, is the precarious respectability of the actress. When Lord Arthur courts Violet, Julia knowingly observes: '*I* know what the deep interest of young officers for young actresses always leads to.'[15] Grimaldi narrowly prevents Lord Arthur from eloping with Violet, enlisting him instead as Violet's protector, but Violet's vulnerability is further underscored by the melodramatic plot, in which she is abducted on her debut evening by a villainous seducer, appropriately named Maltravers, who is also the attacker who killed her dog. He seeks to interrupt the authentic emotional bond between Violet and Grimaldi, citing his view that wealth is the wellspring of authenticity: 'I am rich, and can prove my sincerity by sharing with you my wealth.'[16] After an action-filled rescue, Grimaldi reflects on her unjustly ruined reputation as he 'take[s] her back to infamy': 'The fine young officer run away wid de actrice! ... an old story dat – who cares! actors have no character, actresses have no reputation. Bah! you will laugh it off, and we shall make the best of it.'[17] Even when, under threat, Maltravers provides a written confession to his crime, he tells Grimaldi, 'you will find that even that paper and the oaths of two low actors will not avail against the word of a gentleman'.[18] This penultimate act ends with a cliffhanger as Arthur, after asking Violet to marry him so that he may save her reputation, is shot by Maltravers.

The audience's and critics' strenuous objections to this material reveal how even when the actress herself is a virtuous victim, her sexual vulnerability itself is objectionable to polite society. The *Era* referred to the play as 'one of the most morally objectionable pieces we can remember ever to have witnessed, the very excellence of the acting making the innuendos and situations more repellent'.[19] The *Morning Post* described how the audience expressed its 'reprobation ... in ... strong and earnest accents', particularly about act 4:

> The fell purpose of the seducer was here brought out with heinous distinctness; and when the poor girl, who had been hunted like a hare to gratify the most ignoble of passions, sunk to the ground heartbroken and inanimate, a murmur of disapproval ran through the house, and it was manifestly felt that such an exhibition is scarcely a desirable subject for representation on the stage, and that the interests of virtue are not effectively promoted by the portraiture, however skilful, of events so painful and humiliating.[20]

As we have seen in earlier plays, wealth and success do not gain the actress social respectability. In the play's final scene, set in the gardens of a Duke's villa, Julia describes Violet's stratospheric rise from obscurity to fame: 'And now the aristocracy fight for her smiles. Countesses vie with each other who shall exhibit her in their opera boxes. Riches, honours, coronets fall at her feet – who last year begged her bread in the streets of Nottingham.'[21] Nevertheless, Violet is not accepted as one of the aristocracy. Although she is rumoured to be secretly married to Arthur, his mother does not accept her and has arrived in London 'to vindicate her son from the charge of having allied the noblest family in Britain with the blood of a vagabond'.[22] On arriving, the Countess offers Violet 10,000 pounds 'if [she] will consent at once to marry some person in [her] own profession'.[23] Violet responds by asserting the dignity of her profession: 'There is no person, madame, in my profession, who would consent to marry a nobleman's mistress for the price of her infamy!'[24] She also staunchly defends the family relationship that she has built with Grimaldi: 'No! despise me! crush me if you will! you are Arthur's mother – but the profession I have been taught to love and respect. When you trample upon that, you insult my father, and you pollute the daily bread that God has given me!' The Countess deflates this as 'a performance of indignant virtue' and tells her host: 'You forget, Duke, that we are dealing with actors, people whose sentiments are manufactured for them, and whose characters are fictitious.'[25] Julia responds with the language of the heart, which we saw in Reade and Taylor's *Peg Woffington*, to assert her own authenticity:

> No, madam, you are dealing with those in whose hearts there has ever been more true nobility than in your own titled caste. . . . [W]hen we hear our noble profession insulted, we cast aside all petty rivalry, and heart to heart we repel the aggression with derision and contempt.[26]

Even after Arthur's sudden appearance and declaration that Violet is indeed his wife, which Grimaldi observes is like a scene in a play, the Countess refuses to accept Violet, asserting that it is not poverty that the Countess despises, because their 'wealth' can remedy that, but rather Violet's status as 'an outcast'.[27]

In a melodramatic twist, Grimaldi reveals himself as the Duke of St Elmo, explains that the laws of Italy allow a noble house to adopt when it has no child, and declares that Violet now bears his aristocratic title. He also reveals that thirty years earlier he and the Countess loved each other and he went to jail for her, as he was committed to the cause of England and a failed revolution. Upon release, he chose to become an artist rather than claim his title and live as 'a beggar duke'.[28] Even though Grimaldi's aristocratic status is the vehicle through which all is resolved, his sudden elevation to social prestige undercuts, rather than supports, traditional class hierarchies. It is the domestic bond between Grimaldi and Violet, regardless of origin or birth, that grants Violet respectability both through the play's improbable plot and in the eyes of the audience, and the play insists on the respect that is due to the profession of the stage. At the end, as the Countess expects that Violet will quit the stage, Grimaldi and Violet turn to the audience and say: 'you shall tell her that you can also confer nobility'.[29] The play thus invests power in popular audiences.

Contrived though the ending is, it effects a conclusion in which Violet remains on the stage even as she has attained the highest social standing. Other works that use the actress in order to criticise and undermine traditional class identities in a more pointed or focused way conclude by bringing her into a position of greater social conformity, making her a more typical woman rather than an outsider, subduing through domestication the threat that each of their heroines poses to normative feminine social roles.

No Name and Its Chastened Magdalen

The novelists Wilkie Collins and Charles Reade enjoyed a close professional friendship and may have influenced each other's works.[30] While Reade adapted his actress Peg Woffington from the stage to the page, as we have seen in Chapter 1, because the novel allowed for a fuller realisation of her reclamation, Wilkie Collins created a fictional actress in his novel *No Name* (1862–3) only to struggle in adapting her story for the stage. Their anxious attempts to reclaim the actress from her theatrical changeability are particularly obvious when they revisit their actresses in a second genre. The conditions of the theatre caused Collins, in adapting his novel for the stage, to make drastic changes to his narrative – changes that represent his actress, Magdalen, as more genuine on stage than she is in the novel. Richard Pearson has pointed out that Collins's approach to adapting his novels stands in contrast to and even challenges common understandings of Victorian adaptation, such as that of Dickens's *Nicholas Nickleby* that we touched on in the introduction:

> The notion of adaptation as a unique act of creativity – not just a reformation but an origination – characterises Collins' dramatic engagement with his own fiction and represents a sharp distinction from the quick-and-dirty adaptations proliferating around him. Both Dickens and Collins refer to adaptation as 'theft'; but to counteract this, Collins viewed his play scripts as offering alternative modes of narration.[31]

Both Reade and Collins grapple with the problem of maintaining identities in a world of mutable class by emphasising the psychic bonds of one's origins. They each focus on an actress with a talent for mimicry who, through acting, is able to defy class boundaries. Nevertheless, while Reade, as we have seen, affirms class identities, Collins recasts the theatrical woman in order to criticise class distinctions, and this ideological difference may account for what Andrew Gasson characterises as Reade's critical view of *No Name*.[32]

Set in the nineteenth century, *No Name* explicitly criticises traditional landed wealth and emphasises the acted nature of class. While Reade's novel maintains class identities by asserting Peg's connection to her origins, *No Name* rejects class identities and employs family to establish how individuals can have grounded, stable selves without being firmly fixed in a class structure. It stresses family relationships and domestic life as the basis of individual identity. Like the chastened harlot for whom she is named, the novel's heroine, Magdalen, prostitutes herself both as an actress and by marrying, under a false identity, for mercenary reasons. Magdalen's fall is precipitated by a loss of family and inheritance; her redemption is effected by a symbolic return to her family. Alexander Smith, in 1863, characterised Collins by writing: 'to this writer plot and incident are all in all, character nothing', and Jenny Bourne Taylor, writing in 1988, further argued: '*No Name* does not explore an internalized subjectivity.'[33] In actuality, however, the central mission of *No Name* is to establish the basis of Magdalen's internalised subjectivity. *No Name* traces an elaborate plot of its heroine's identity loss – Magdalen loses herself as she constantly mimics identities that are not her own – only to restore her to her true character. Magdalen's loss of her own feelings as she becomes an increasingly proficient mimic echoes the first speaker's assertion, in Diderot's *The Paradox of Acting*:

> Great poets, great actors, and, I may add, all great copyists of Nature, in whatever art, beings gifted with fine imagination, with broad judgement, with exquisite tact, with a sure touch of taste, are the least sensitive of all creatures. They are too apt for too many things, too busy with observing, considering, and reproducing, to have their inmost hearts affected with any liveliness.[34]

The speaker continues this analysis by aligning 'sensibility' with women and 'imitation' with men, and Magdalen's acting also constitutes her unsexing.[35] When Magdalen's salvation, in the end, comes with her re-domestication, it also effects her re-feminisation.

Although centred on an inheritance, *No Name*, like other sensation novels including Mary Elizabeth Braddon's *Lady Audley's Secret*, differs from *Peg Woffington*'s eighteenth-century class structure by emphasising how Victorian society uses money rather than birth as a class determinant. Magdalen Vanstone and her sister live with their parents in respectable gentility until their father's death, when a family secret deprives them of wealth and social standing. Their father had been married when he was much younger, and only recently married their mother upon the death of his estranged first wife. He dies in a railway accident without having made a will subsequent to his second marriage and, since his earlier will that provided for his daughters is nullified by his second marriage, Magdalen and her sister are left as bastard children. They lose all social status and connections and have 'no name'. The potentially scandalous revelation of their birth out of wedlock is minimised in Collins's criticism of the arbitrariness of laws governing inheritance. If their father had arrived safely home to make a new will, his daughters would have had the rights of legitimate children. Magdalen becomes obsessed with regaining her father's money in order to recover her family name and status. Once she has achieved financial independence through acting, Magdalen uses her theatrical talent to deceive and marry her cousin Noel Vanstone, who has legally but wrongly inherited the fortune that should have gone to her and her sister. When her marriage and subsequent widowhood fail to provide her with the fortune, she disguises herself as a servant in order to discover a Secret Trust that names the new heir to the Vanstone fortune.

No Name disparages not only legal forms as arbitrary, but also inherited gentility. In describing Francis (Frank) Clare, whose father is a member of 'the younger branch of a family of great antiquity', it criticises family lineage by suggesting the degeneration that occurs in a family over time: 'no close observer could look at him, without suspecting that the stout old family stock had begun to wear out in the later generations, and that Mr Francis Clare had more in him of the shadow of his ancestors than of the substance'.[36] Similarly, Noel Vanstone, whose grandfather was a wealthy manufacturer, wears his father's dressing gown only to reveal that he is too small in stature for it to fit properly, and he suffers from a heart disease that his housekeeper Mrs Lecount describes as 'a fatty degeneration'.[37] Although Noel asserts his family lineage, 'I am my father's son!', the narrator emphasises how Noel is a diminished heir who 'had inherited his father's sordid love of money, without inheriting his father's hard-headed capacity for seeing the uses to which money can be put'.[38]

In contrast, Frank's father, Mr Clare, argues in favour of the self-made man in a world in which social stature depends on material wealth: 'The only excuse which a poor gentleman has for presuming to exist in the nineteenth century, is the excuse of extraordinary ability.'[39] The talent of actresses that we have seen in earlier works – Peg, Stella and Violet – can provide them with great wealth, but not genteel status. But birth and family background are subsumed to wealth in the social world that *No Name* depicts and criticises. Characterising the odd match between Magdalen and Frank that results from their participation as actors in a private theatrical performance at a friend's home, the novel discusses lineage only insofar as it provides wealth:

> Here, on one side, was a girl – with great personal attractions, with rare pecuniary prospects, with a social position which might have justified the best gentleman in the neighbourhood in making her an offer of marriage – perversely casting herself away on a penniless idle young fellow, who had failed at his first start in life, and who, even if he succeeded in his second attempt, must be for years to come in no position to marry a young lady of fortune on equal terms.[40]

Regardless of his genteel family background, Frank is an unsuitable match for the wealthy Magdalen because he does not have the ability to become a financially self-made man. Because the disparate match of Frank and Magdalen occurs as a result of theatrical activity, the theatre is represented as a vehicle for overcoming the financially based class boundaries that continue to exist in a world in which money allows traditional class boundaries to be permeable.

In the success of the dishonest Horatio Wragge, *No Name* evinces mistrust in a world of class fluidity even as it criticises traditional social classes. The character of Wragge suggests that in the economic world, theatricality is an important aspect of success. Wragge begins as a con man, independent theatre agent and drama instructor. In the end, he has become a respectable swindler: a self-made man in the world of consumer goods, selling quack medicine. Collins implies that success in business requires the skills of a con man; the self-made man is not a pillar of genuine selfhood but an adaptable actor who can play to audiences. The close tie between the theatre and Wragge's success in business is underscored by the fact that his 'pill' is advertised at the theatre, among other places, and by Wragge's own description of the spectacle of his entrepreneurship:

> The place in which my Pill is made, is an advertisement in itself. I have got one of the largest shops in London. Behind one counter (visible to the public through the lucid medium of plate-glass), are four-and-twenty

young men in white aprons, making the Pill. Behind another counter, are four-and-twenty young men, in white cravats, making the boxes. At the bottom of the shop are three elderly accountants, posting the vast financial transactions accruing from the Pill. Over the door are my name, portrait, and autograph, expanded to colossal proportions, and surrounded, in flowing letters, by the motto of the establishment....[41]

This mistrust of the theatricality of the Victorian business world is also expressed in Charles Reade's sensation novel *Hard Cash* (1863), which, published in the same year that *No Name*'s serial publication concluded, shows how unscrupulous bankers swindle unsuspecting investors out of their money by maintaining an appearance that inspires confidence.

Nevertheless, while *Masks and Faces* and *Peg Woffington* reinscribe the class affiliations into which characters are born, *No Name* embraces greater class fluidity. The scene in which Magdalen and her maid Louisa switch roles as mistress and maid is similar to that in which the lowborn Peg is able to pass for Mabel Vane. Yet *No Name*, like other sensation novels that employ such doublings in order to foreground the performance of class, does not suggest that origins provide firm class identities. Class identities, Collins implies, are mutable and are often at least partially based on personal achievement. The novel's criticism of the law that disinherits the sisters suggests that birth, as understood and defined by the law and society, is not a determinant of one's rightful class status. The reader believes that Magdalen, by virtue of the true family ties that the law does not recognise, deserves her parents' fortune even though she was not legitimately born to it. Magdalen tells Louisa that money and performance constitute class:

> Shall I tell you what a lady is? A lady is a woman who wears a silk gown, and has a sense of her own importance. I shall put the gown on your back, and the sense in your head. You speak good English – you are naturally quiet, and self-restrained – if you can only conquer your timidity, I have not the least fear of you. There will be time enough ... for you to practise your character, and for me to practise mine.[42]

Magdalen's emphasis that class is changeable through money is echoed by Mrs Wragge: 'When you have a trifle of money left you that you didn't expect, if that don't make a lady of you, what does?'[43] Mrs Wragge, however, as her flawed grammar reveals, lacks Magdalen's and Louisa's performative abilities to play a different class role convincingly.

Magdalen and Louisa's discussion of their role-reversal is followed by a moment of intimacy between the two women that echoes the bond between Mabel Vane and Peg Woffington. Louisa, herself a fallen woman who has had a child out of wedlock, approaches Magdalen and kisses her hand. While the bond between Mabel and Peg reinforces class differentiation, the bond between Louisa and Magdalen undermines it. Despite their disparate origins, both have fallen, although in different ways. Louisa's story about being separated from a man she loves leads Magdalen to a 'remembrance of her own loveless marriage' and she tells Louisa: 'For God's sake, don't kneel to *me*! . . . If there is a degraded woman in this room, I am the woman – not you!'[44] Like Mrs Henry Wood's sensational *East Lynne* (1860), in which Lady Isabel Vane disguises herself as a governess to care for her children after scandalously abandoning them, *No Name* depicts Magdalen's mimicry of a servant while emphasising her degradation. Each novel employs its heroine's role-playing a lower-class position to underscore the point that there is nothing inherently different about an aristocratic or genteel woman: she shares the same vulnerabilities as women of other classes.

At the same time that Magdalen's elevated class status is deflated, Louisa is shown that her own class status is mutable. Louisa, an unmarried mother because the father of her child cannot earn enough money in London for them to live together, provides an example of how money shapes non-financial indices of respectability. Magdalen promises that she will provide Louisa with a wedding dress and enough money so that she, her child and the father of her child can emigrate to Australia, where they can afford to live in comfort as a family. Mary Elizabeth Braddon's Lady Audley and her lookalike maid Phoebe share a similar bond because Lady Audley, a governess who married into the aristocracy and is emblematic of the ability of servants to attain higher class status, enables Phoebe and her fiancé to attain financial independence. In both *Lady Audley's Secret* and *No Name*, the servant, as well as the mistress, occupies a position of power: servant and mistress serve each other's needs.

Like Peg Woffington's acting, Magdalen's talent for mimicry enables her to pass as a member of any social class, which makes it more difficult to instil in her the single social role that she is expected to play. For this reason Miss Garth, Magdalen's governess, is horrified when the hired manager for the private theatrical points out Magdalen's aptitude for acting:

> Her worst apprehension of results in connection with the theatrical enterprise, had foreboded levity of conduct with some of the gentlemen – she had not bargained for this. Magdalen, in the capacity of a thoughtless girl, was comparatively easy to deal with. Magdalen, in the character of a born actress, threatened serious future difficulties.[45]

Miss Garth's initial fear of private theatricals – that they provide a degree of intimacy with the opposite sex – echoes earlier representations of private theatricals in novels such as Jane Austen's *Mansfield Park* (1813). Jonas Barish argues that this concrete but trivial fear in *Mansfield Park* was used by novelists to warn against participation in theatrical activities because more deep-seated philosophical or theological discomforts with the concept of role-playing were difficult to present in compelling, concrete terms.[46] In this case, Miss Garth's concern gives voice to the more abstract fear of naturally fluid identities, a fear that is played out sensationally when Magdalen's acting in the private theatrical effects a startlingly concrete loss of identity. While her success is the source of her idea that she can become a professional actress and achieve financial independence that will enable her to pursue her inheritance, her performance leads more immediately to her engagement to Frank. Her engagement, in turn, prompts her father's admission to Frank's father that Magdalen and Norah were born out of wedlock. When Frank's father informs Andrew Vanstone that his recent marriage to Magdalen and Norah's mother has nullified his pre-existing will, Vanstone fatefully decides to make a business trip on a Friday so that he can ask his lawyer to visit to make a new will on Saturday. It is this change in travel plans that causes Andrew Vanstone to fall victim to a fatal train accident before he can make a new will. Magdalen's father's death, in turn, causes the premature birth of Magdalen and Norah's brother and the death of their mother without a valid will. The subsequent death of the newborn legitimate child causes Mrs Vanstone's portion of Andrew Vanstone's estate to revert to Andrew Vanstone's brother. In the logic of this sensational plot, then, the ultimate result of the private theatrical is the loss of Magdalen and Norah's inheritance and social identity.

In his examination of *Mansfield Park*, Barish argues that characters who are most successful in assuming other personas in private theatricals do so because they do not possess a stable, immutable personality of their own.[47] Auerbach similarly argues that '[f]or Magdalen the fallen woman, orphan, bastard, and actress must lack an essential self; her dangerous psychic void creates the fascination of the novel which denounces her.'[48] Both Barish and Auerbach thus echo Diderot's claim: 'It has been said that actors have no character, because in playing all characters they lose that which Nature gave them, and they become false just as the doctor, the surgeon, and the butcher, become hardened. I fancy that here cause is confounded with effect, and that they are fit to play all characters because they have none.'[49] Magdalen's lack of an 'essential self' is not innate, however. Rather, her pursuit of her purpose, impelled by her loss of wealth and class, requires the dissolution of her identity. She wavers between a stable self and a protean theatricality. Her tears, which the narrator calls 'Magdalen's return to her better self', are like Peg's flush and tear in that they signal Magdalen's experience of heartfelt emotion.[50]

It is Magdalen's family origins that provide her with a self-identity. Thackeray's notorious mimic Becky Sharp was an orphan, and *No Name* implies that a lack of family may be necessary for effective acting. More theatrical than her sister, Magdalen is symbolically detached from her family. The narrator introduces Magdalen as a character who bears no resemblance to her parents, in contrast to Norah, who is described as a faded replica of her mother.[51] When she and Norah are declared 'Nobody's Children', Magdalen's loss of family not only frees her to act professionally but impels her to pursue a scheme that depends on her ability to mimic.[52] Dispossessed of her family name, Magdalen explains to her sister:

> we must get our living for ourselves; I have only gone to get mine in the manner which is fittest for me. Whether I succeed, or whether I fail, I can do myself no harm, either way. I have no position to lose, and no name to degrade.[53]

Relying on her distance from her own family and identity, Magdalen's theatrical profession also places her outside of respectable domesticity. Norah leaves her position as a governess when her employers ask her to prevent Magdalen, 'a public performer, roaming from place [sic] in the country' from having contact with the house or the children.[54]

It is precisely their relationships to the domestic world that differentiate the governess and actress, who otherwise appear similar in their potential to disrupt class distinctions. Mary Poovey argues, 'The governess represents class instability because women were often driven to serve as governesses as a result of the failure of their father's financial future', and M. Jeanne Peterson points out that the position of governess was perceived as one for potential social climbing.[55] The indeterminacy of Miss Garth's class is evident in her description of how, although she is a servant, the Vanstones treated her 'as their companion and their friend' and in the fact that she is economically independent because of her financial stake in her sister's school.[56] Yet even though the governess and the actress can both blur social class boundaries, the governess is considered respectable while the actress is not. When Miss Garth says, 'If Norah's and Magdalen's altered prospects oblige them to earn their own independence, I can help them to earn it, as a gentleman's daughters should', she means helping them to become governesses.[57] In contrast, Miss Garth informs Magdalen that, even if she is not sexually fallen, as an actress: 'Your way of life, however pure your conduct may be – and I will do you the justice to believe it pure – is a suspicious way of life to all respectable people.'[58] The difference between the actress and the governess is that the governess works privately within the home while the actress works in public and, Collins suggests, can only do so because she is detached from her home and family. The actress is, therefore, considered a threat to a reputable household.

While her acting relies on separation from her family and places her outside of wholesome domestic life, ties to her family provide Magdalen with a stable emotional identity that interferes with her theatricality and the pursuit of her unsavoury purpose. She writes to her sister that Frank's dissolution of their engagement has left her self-less:

> The shock I have suffered has left a strange quietness in me. I feel as if I had parted from my former self – as if the hopes, once so dear to me, had all gone back to some past time, from which I am now far removed. I can look at the wreck of my life more calmly, Norah, than you could look at it, if we were both together again.[59]

Magdalen herself identifies the danger of this detachment: 'Better have been Frank's wretched wife than the free woman I am now!'[60] This freedom is curbed by Magdalen's family, which prompts her to experience her own, genuine emotions and renders her too grounded in her self to mimic. Anticipating her debut as a professional actress, Wragge writes in his journal: 'I have not the least doubt she will do wonders if she is only left to herself on the first night. But if the day's post is mischievous enough to upset her by a letter from her sister, I tremble for the consequences.'[61] Wragge's concerns echo Diderot's observation of 'the unequal acting of players who play from the heart. From them you must expect no unity. Their playing is alternately strong and feeble, fiery and cold, dull and sublime.'[62] Thinking of her family, Magdalen breaks down as she is about to begin her performance that evening, exclaiming: 'Oh, poor papa! Poor papa! Oh, my God, if he saw me now!'[63] Elsewhere, she writes to Norah that thinking of her leads her to feel emotions that restore her self-identity: 'When I think of your hard life, I can almost feel the tears once more in my weary eyes. I can almost think I have come back to my former self.'[64] When Magdalen, disguised and exercising mimicry to gain access to Noel Vanstone, encounters Norah, working as a governess, in a park, Magdalen's loyalty to her sister calls forth an emotional response: a desire to defend her sister against the bratty children whom she serves. That emotional response, resulting from a sense of connectedness to her only living family member, momentarily interrupts her ability to mimic and unifies external and internal: 'A horror of the vile disguise that concealed her; a yearning to burst its trammels and hide her shameful painted face on Norah's bosom, took possession of her, body and soul.'[65] Yet while loyalty to origins threatens her ability to act, both in the sense of theatrical performance on or off the stage and in the sense of activities to regain her family fortune, Magdalen's realisation that she has lost her origins causes her to renew her commitment to her plan and resume her mimicry. In the next moment after seeing Norah in the park,

> The thought of her sister, which had turned her from the scene of her meditated deception, which had made the consciousness of her own disguise hateful to her – was now the thought which sanctioned that means, or any means, to compass her end; the thought which set wings to her feet, and hurried her back nearer and nearer to the fatal house.[66]

Later, as Magdalen is about to flee her imminent marriage to Noel Vanstone, she stumbles upon the words she had copied from her family's lawyer, 'Mr Vanstone's daughters are Nobody's Children', and determines to continue with her deceitful scheme.[67] Magdalen thus embodies what Lewes describes as the 'antinomy' of acting: 'If the actor lose all power over his art under the disturbing influence of emotion, he also loses all power over his art in proportion to his deadness of emotion. If he really feel, he cannot act; but he cannot act unless he feel.'[68] It is through the 'memory of past feelings', distanced by her loss of identity and sublimated into performance, that Magdalen is such an effective actress.[69]

While family in *No Name* is not itself an anchor of class identity – social hierarchy is determined by money – family is an anchor for the self. Magdalen is ultimately saved by Captain Kirke, a man whose seafaring life serves as an apt metaphor for the wandering, untethered individual who nevertheless returns to a safe harbour. This man, whose own honesty restores Magdalen to her family and her former self, has ties to her origins: Kirke's father was the military officer who saved her father from disgrace and suicide as a result of his first marriage to an American fortune-seeker, a woman who embodies the contrast between materialism and the wholesome bonds of a loving family. Kirke, an upstanding man of action, rather than the indolent Frank, who is descended from an old family, is rewarded with Magdalen's love. Thus, although *No Name* explores the dangers of a world in which class status is often a matter of theatrical performance, it does not argue for a return to a strictly defined inherited class system.

It was precisely the representation of Magdalen as a role-player who ultimately returns to her own identity, so central to the novel, that Collins eliminated when he adapted the novel for the stage in 1870. Alexander Smith's review of the novel in the *North British Review* criticised its lack of verisimilitude, which it characterised as theatricality:

> There never was a young lady like Magdalen, there never was a scoundrel like Wragge, a fool like Vanstone, a housekeeper like Mrs Lecount. Such people have no representatives in the living world. Their proper place is the glare of blue lights on a stage sacred to the sensation drama.[70]

Even though Smith's criticism suggests an affinity between the genre of the sensation novel and sensation drama, Collins's stage version of *No Name* completely evacuated the narrative of Magdalen's theatrical career and sensational role-playing. The fact that, in comparison, the 1863 adaptation by William Bayle Bernard was more faithful to the novel suggests that Collins deliberately decided that the character of Magdalen required substantial alterations for the stage. Specifically, because the stage, on which all that appears genuine is an act, made it difficult to claim a genuine emotional selfhood for Magdalen, Collins's play represents her as a stable character, so that the question of performance never interferes with her authentic identity.

Although Kenneth Robinson calls Bernard's five-act play 'a collaboration' with Collins, a letter from Collins to W. H. Wills on 21 November 1862 indicates that Collins was paying Bernard to draft an adaptation of the novel before Collins had even completed the manuscript, because Collins sought 'legal protection from the British Manager and Dramatist' for his copyright for the story.[71] While the letter alludes to Collins's struggles to write the conclusion of *No Name*, the history of its adaptation for the stage was also a source of irritation for Collins. Collins hoped Bernard's adaptation would be produced at the Olympic Theatre, which had staged dramatisations of several of Collins's works, but even after writing his own dramatisation Collins continued to be dissatisfied and 'refused an Edinburgh Repertory Theatre permission to produce the play. Finally he invited his friend, Wybert Reeve, the actor-manager, to try his hand, giving him *carte blanche*. Wilkie was so pleased with Reeve's adaptation that he abandoned all idea of further tinkering with his own versions and gave it his blessing.'[72] Although it is more accurate to say that Reeve became one of Collins's collaborators on the adaptation, this vexed adaptation history may account for widespread inaccuracies in chronicles of *No Name*'s performance history. Bernard's adaptation, published in 1863, appears never to have been performed. Collins's own four-act play, which he published privately in 1870, was altered in collaboration with Augustin Daly before it was produced by Daly at the Fifth Avenue Theatre in New York on 7 June 1871 and was later produced at Newcastle-on-Tyne, with Reeve listed as its author, and in Australia.[73] The lack of clarity about authorship accords with Pearson's point that 'the Foucauldian model of the author, a homogenous entity . . . is very much at odds with the dramatic practices of the nineteenth century when any writer could translate, adapt, or rewrite the work of any other', and that this is the world in which Collins was operating.[74]

Bernard's play does not make significant changes to the plot of the novel. It streamlines the plot, using dialogue between characters to inform the audience of what has transpired off stage. It shortens the action of the novel by omitting Madame 'Lecompte's' (the play makes her name more foreign) clipping Magdalen's alpaca gown, the episode in which Magdalen is suspected of plotting to murder Noel with the poison she had purchased for her suicide, and Magdalen's attempt to retrieve the Secret Trust from St Crux.[75] Although we never witness the Vanstone daughters with their parents – the action begins with the lawyer informing Miss Garth of the daughters' legal status – it maintains an emphasis on Magdalen's loss of herself and her final return to family through Kirke. The play omits both daughters' professional activities. Magdalen's amateur theatrical as the incident which precipitates the plot, as well as her career as a professional actress, are not included in Bernard's play. When Wragge, having read of her aspirations for the stage on the handbill advertising Magdalen's disappearance, offers to help launch her career, she informs him that acting was merely a 'screen' for her plan to pursue her inheritance.[76] Although she is not an actress, Bernard's Magdalen nevertheless remains true to the novel's view of her by exercising a great deal of agency. Rather than allowing Wragge to profit by swindling her out of her earnings as an actress, as he does in the novel, she initiates her own scheme and recruits him and his wife to serve her needs. The play also maintains the multi-voiced effect of what Jenny Bourne Taylor describes as the novel's 'third-person narrative ... broken up by letters ... and by Wragge's chronicle that works on a different time-scale from the dominant narrative as well as disrupting its omniscience and qualifying its authority over Magdalen' by including asides in which characters tell the audience their thoughts.[77] A notable example is when Madame Lecompte, instead of clipping Magdalen's dress, tells the audience that she recognises Magdalen in her disguise as Miss Garth.

Paradoxically, it appears that Bernard's faithfulness to the novel's characterisation of Magdalen is precisely what Collins objected to in the play. Pearson urges us: 'While we might think of productions of plays as re-interpreting the original text, we might also see that the play was generated in relation to other earlier adaptations and was more properly an adaptation of an adaptation.'[78] This is true of Collins's *No Name*, even though he was adapting what was originally his own work. Pearson further points out that the existence of multiple stage adaptations of the same story 'is a consequence of the burgeoning of theatre'.[79] In his own stage version of *No Name*, Collins radically changed his heroine in order to make her easier to reclaim. Collins's play is similar to Bernard's in that Magdalen never becomes a professional actress, nor does she participate in the private theatrical that, in the novel, launches the trajectory of events. Collins, however, also eliminates her disguise as Miss Garth in order to gain entry to Noel Vanstone's home, thereby excising the explicit representation of her deceitful practices as theatrical behaviour. Moreover, Magdalen exhibits very little agency. Twice in the four-act play she leaves her family, which consists of Miss Garth, an offstage Norah who is a 'bedridden invalid', and her cousin George Bartram, who adores Magdalen and, when Frank jilts her in the play immediately after she loses her inheritance, hopes to marry her.[80] In both cases she leaves her family not as the result of her own initiative but because Wragge twice impels her to attempt to regain her fortune, first by marrying Noel and then by pursuing the Secret Trust. Even as Magdalen participates in Wragge's scheme, she decries his deceptive strategies. For example, in response to his pretense of scientific knowledge in order to engage Madame Lecount, Magdalen says, 'More deception! More falsehoods! ... Let me do something innocent and harmless, or my horror of myself will be more than I can bear!'[81] Magdalen maintains her morality and identity apart from her involvement with the con man.

The play does not represent Magdalen as a woman who becomes more and more mutable as she is detached from her origins. The audience witnesses no fall from origins because the play begins after her parents' deaths, and viewers only meet Magdalen for the first time in her response to the contents of the will. George Bartram, rather than her immediate family, is responsible for her wavering in her determination to carry out her schemes. Magdalen is less an agent situated between good and evil, and between a stable identity grounded by family and a protean theatricality, than she is a woman torn between the influences of two different men: Wragge and George. When Wragge approaches her a second time and suggests that she disguise herself as a parlour-maid to gain access to the Secret Trust, it is the thought of George that causes Magdalen to hesitate.[82] Like Svengali, the mesmerist who impels the performances of the eponymous heroine of George Du Maurier's novel *Trilby* (1894), Wragge is the villainous character under whose control Magdalen falls and the central agent of duplicity in the play. A scene in which he holds his wife up to an audience of consumers as an example of the wondrous effects of his pill signifies his position as a puppet master. In Collins's play theatricality is not indeterminate identity, but the control of another person.

Because in this version she exercises little agency in her corruption, Magdalen is easily redeemed. When she is restored to her family after her marriage to Noel Vanstone, she sees herself as a fallen woman who cannot accept George's proposal of marriage. Her second attempt, under Wragge's control, to regain her lost fortune ends in the play's final scene, which represents Magdalen's refusal to carry out their dishonest scheme while Wragge does not hesitate to pursue the Secret Trust. When George discovers the two, he drops to his knees, declaring, 'Disguised in a servant's dress! Found near an open bureau! . . . What does it mean?'[83] Wragge acknowledges all responsibility, enabling Magdalen and George to be united, and tidily speaks the last lines of the play: 'Accept my best congratulations. Good evening!'[84]

By stripping Magdalen of both agency and theatricality, Collins's play loses the verve of the novel. Unlike Taylor and Reade, whose *Masks and Faces* allows the viewer to see and to see through the performances that deceive the novel-reader, Collins, in adapting his story for the stage, eliminates the novel's scenes of Magdalen's most sensational role-playing. While the novel suggests the danger and excitement of Magdalen's acting, the play lacks any sense of this. The novel's theatrical Magdalen would have been difficult to redeem in the way that Collins redeems her in the novel, and in the way that Reade redeems Peg Woffington in the novel he based on his own co-authored play. Taylor and Reade allowed Peg Woffington to remain the unreclaimed theatrical woman in their play while they asserted her class identity as distinct from Mabel Vane's. Collins, embracing greater class fluidity, must reclaim Magdalen from her theatrical changeability in order to establish a basis for a stable self-identity in a world in which class is mutable. The stage, on which all that appears genuine is an act, would have made it difficult to claim any genuine emotional selfhood for Magdalen. As Collins points out in his novel, Magdalen's only problem acting in the private theatrical occurs when she must present 'stage artifice' rather than an illusion of reality.[85] The theatre makes it difficult to distinguish between artifice and genuineness, though such a distinction is crucial for Collins's reclaiming of Magdalen in the novel. For this reason, the play does not represent Magdalen as a woman who wilfully assumes different roles and ultimately returns to her own identity, a transformation that Margaret Oliphant, writing about *No Name* in *Blackwood's*, criticised for the way in which Magdalen leaves her 'career of vulgar and aimless trickery and wickedness' and 'emerges, at the cheap cost of a fever, as pure, as high-minded, and as spotless as the most dazzling white of heroines'.[86] In his play Collins eliminates this extreme conversion by representing Magdalen, with a stable sense of her own identity and moral worldview, as more reluctant to pursue trickery and, therefore, more consistently innocent. While in the novel Magdalen narrowly avoids attempting suicide, in the play Magdalen actually tries to poison herself in order to maintain her integrity and avoid consummating her marriage to Noel. When Collins's play was produced at the Fifth Avenue Theatre in New York City, where it ran for thirteen nights, the *New York Times* praised the actress who played Magdalen but found her 'much too elaborate and artificial as the heroine'.[87] The reception of her apparent attempt to convey Magdalen's own theatricality illustrates the difficulty of performing the contrast between artifice and authenticity on stage. Good acting makes performance indistinguishable from 'nature', and an audience can easily mistake stage artifice for bad acting.

While Reade asserts Peg Woffington's class origins as the vehicle through which he reclaims her from the changeability of performing, Collins relies on the home and family to reclaim Magdalen or, in the case of his play, to maintain her integrity. In fact, his play transposes the novel's revenge plot into a domestic drama: the second time that Magdalen falls under Wragge's spell she does so in a desperate attempt to gain money so that her sister can be cured of a fatal illness. Pearson suggests that other Collins adaptations of his own works '[shrank] the range or reach of the narrative to the confines of the middle-class house', and that this reflected the theatrical modes of the time – modes that were shaped in part by the plays of T. W. Robertson.[88] Pearson identifies Collins's adaptations of the 1870s as part of 'a rising intellectual theatre from the visually-oriented melodramas of the earlier Victorian stage, creating a critical space between a popular theatre for the masses and what was styled as a more refined experience for the sophisticated playgoer'.[89] We turn our attention now to the playwright who is identified as being central to this shift: T. W. Robertson.

Robertson's Theatre of Realism and Respectability

The actress, both off stage and as a figure in drama, helped drive the theatrical change that Pearson describes. The 1860s were pivotal for Victorian drama's renaissance as the commercial strategies of theatre managers such as Marie Wilton, who was also known as Mrs Bancroft, combined with the output of increasingly realistic playwrights such as T. W. Robertson to lure the respectable novel-reading public back to the theatre. Wilton, the actress-manager who would play Tom Taylor and Charles Reade's Woffington at the Prince of Wales's Theatre in 1875 with her husband Squire Bancroft in the role of Triplet, and who with her husband testified in William Archer's *Masks or Faces? A Study in the Psychology of Acting* that outstanding acting requires the actor to feel, made theatrical business success out of respectable domesticity.[90] In addition to her collaboration with Robertson, in managing the Prince of Wales's she converted an 'unfashionable' playhouse that had been known as a '"dusthole"' to a pink-chintzed and carpeted auditorium, and she reduced the evening's bill to a single play, eliminating the 'salacious interludes'.[91] Jim Davis and Victor Emeljanow argue that theatre history has overstated this transformation and explain: 'the myth of the Prince of Wales's Theatre is a myth of reclamation involving a theatre, the drama, an actress, and an audience. In reclaiming the Prince of Wales's Theatre, Marie Wilton also reclaimed herself.'[92] Recognising Wilton's success as more a matter of image than quantifiable change – the image that she made for the theatre and the actress – *The Victorian Actress* demonstrates the influence that such image-making exerted.

Tracy Davis points out that the use of the 'box set' – a detailed, naturalistic, self-enclosed domestic set comprising three walls that prevented audience members from seeing into the wings – increased the 'existential' as well as 'physical' distance between the stage and the auditorium, restoring the '"proper" demarcation of public and private realms'.[93] Robertson's plays at the Prince of Wales's popularised the box set, and his marriage of the box set to domestic themes accomplished what Allardyce Nicoll calls 'spiritual reality' and 'a deliberate attempt, through the medium of art, at dealing with the major problems of the day'.[94] The *Daily News* called Robertson's *Caste* a 'play "with a purpose"', and 'more than a mere attempt to amuse the groundlings'.[95] At the same time that Robertson's 'conception of theme value' targeted an audience of greater sophistication than most nineteenth-century theatre had done before, it challenged the widespread cultural belief, expressed forcibly in most of the works that we have examined, that actresses were outsiders and threats to the respectable home.[96] Actresses, whose public performances transgressed gender expectations, were far more socially problematic than actors. Reclaiming the theatre, therefore, included refiguring the actress as compatible with the domestic sphere. In addition to the actress's metonymic relation to the theatre, the actress figures prominently in the competition between the novel and the stage because her ability to feign challenges one of the most fundamental principles of what Ian Watt has termed '[m]odern realism': 'the position that truth can be discovered by the individual through his senses' or, 'that the external world is real, and that our senses give us a true report of it'.[97] While actresses or actress-like women appear in sensation novels precisely because they challenge the notion that things are as they appear, more realistic works unmask the actress's performance in order to establish a genuine reality. *Caste* reaches towards both respectability and realism by presenting the actress, off stage, as a mother.

The homophonic title of Robertson's *Caste* refers both to social classes and to the assignment of theatrical roles. By underscoring the theatricality of social distinctions, this play on words suggests that respectable society and the socially marginalised world of the theatre are not as dissimilar as a caste system tries to make them. As the actors portray a wide spectrum of classes from labourers to the aristocracy, *Caste* echoes the final act of Boucicault's *The Life of an Actress* as it claims that its actress heroine, Esther Eccles, can achieve domestic happiness by marrying the Honourable George D'Alroy against the wishes of his mother, the Marquise de St Maur. Esther's sister, Polly, asserts a distinction between the art that she and her sister practise on stage and her beau's trade:

> Better paint our *cheeks* than paint *nasty old doors* as you do. How can you understand art? You're only a mechanic! you're not a professional. You're in trade. You are not of the same station that we are. When the manager speaks to you, you touch your hat, and say, 'Yes, sir', because he's your superior. . . . Actors are not like mechanics. They wear cloth coats, and not fustian jackets.[98]

But while Polly delineates the actress as a professional, the play asserts the respectability of actresses by tracing Esther's absorption into non-professional, domestic life, and the actress's motherhood is central to this claim. *Caste* thus falls into the category of texts that Davis defines as 'public relations attempts to depict actresses as home-centred, modest, self-respecting females redolent of middle-class virtues', at the same time that it acknowledges and answers the phenomenon of actresses whose 'visibility and notoriety in the public realm led to persistent and empirically unfounded prejudices and very real sexual dangers in their work places'.[99] The sexual dangers of Esther's career are evident in the play's first dialogue, in which Hawtree assumes that his friend George's interest in the actress is a typical dalliance: 'I know – pastry-cooks – Richmond dinner – and all that.'[100] When Hawtree himself flirts with Polly, her mechanic beau, Sam, points out: 'What can a long fool of a swell dressed up to the nines within an inch of his life want with two girls of your class? Look at the difference of your stations! 'E don't come 'ere after any good.'[101] The central problem of *Caste* is the respectability of Esther and her sister Polly as Esther marries above her station, is rejected by her mother-in-law and returns to the stage to support her child when her husband goes off to war and is believed to be killed.

Although the *Daily News* suggested that *Caste* infringed on the novelistic by attempting a complexity uncommon for the stage and by 'combin[ing] the geniality of Mr Dickens with the cynicism of Thackeray', the play's contrived and common plot about a supposedly dead man's return from India actually differs a great deal from Robertson's short story 'The Poor Rate Unfolds a Tale' (1866), on which the play was based. Like Pearson's argument that Collins viewed stage adaptation as requiring a separate act of creation, Robertson clearly viewed the stage as having different exigencies and affordances than the page. The short story ends with the deaths not only of Fairfax Daubray (the story's George D'Alroy) in battle but also of his wife

Polly (the Esther figure), who, on her deathbed, entrusts her son to the care of her mother-in-law Lady Clardonax. We are not aware until the very end of the story that it has been told by an unannounced narrator, the Tax Collector, who explains how Fairfax and Polly's son was the spoiled heir of Lady Clardonax, Fairfax's friend Major Swynton became less socially elitist, and Esther's father 'went somewhere – to the bad, of course, in a general sort of way'.[102] Whereas the story bitterly observes that society does not reward merit with the wealth on which class hierarchies are based, the play insists on the need to recognise the merits of individuals regardless of birth. Unlike Reade, who adapted his collaborative play into a novel because he felt that the theatre could not convey his theme, Robertson, while recognising that his story could not retain its novelistic realism amid the convention-bound expectations of a theatrical audience, nevertheless believed that a social theme could be explored on stage and set about to define a new form of stage realism.

Although it changes the story's ending, the play contrasts its own relatively realistic treatment of a social theme with the cross-class romantic plots of other novels and plays. 'All those marriages of people with common people', Hawtree tells George,

> are all very well in novels and in plays on the stage, because the real people don't exist, and have no relatives who exist, and no connections, and so no harm's done, and it's rather interesting to look at; but in real life with real relations, and real mothers, and so forth, it's absolute bosh. It's worse – it's utter social and personal annihilation and damnation.[103]

Similarly, Esther's sentimental description of her courtship as 'like in a novel from the library, only better. You, a fine, rich, high-born gentleman, coming to our humble little house to court poor me', and her reference to 'Jeanne la Folle; or, the Return of the Soldier', a play with a similar plot to Robertson's, provide points of contrast for Robertson's focus on social class and the necessities of daily life.[104] When Esther's sister alludes to 'Jeanne la Folle' in an attempt to prepare Esther for George's return, the melodramatic details that she touches on – the groom's forced conscription on his wedding day and the madness of his bride in his absence – serve to emphasise Robertson's relative realism.[105] Robertson's heroine does not go mad but pragmatically attempts to support herself and her child.

Central to *Caste*'s true-to-life quality is its depiction of the actress at home. Robertson's play excludes his short story's fairly long flashback about 'The Sara', the hero's first stage infatuation, because *Caste* is concerned not with glamorous divas like Peg Woffington but with the mundane life behind the illusion of Esther's performances. Her acting is respectable because, prior to her marriage, she works outside the home only to maintain her home, a domestic setting realised on stage in detailed three-dimensional verisimilitude:

> A plain set chamber, paper soiled. A window, C., with practicable blind; street backing and iron railings. Door practicable, R.3E.; when opened showing street door (practicable). Fire-place, L.; two-hinged gas-burners on each side of mantelpiece. Sideboard cupboard in recess, L.3E.; tea-things, teapot, tea-caddy, tea-tray, &c., on it. Long table, L.C., before fire; old piece of carpet and rug down; plain chairs; book-shelf back L.; a small table under it with ballet-shoe and skirt on it; bunch of benefit bills hanging under book-shelf. Theatrical printed portraits, framed, hanging about; chimney glass clock; box of lucifers and ornaments on mantelshelf; kettle on hob, and fire laid; door-mats on the outside of door. Bureau, R.[106]

These solid realities of domestic life give the lie to the romanticisation of the actress, mocked by Hawtree: 'And this is the fairy's bower!'[107] Later Esther's motherhood and domesticity are constituted as touchstones for authenticity, in contrast to the theatricality of her father, whose lack of stability is reflected in his alcoholism. After he tries to steal her son's coral (used for teething) to pawn it for alcohol, Esther rejects his theatrical excuses, which draw on textual and rhetorical references, by declaring her own identity within the home: 'I am a woman – I am a wife – a widow – a *mother*! Do you think I will let you outrage *him*? [*Pointing to cradle.*] *Touch me if you dare*!'[108] Her mutually reinforcing domestic identities, expressed most forcefully in motherhood, invoke stability rather than Peg Woffington's protean role-playing.

That Robertson dedicated the published copy of his play to 'Miss Marie Wilton (Mrs Bancroft)', referring to himself as 'her grateful friend and fellow labourer', emphasises both how Wilton had achieved professional success and public stature on par with men, and how her professional status depended at least in part upon the domestic respectability conferred by her marital status. In analysing the autobiographies of actresses including Wilton, Mary Jean Corbett argues that 'the ideology of domestic femininity persistently shaped the written lives of Victorian and Edwardian women' and that 'the discourse of femininity was something many public women consciously appropriated as a means of legitimating their public identities, of achieving professional success, of making political change'.[109] In fact, as Corbett demonstrates,

Robertson's youngest of twenty-one siblings, Madge Kendal, possessed a 'queenly preeminence' that 'depended on the close fit between her staged public performances and her known "private" character as an exemplary wife and mother who was as devoted to imposing a salutary feminine influence on the theater as to upholding familial values and virtues'.[110] It is even more appropriate that Robertson dedicated *Caste* to Wilton, because her originating the role of Esther provides a prime example of how Wilton used domesticity in order to claim respectability for actresses, including herself, and in doing so contributed to the development of a new form of stage realism.

An illustration of Esther's act 2 marital home reflects the thematic importance of Robertson's sets (Fig. 2.1). Within this setting, which evinces the conspicuous consumption of a leisured class, Esther, collapsing in a heap on the floor, mars her tidy surroundings and contrasts starkly with the upright figure of her mother-in-law. The swirling fabric of Esther's skirt is out of place amid the vertical lines that, in the door frames, doors, book cases, wallpaper and tablecloth, dominate the upper half of the illustration, and amid the horizontal lines that, in the floor, piano keys and sword, define the lower half. Her supine form thus embodies the central problem of the play: will Esther be able to fit into her husband's class and gain the acceptance of her mother-in-law? Within the logic of the play, Esther's susceptibility to emotion is precisely what enables her to live a domestic life. Robertson relies on the melodramatic convention of the legibility of bodily expression: Esther's emotionality signals her genuineness. Like Peg Woffington's, her tears prove her to be better than an actress and, in this case, better than members of the aristocracy, who are depicted in well-worn social roles. Indeed, the *Daily News* praised the working-class characters as 'real characters who think, speak, and act like human beings, and yet are intensely amusing and interesting', but criticised '[t]he aristocratic portraits' for being 'comparatively weak, more or less wooden, conventional, and stagey, and highly coloured for the sake of contrast'.[111] Although the Marquise points out that Esther's feelings mark her class by preventing her from living up to the aristocratic tradition of women arming their men for war, Esther's fainting expresses her true distress and true possession of the feelings of a good wife.

Equating the actress's genuineness with her domesticity, asserting both that Esther's genuine emotions allow her to fulfil domestic duties and that her domesticity testifies to her authenticity, permitted Robertson to contrast his play's realism with the artifice of other plays and novels and to achieve renown both in his own time and

Figure 2.1 Act 2 of *Caste*. 'Scene from *Caste* by T. W. Robertson, Prince of Wales Theatre, probably 1867' (© Victoria and Albert Museum, London)

today as a pivotal figure in Victorian drama. Because it was common for Victorian critics and novelists, such as Dickens in *Nicholas Nickleby* (1838–9) and Collins in 'Dramatic Grub Street',[112] to lament that high drama in England consisted of translations of French plays, the *Illustrated London News* identified *Caste* as an epochal play, indicating that 'an English school of dramatic writing is among the possibilities of no very remote future':

> Mr Robertson has not recently been fortunate in his ventures, particularly in one derived from the French; but in the present he has trusted to his own invention, and conceived and executed his subject in a thoroughly English spirit. The true Saxon vein is appreciable in every scene, speech, and line of a piece thoroughly moral, frequently satirical – its satire being life – and boldly independent in its view of men and things.[113]

Nicoll calls Robertson 'no first in merit among playwrights of the past but first in time among the dramatic writers of the present'.[114] As we shall see in Chapters 4 and 5, however, this view of Robertson would be challenged by future novelists and playwrights to whom Robertson's innovations had become conventions. Nevertheless, as

Chapter 4 will demonstrate, the theatrical innovations of Robertson would also influence the development of the late Victorian novel.

Like Collins's *No Name*, in which the home is a source of authentic identity for Magdalen, in *Caste* the actress's compatibility with the domestic world requires virtue and signals respectability. In both of these works, however, this respectability ultimately removes the actress from the stage and therefore from her source of financial independence. Gail Marshall's description of how nineteenth-century responses to Diderot curtailed the actress's power points to another way in which these works curtailed the actress's powers, even as they used her as a figure that disrupted rigid class hierarchies:

> Diderot's self-appointed nineteenth-century opponents ... saw their opposition as necessary in order to counteract the implication in Diderot that the best actor might be a calculating creature whose theatrical standing relied on a lack of common humanity. This was an implication particularly unbecoming to the actress and one which had to be refuted if she was to remain desirable in, and subject to, the audience's gaze. Further, if Diderot's contention is allowed to stand, it makes of the actress one capable of manipulating her audiences, controlling rather than being subject to their desire, and hence wresting the power of dramatic determination from them and the playwright. Such a possibility was strongly resisted.[115]

Even when the actress was used in order to challenge traditional class structures, her powers remained checked by the audience, as Violet's final lines in *The Life of an Actress* illustrate:

> Am I to quit the stage? What do you say –
> Forbid with a smile, and I'll obey.[116]

Even as Violet attains both professional success and social acceptance, the power that her acting represents is ultimately kept in check by the audience. A power negotiation between actress and audience is the subject of Chapter 3, which examines how George Eliot grappled with this problem as she employed the actress as a figure for the female artist.

Notes

1. Tom Taylor and Charles Reade, *Masks and Faces*, p. 161.
2. 'The Theatres', *The Illustrated London News*, 8 March 1862, p. 245.
3. Fawkes, *Dion Boucicault*, pp. 86, 92.

4. 'Drama', *The London Daily News*, 3 March 1862, p. 2.
5. 'The Theatres', *The Era*, 9 March 1862, p. 10.
6. Ibid. p. 10.
7. Boucicault, *The Life of an Actress*, p. 4.
8. Ibid. p. 4.
9. Ibid. p. 3.
10. Ibid. p. 5.
11. Ibid. p. 5.
12. Ibid. p. 5.
13. Ibid. p. 6.
14. Ibid. p. 9.
15. Ibid. p. 8.
16. Ibid. p. 8.
17. Ibid. p. 14.
18. Ibid. p. 14.
19. 'The Theatres', *The Era*, 9 March 1862, p. 10.
20. 'The New Adelphi Theatre', *The Morning Post*, 3 March 1862, p. 6.
21. Boucicault, *The Life of an Actress*, p. 15.
22. Ibid. p. 15.
23. Ibid. p. 16.
24. Ibid. p. 16.
25. Ibid. p. 17.
26. Ibid. p. 17.
27. Ibid. p. 17.
28. Ibid. p. 18.
29. Ibid. p. 18.
30. For accounts of Reade and Collins's relationship, see Malcolm Elwin, *Charles Reade*; Thomas D. Clareson, 'Wilkie Collins to Charles Reade'; and Walter de la Mare, 'The Early Novels of Wilkie Collins'.
31. Pearson, *Victorian Writers and the Stage*, p. 152.
32. Gasson, *Wilkie Collins: An Illustrated Guide*, p. 131.
33. [Smith], 'Art. VI. – Novels and Novelists of the Day', *North British Review*, p. 183; Jenny Bourne Taylor, *In the Secret Theatre of Home*, p. 148.
34. Diderot, *The Paradox of Acting*, p. 13.
35. Ibid. p. 14.
36. Collins, *No Name* [1862–3], pp. 26, 30.
37. Ibid. pp. 98–100, 227.
38. Ibid. p. 244.
39. Ibid. p. 27.
40. Ibid. p. 60.
41. Ibid. p. 586.
42. Ibid. p. 503.
43. Ibid. p. 165.
44. Ibid. p. 497.
45. Ibid. p. 44.

46. Barish, *The Antitheatrical Prejudice*, p. 305.
47. Ibid. p. 306.
48. Auerbach, *Romantic Imprisonment*, p. 255.
49. Diderot, *The Paradox of Acting*, pp. 64–5.
50. Collins, *No Name*, p. 117.
51. Ibid. pp. 8, 6.
52. Ibid. p. 109.
53. Ibid. p. 144.
54. Ibid. p. 254.
55. Poovey, *Uneven Developments*, p. 147; Peterson, 'The Victorian Governess', pp. 6–7.
56. Collins, *No Name*, p. 129.
57. Ibid. p. 122.
58. Ibid. p. 254.
59. Ibid. p. 258.
60. Ibid. p. 258.
61. Ibid. p. 194.
62. Diderot, *The Paradox of Acting*, p. 8.
63. Collins, *No Name*, p. 194.
64. Ibid. p. 259.
65. Ibid. p. 221.
66. Ibid. p. 222.
67. Ibid. p. 399.
68. Lewes, *On Actors and the Art of Acting*, pp. 100–1.
69. Ibid. p. 102.
70. [Smith], 'Art. VI. – Novels and Novelists of the Day', p. 185.
71. Collins's unpublished letter to Wills, dated 21 November 1862, can be found in Autographs Miscellaneous English, The Pierpont Morgan Library, New York. Although the play *No Name* remains unnamed in this letter, Robinson points out that Bernard's play 'was published in 1863 by the Office of *All the Year Round*, soon after the appearance of the novel'. It is, therefore, a reasonable conclusion that the play Bernard was writing is the dramatisation of the novel *No Name* that Collins describes himself as in the process of completing. See Robinson, *Wilkie Collins: A Biography*, p. 158.
72. Gasson, *Wilkie Collins*, p. 119; Robinson, *Wilkie Collins*, pp. 158–9.
73. Robinson, among other sources, incorrectly states that Reeve's production in Melbourne is the only recorded staging of *No Name* (p. 159), while Gasson, also incorrectly, states that no version was produced in England, and notes only foreign performances of Collins's version. According to Gasson, Collins's version, 'altered' by Wybert Reeve and produced by Augustin Daly, opened at the Fifth Avenue Theatre in New York on 7 June 1871 before being taken, by Reeve, to Melbourne, Australia, in 1879, where it was performed under the title *Great Temptation* (pp. 115, 131). A cast list for Augustin Daly's New York production of *No Name* at the Fifth Avenue Theatre on 7 June 1871 confirms Gasson's

assertion, as well as Robert P. Ashley's, in 'Wilkie Collins and the American Theater', pp. 241–55, that the production was based on Collins's, rather than Bernard's adaptation: George and Admiral Bartram are included, as is an 'Attendant at Crux Abbey', while Kirke is not. For the cast list, see George C. D. Odell's *Annals of the New York Stage*, vol. 9, p. 18. The *New York Tribune*'s review of *No Name* at the Fifth Avenue Theatre in New York (8 June 1871, p. 8) describes the play performed there as consisting of five acts, however, indicating that the play performed was not identical to the four-act print version. The *Times* review notes: 'On the bills of the Fifth–avenue Theatre, where the drama was first given last night, it is attributed to Mr Wilkie Collins and Mr Augustin Daly. The name of the latter gentleman is employed, we presume, as a protective measure' (p. 4).

Gasson, however, overlooked the opening of Collins's four-act version, bearing Reeve's name, at the Newcastle-on-Tyne Theatre Royal on 26 October 1877, a production that appears in both Reginald Clarence's *'The Stage' Cyclopaedia: A Bibliography of Plays*, p. 320; and Allardyce Nicoll's *Late Nineteenth Century Drama*, vol. 5 of *A History of English Drama*, p. 540. Although the play bears Reeve's name, it is likely that production circumstances led Collins to have his name removed from the playbills. Ashley's chronicle of Collins's novels on the American stage describes how Collins became more and more unwilling to allow plays to be staged without his involvement. More specifically, Ashley cites an 1871 letter in which Collins explains that he is unwilling to allow *The Woman in White* to be staged without his tutoring the actor who would play Fosco, 'after the experience of *No Name*' (p. 252). In his 1870 dealings with Daly, Collins asked that his name be removed from Daly's production of an adaptation of Collins's *Man and Wife* because Collins did not want 'his name linked with an adaptation over which he had no control' (Ashley, p. 244). A copy of Collins's published adaptation of *No Name* held by Indiana University's Lilly Library includes a cast list for a performance at the Theatre Royal in Newcastle-on-Tyne. The cast of characters, with the exception of the substitution of a character named 'Merrick' for Admiral Bartram, is identical to that of Collins's adaptation.

In his list of 'Collins's Plays', Ashley also mistakes the publication date of Collins's adaptation of *No Name*, using the 1863 date of Bernard's play, rather than its publication date of 1870 (p. 255).

74. Pearson, *Victorian Writers and the Stage*, p. 149.
75. The list of acts at the beginning of the *All the Year Round* 1863 edition of Bernard's play inexplicably lists act 5 as taking place at St Crux, Essex. The text of act 5 indicates that it in fact takes place at Aaron's Buildings, Regents Park, where Kirke has been caring for Magdalen. This mistake was corrected in the 1880s edition of the play. [Bernard], *No Name: A Drama, in Five Acts* (London: G. Holsworth, at the Office of 'All the Year Round', 1863); [Bernard], *No Name: A Drama, in Five Acts* (Chicago: The Dramatic Publishing Company, [188–?]).

76. [Bernard], *No Name* (1863), p. 25.
77. Jennie Bourne Taylor, *In the Secret Theatre of Home*, p. 148.
78. Pearson, *Victorian Writers and the Stage*, p. 150.
79. Ibid. p. 150.
80. Collins, *No Name: A Drama, In Four Acts*, p. 10.
81. Ibid. pp. 45–6.
82. Ibid. p. 67.
83. Ibid. p. 81.
84. Ibid. p. 82.
85. Collins, *No Name*, p. 43.
86. [Oliphant], 'Novels', *Blackwood's Edinburgh Magazine* 94 (1863), p. 170.
87. *New York Times*, 8 June 1871, p. 4. For a description of the play's run, see Odell, *Annals of the New York Stage*, p. 18.
88. Pearson, *Victorian Writers and the Stage*, p. 163.
89. Ibid. p. 163.
90. Archer, *Masks or Faces?*, pp. 52–3.
91. Rowell, *The Victorian Theater 1792–1914*, pp. 82–3; Tracy C. Davis, *Actresses as Working Women*, p. 150.
92. Jim Davis and Victor Emeljanow, *Reflecting the Audience*, pp. 161–2.
93. Tracy C. Davis, *Actresses as Working Women*, p. 149.
94. Nicoll, *Late Nineteenth Century Drama*, pp. 122, 131. According to George Rowell the box set was first used by Madame Vestris and Charles Mathews at the Olympic Theatre and Covent Garden two decades before Robertson, but 'they could find no Robertson to evolve a new school of comedy on which to lavish their scenic reforms' (*The Victorian Theater*, pp. 79, 19).
95. Review of *Caste*, *Daily News* [London], 8 April 1867, p. 2.
96. Nicoll, *Late Nineteenth Century Drama*, p. 126.
97. Watt, *The Rise of the Novel*, p. 12.
98. Robertson, *Caste*, p. 360.
99. Davis, *Actresses as Working Women*, p. xiv.
100. Robertson, *Caste*, p. 348.
101. Ibid. p. 359.
102. Robertson, 'The Poor Rate Unfolds a Tale', p. 184.
103. Robertson, *Caste*, p. 349.
104. Ibid. p. 363.
105. Ibid. pp. 401–2.
106. Ibid. p. 347.
107. Ibid. p. 347.
108. Ibid. p. 384.
109. Corbett, *Representing Femininity*, p. 15.
110. Ibid. p. 121.
111. Review of *Caste*, *Daily News* [London], 8 April 1867, p. 2.

112. [Collins], 'Dramatic Grub Street: Explored in Two Letters', *Household Words* 17 (1858): pp. 265–70.
113. Review of *Caste*, by T. W. Robertson, *Illustrated London News*, 13 April 1867, p. 370.
114. Nicoll, *Late Nineteenth Century Drama*, p. 131.
115. Gail Marshall, *Actresses on the Victorian* Stage, p. 123.
116. Boucicault, *The Life of an Actress*, p. 18.

Chapter 3

The Actress and Her Audience: Performance, Authorship and the Exceptional Woman in George Eliot

Many of George Eliot's female characters – Mirah, the Alcharisi, Gwendolen, Dinah, Hetty and Rosamund – are in different ways and to various degrees performing women. Eliot's grandest diva, however, is also her least studied. The opera singer Armgart takes centre stage in the poetic closet drama of the same name. A focused study of an exceptional woman, *Armgart* (1871) conveys both Eliot's belief in the dangers of the influence of public opinion and her belief that exceptionally talented women can gain power – albeit tenuously – through interacting with audiences. My analysis of *Armgart* builds on recent books by Susan David Bernstein and Kathleen McCormack, which focus respectively on Eliot's work in the British Museum and her entertaining in her home. These works contradict the understanding of Eliot's preference for privacy, as each examines how Eliot negotiated between public and private, attempting to fulfil her need for a 'productive exteriority' even as her relationship to it was vexed.[1] Additionally, *Armgart* demonstrates that Eliot advocated for community among exceptional women and ordinary women, and it continues to develop a performed sympathetic bond that moves beyond the emotional and spectacular bond of melodrama we saw in *Peg Woffington* and *No Name*. Finally, *Armgart*'s examination of the talented female performer allowed Eliot to consider the role of the woman writer.

Armgart depicts an opera star in her glory and then in her desolation after she has lost her voice due to medication she received during a life-threatening illness. In order to pursue her career, Armgart spurns the attentions of a noble suitor, Graf Dornberg. Ultimately, she is left alone with only her cousin and companion, the lame Walpurga. Criticism of *Armgart* places it within a tradition of operatic diva heroines created by women writers and focuses on how voice provides self-expression, agency and spiritual meaning.[2] In emphasising Armgart's vocation as a singer, such analyses have neglected a key element of Armgart's power that results from her theatrical performance. After Armgart has lost her voice, Walpurga describes the dual benefits of the stage as,

> The prouder queenly work that paid itself,
> And yet was overpaid with men's applause.[3]

The second of these benefits, that of an audience's applause, is discussed at length in Eliot's drama and identified as a source of power for the performing woman. *Armgart* shows how, despite the power that the audience wields over performers and, particularly, female performers, interacting with an audience is an empowering alternative to a domestic life.[4] Indeed, Gillian Beer has pointed out, Eliot's 'chosen figure for the creative woman is not the writer. . . . Instead it is the musician, and in particular the singer.'[5] Eliot's translation of authorship into theatre emphasises the importance of performing for an audience and the power dynamic between the female performer and her audience. This chapter considers Armgart in the context of other performing women created by Eliot – most notably Mirah, the Alcharisi and Gwendolen in *Daniel Deronda* (1876) – in order to examine Eliot's emphasis on women's talent not as a mode of self-expression or spirituality but as a vehicle through which women can broaden their influence and play a role in the public sphere.[6] In juxtaposition to Wilkie Collins and T. W. Robertson, who locate a stable, authentic identity in family relationships and the home, Eliot's female performers derive self-importance and self-determination from their influence that extends beyond family life and even precludes wifehood and motherhood.

Louise Hudd has noted that *Armgart* 'restages the themes of *Aurora Leigh*, continuing [Elizabeth] Barrett Browning's disquisition upon the place of the female artist in Victorian society' and 'explores the obligations of the exceptional woman to her society and to other women, raising the issue of what it means to be marginalised in the interests of a political action which might liberate only the exceptional few rather than the many'.[7] Suggesting that Eliot manifested a feminism that united women across class and talent lines, Hudd views Walpurga's criticism of Armgart's self-centredness as a response to Barrett Browning's eliminating the fallen working-class woman Marian Erle from the plot of *Aurora Leigh* (1856) in order to focus on Aurora and Romney.[8] In Eliot, however, the connection between women divided by talent or class is not effected through an affective moment, as it is in *Peg Woffington* or *No Name*, but rather requires an effort to comprehend the condition of other women.

This chapter examines the contrast between *Aurora Leigh*'s characterisation of the female artist as a transcendent, quasi-religious prophet who eschews public exposure and *Armgart*'s notion of the female artist's greatness – her exceptionalness – as inseparable from her interaction with audiences. Beer asserts that '[t]he hidden resistances and enforcements of [Eliot's] works can be understood more subtly if we do not concentrate our attention within the 'great woman' model, but see the text as containing and resisting other writing by which it was surrounded.' Considering *Middlemarch* (1871–2) within a frame of writings supporting women's rights and enfranchisement, Beer contradicts critics who have accused Eliot of avoiding feminism. She argues that Eliot 'did engage with issues vital in the life of the women's movement'.[9] Examining *Armgart* as a response to *Aurora Leigh* illuminates Eliot by considering her work within the context of cultural texts that influenced her, as Beer has done, but also establishes Eliot's place in the developing understanding of women, theatricality and the public world and, in doing so, demonstrates that Eliot was a precursor of the twentieth-century suffrage movement.

Poetry, Music and the Body in *Aurora Leigh* and *Armgart*

Eliot's review of *Aurora Leigh* in the *Westminster Review* reveals how the poem fascinated her: 'no poem embraces so wide a range of thought and emotion, or takes such complete possession of our nature'. Her description of the poem as 'a full mind pouring itself out in song as its natural and easiest medium' emphasises a relationship between the artist's mind and music that she would explore more fully in *Armgart*.[10] Joseph Litvak has argued that Eliot, for whom music represents a poetry that contrasts with the theatricality of sensation novels, weighs Barrett Browning's poem by considering the degree to which it avoids sensational strategies.[11] She praises it by noting, 'The *story* of "Aurora Leigh" has no other merit than that of offering certain elements of life, and certain situations which are peculiarly fitted to call forth the writer's rich thought and experience. It has nothing either fresh or felicitous in structure of incident.'[12] This emphasis on situation, rather than plot, parallels *Armgart*, which has little action but consists of Armgart musing on her fame and, after she has lost her voice, her helplessness. Eliot criticises *Aurora Leigh* when it employs a sensational incident, notably the 'maiming' and 'blindness' of Romney: 'we think the lavish mutilation of heroes' bodies, which has become the habit of novelists, while it happily does not represent probabilities in the present state of things, weakens instead the tragic effect'.[13] But, while Eliot here refuses the theatricality of sensation, music in *Armgart* does not function as antitheatrical poetry, as Litvak argues in his examination of other works by Eliot. A fundamental difference between *Aurora Leigh* and *Armgart* is Eliot's emphasis on audience.[14]

Aurora and Armgart share a belief in women's right to pursue an artistic vocation and each heroine, at least initially, eschews marriage in order to devote herself to art. Aurora's use of a musical metaphor for her talent, which she sees as a divine gift, emphasises the voice that her poetry has provided her:

> My own best poets. . . .
> When my joy and pain,
> My thought and aspiration, like the stops
> Of pipe or flute, are absolutely dumb
> Unless melodious, do you play on me
> My pipers – and if, sooth, you did not blow,
> Would no sound come? or is the music mine,
> As a man's voice or breath is called his own,
> Inbreathed by the Life-breather?[15]

Aurora is doubtful whether the talent that elevates her is something that she controls. Such doubt assumes extreme proportions decades later in George Du Maurier's *Trilby* (1894), in which a woman with a naturally powerful voice can only overcome her tone-deafness while under the spell of the mesmerist Svengali. Armgart is herself an embodiment of Aurora's metaphor of voice for women's art, and Armgart's voice is something that she does not fully control – she loses her ability to sing as a result of her doctor's life-saving cure. Armgart's voice is not only other than herself but, at times, at odds with her body.

Despite her identification with music, Aurora is no performer. She declares that she will not write for the stage because audience control debases art:

> . . . whosoever writes good poetry,
> Looks just to art. He does not write for you
> Or me – for London or for Edinburgh;
> He will not suffer the best critic known
> To step into his sunshine of free thought
> And self-absorbed conception and exact

> An inch-long swerving of the holy lines.
> If virtue, done for popularity
> Defiles like vice, can art, for praise or hire,
> Still keep its splendour and remain pure art?
> Eschew such serfdom.[16]

In contrast to poetry, drama

> Makes lower appeals, submits more menially,
> Adopts the standards of the public taste
> To chalk its height on, wears a dog-chain round
> Its regal neck, and learns to carry and fetch
> The fashions of the day to please the day,
> Fawns close on pit and boxes, who clap hands
> Commending chiefly its docility
> And humour in stage-tricks – or else indeed
> Gets hissed at, howled at, stamped at like a dog,
> Or worse, we'll say.[17]

Aurora specifically describes how the success of performers is determined by audience response and, elsewhere, illustrates the distinction between her own gravity and the frivolity of stage performers:

> I would rather dance
> At fairs on tight-rope, till the babies dropped
> Their gingerbread for joy – than shift the types
> For tolerable verse, intolerable
> To men who act and suffer. Better far
> Pursue a frivolous trade by serious means
> Than a sublime art frivolously.[18]

Additionally, Aurora is disinherited of her Leigh birthright because of

> that clause in the entail
> Excluding offspring by a foreign wife
> (The clause set up a hundred years ago
> By a Leigh who wedded a French dancing-girl
> and had his heart danced over in return.[19]

Aurora Leigh emphasises the faulty logic in the elision of foreignness, female stage performers, and light morals – a combination of characteristics that appears in *Jane Eyre*'s (1847) Céline Varens and *Middlemarch*'s (1871–2) Madame Laure, both of whom deceive English gentlemen, and, as we have seen, in *Vanity Fair*'s (1847–8) deceptive and theatrical Becky Sharp. Jane's beloved Rochester is haunted not only by the mad wife he has confined in the attic of Thornfield Hall but also by his former inconstant mistress, the French opera-dancer whose daughter Adèle, 'a miniature of Céline Varens, as she used to appear on the boards', is Rochester's ward and Jane's charge.[20] Adèle's theatricality is elided with foreignness – her 'superficiality of character, inherited probably from her mother, [is] hardly congenial to an English mind'.[21] After his mutilation, Rochester is able to achieve domestic stability with the untheatrical Jane who, unlike Céline, does not untruthfully flatter Rochester about his appearance and who, when refusing his premarital gifts, says, 'I will not be your English Céline Varens.'[22] Jane Eyre's comment on the formulaic nature of Rochester's experience suggests that the figure of the French female performer had become a shorthand for sexual licence and inconstancy: 'As he had said, there was probably nothing at all extraordinary in the substance of the narrative itself: a wealthy Englishman's passion for a French dancer, and her treachery to him, were everyday matters enough, no doubt, in society.'[23] Litvak points out that '*Middlemarch*, like *Jane Eyre*, attempts to get beyond its (equally French) theatrical prehistory.'[24] Similarly, *Aurora Leigh* uses the French dancer to differentiate its poetry-writing heroine from the stage performer. Mary Jean Corbett notes that *Aurora Leigh* is an autobiographical work that does not stage a 'public authorial persona' as do works by Wordsworth and Carlyle, but rather it separates and shields its author from 'public circulation'. Corbett accounts for this by arguing that Barrett Browning felt a 'bodily terror about publicizing the self' that 'is linked to the cultural division of masculine and feminine spheres'.[25] Eliot's comment that 'Mrs Browning has added one more to the imitations of the catastrophe in "Jane Eyre", by smiting her hero with blindness before he is made happy in the love of Aurora', suggests that Aurora provides a non-theatrical antidote to the beautiful and deceptive Lady Waldemar just as Jane provides a non-theatrical antidote to Céline Varens.[26]

Litvak points out, however, that Jane is more theatrical than she appears. Chapter 2 of this book showed that *No Name* (1862–3) underscores similarities between the actress and the governess as figures that reveal the theatrical nature of class status. Litvak suggests that *Jane Eyre* follows the tradition of *Vanity Fair* by representing '[t]he Governess as Actress' and, like Charlotte Brontë's *Villette* (1853), 'illustrate[s] a suitably corrosive confrontation between the domestic, the private, and the inward – the world, in short, of "the governess" – and the foreign, the public, and the centrifugal – the world, in short, of "the actress."'[27] *Aurora Leigh* echoes what Litvak calls *Jane Eyre*'s 'Protestations of antitheatricality' that 'proliferate ... throughout the book', and Jane's abandonment of Rochester in order 'to avoid the implicitly theatricalizing fate of becoming the latest in Rochester's series of mistresses'.[28] Aurora refuses a letter of courtship from an admirer, John Eglinton, because she views it as explicitly theatricalising:

> I will not read it: it is stereotyped;
> The same he wrote to – anybody's name,
> Anne Blythe the actress, when she died so true,
> A duchess fainted in a private box:
> Pauline the dancer, after the great *pas*
> In which her little feet winked overhead
> Like other fire-flies, and amazed the pit:
> Or Baldinacci, when her F in alt
> Had touched the silver tops of heaven itself
> With such pungent spirit-dart, the Queen
> Laid softly, each to each, her white-gloved palms,
> And sighed for joy . . .[29]

Aurora's constant reiteration that she is not a performer reveals her, and perhaps Barrett Browning's, anxiety about whether or not artistic creation can be separated from performing for an audience. As Aurora repeatedly attempts to detach her art from public consumption, she voices an anxiety similar to what Litvak describes as 'writing forgo[ing] its associations with the social luster of professional authorship – especially *successful* professional authorship – to assume instead the protective covering of (home)work'.[30]

Sandra Gilbert and Susan Gubar as well as Rosemarie Bodenheimer have argued that Eliot's representations of performing women, including Armgart, demonstrate a similar anxiety about writing for public adulation.[31] Armgart, however, is Aurora's antithesis – the very performer from whom Aurora distinguishes herself, and therefore a very different figure for the female artist. Moreover, Susan Rutherford has examined how *Armgart* depicts the diva at a time when amateur singing in the domestic sphere led 'the boundaries between the private and public world' to be 're-drawn' – in other words, the division between Litvak's '(home)work' and professionalism was blurred – and she attributes the increased respectability of the stage in part to this.[32] Although *Armgart* depicts a similar power dynamic to what Litvak calls *Jane Eyre*'s 'insistent formulation of theatricality as an endless, dizzying dialectic of power and subservience, whereby to act is to be simultaneously empowered and vulnerable', in contrast to Jane's assertion of non-theatricality, Armgart glories in the individual greatness that occurs by gaining control over an audience.[33] Aurora echoes Jane's insistence on non-theatrical genuineness or 'absorption'.[34] Armgart revels in the audience's attention. While 'Brontë's disciplining of the self that writes has the peculiar consequence of transforming what ought to look like a subjection to social control into what looks instead like a savingly asocial or at least antisocial condition', Armgart's theatrical performance signals submitting to social control and gaining power over it.[35]

In its insistence that artists should avoid subjecting their art to public opinion, *Aurora Leigh* anticipates John Stuart Mill's characterisation, in *On Liberty* (1859), of the power that public opinion has to enforce conformity. Mill's comment, in his letters, that 'almost all the projects of social reformers these days are really *liberticide* – Comte, particularly so', echoes *Aurora Leigh*'s criticism of Romney's Comte-ian and highly controlled commune.[36] Romney ends up renouncing his failed reform plan, saying,

> Fewer programmes. . . .
> Fewer systems. . . .
> Less mapping out of masses to be saved,
> By nations or by sexes. Fourier's void,
> And Comte absurd – and Cabet puerile.
> Subsist no rules of life outside of life,
> No perfect manners without Christian souls:
> The Christ himself had been no Lawgiver
> Unless He had given the life, too, with the law.[37]

In *On Liberty*, however, Mill considers how religion and reform operate in similar ways: 'And some of those reformers who have placed themselves in strongest opposition to the religions of the past have been noway behind either churches or sects in their assertion of the right of spiritual domination: M. Comte, in particular.'[38] Mill's criticism of social reform stems from his concern about the control of society over the individual: 'The spirit of improvement is not always a spirit of liberty, for it may aim at forcing improvements on an unwilling people'.[39] He states that 'English philanthropists are so industriously working at . . . making a people all alike, all governing their thoughts and conduct by the same maxims and rules. . . . The modern régime of public opinion is, in an unorganized form, what the Chinese educational and political systems are in an organized.'[40]

Hudd has pointed out how *Armgart* 'question[s]' Barrett Browning's 'attack upon the type of practical social reform desired by Romney Leigh'.[41] It is likely, however, that Eliot's exploration of the audience's power was influenced by Mill's concern about the power of public opinion. In a letter dated 10 July 1865, Eliot likens public applause to music, emphasising the critical role of the audience rather than the primacy of a performance's content, since the audience's response itself can have the impact of great art:

> The expression of a common feeling by a large mass of men, when the feeling is one of good-will, moves me like music. A public tribute to any man who has done the world a service with brain or hand, has on me the effect of a great religious rite, with pealing organ and full-voiced choir.[42]

Eliot proceeds immediately to comment on Mill and her recent reading of his works, suggesting Mill's association with Eliot's contemplation of audience. The suffragettes of the Edwardian period are commonly understood to be direct descendants of earlier movements in favour of the vote, including Mill's proposal to amend the 1867 Reform Act, which extended the franchise to portions of the working classes, so that 'person' would replace 'man', and his *The Subjection of Women* (1869).[43] The theatrical tactics of the early twentieth-century women's suffrage movement have their intellectual roots not only in Mill's view of the power of public opinion but also in Eliot's view of how female performers can engage audiences.

Eliot and Barrett Browning present tellingly different definitions of greatness. Aurora criticises the propensity of women to

> strain [their] natures at doing something great,
> Far less because it's something great to do,
> Than haply that [they], so, content [them]selves
> As being not small, and more appreciable
> to some one friend[44]

and resolves:

> .... Fame itself,
> That approbation of the general race,
> Presents a poor end (though the arrow speed,
> Shot straight with vigorous finger to the white),
> And the highest fame was never reached except
> By what was aimed above it. Art for art,
> And good for God Himself, the essential Good!
> We'll keep our aims sublime, our eyes erect,
> Although our woman-hands should shake and fail;
> And if we fail ... But must we? –[45]

In contrast to Barrett Browning, Eliot, although cautious about the effects of ambitious goals, recognises the value of an audience. Emily Davies, who founded Cambridge's Girton College as the first college for women, related a conversation in which Eliot expressed concern about educated women: 'She said, was there not a great deal among girls of wanting to do some great thing and thinking it not worth while to do anything because they cannot do that?'[46] As Davies relates it, Eliot echoes Aurora's language, and the letter bolsters the common understanding that Eliot espoused a social conservatism that contrasted with her own unorthodox life – an understanding that is evident in Gilbert and Gubar's position that Armgart is punished for her ambition as well as Bodenheimer's argument that the voices of the characters in the play represent Eliot's own conflicted views on ambition, fame and public display as the play tries 'to disconnect ambition and fame from the practice of the artist's life'.[47] Yet Eliot's close friendship with Barbara Bodichon, who co-founded Girton with Davies, connects Eliot directly with the Victorian women's movement: Eliot contributed financial support and curricular suggestions to Girton, which she visited in 1877.[48] Indeed, Eliot's female performers often do 'some great thing' at the cost of personal, domestic relationships. Armgart neglects personal relationships in favour of her fame, and she reluctantly accepts humble private duties only after she has lost her singing voice. The Alcharisi in *Daniel Deronda* gives up her son in order to pursue a stage career. Thus Eliot defines greatness and the goals to which ambitious young women aspire as an escape from the domestic sphere to performing in the public sphere.

In *Armgart*, the stage provides a realm in which women can be competitive. Walpurga describes Armgart's ambition:

> at some such trivial word of mine,
> As that the highest prize might yet be won
> By her who took the second – she was roused,
> 'For me', she said, 'I triumph or I fail.
> I never strove for any second prize.'[49]

Such ambition is positioned in opposition to femininity. When Armgart tells her suitor Graf Dornberg,

> I am an artist as you are a noble:
> I ought to bear the burthen of my rank,

he responds by suggesting that it is not women's place to strive, saying:

> Men rise the higher as their task is high,
> The task being well achieved. A woman's rank
> Lies in the fullness of her womanhood:
> Therein alone she is royal.[50]

Dornberg characterises Armgart's ambition as masculine but points out the limited means by which she can pursue it:

> She bears Caesar's ambition in her delicate breast,
> And nought to still it with but quivering song![51]

Yet Armgart's female voice allows her to transcend traditional feminine social roles. Dornberg wishes that

> [s]he were less apt to soar beyond the reach
> Of woman's foibles, innocent vanities,
> Fondness for trifles like that pretty star
> Twinkling beside her cloud of ebon hair.[52]

Armgart's ambition conflicts with domestic life; she rejects Dornberg's marriage proposal to devote herself to art. Art provides her life with meaning, and in rejecting Dornberg's proposal, she tells him to marry a woman, unlike herself,

> who has not yet found
> A meaning in her life, nor any end
> Beyond fulfilling yours. The type abounds.[53]

When Armgart contrasts her public success with domesticity and, more specifically, motherhood, she explains that women can achieve equality with men on the operatic stage because it requires female voices:

>   Yes, I know
> The oft-taught Gospel: 'Woman, thy desire
> Shall be that all superlatives on earth
> Belong to men, save the one highest kind –
> To be a mother. Thou shalt not desire
> To do aught best save pure subservience:
> Nature has willed it so!' O blessed Nature!
> Let her be arbitress; she gave me voice
> Such as she only gives a woman child,
> Best of its kind, gave me ambition too,
> That sense transcendent which can taste the joy
> Of swaying multitudes, of being adored
> For such achievement, needed excellence,
> As man's best art must wait for, or be dumb.
> Men did not say, when I had sung last night,
> "Twas good, nay, wonderful, considering

She is a woman' – and then turn to add,
'Tenor or baritone had sung her songs
Better, of course: she's but a woman spoiled.'[54]

Although 'woman child' primarily indicates that Armgart was given a vocal gift unique to girls, the construction also suggests that Armgart's voice was given to her for her to nurture in the same way that other women are given children. A public role is, thus, represented as a substitution for motherhood. Armgart further challenges supposedly 'natural' feminine social roles, using growth imagery to emphasise the naturalness of her art and her ambition:

> The great masters write
> For women's voices, and great Music wants me!
> I need not crush myself within a mould
> Of theory called Nature: I have room
> To breath and grow unstunted.[55]

In defining her own natural ambition as the desire to be 'adored' by a large audience, Armgart challenges the belief, voiced by her suitor, that women are unsuited for the public sphere. Hudd has pointed out that Barrett Browning's and Eliot's challenges to the naturalness of domestic femininity echo Mill's *The Subjection of Women* (1869), which refers to 'women of the higher classes' as 'a kind of hothouse plants, shielded from the wholesome vicissitudes of air and temperature'.[56] In characterising her indoctrination into domesticity by her aunt as an attempt to quash her natural instincts, however, Aurora, unlike Armgart, does not emphasise her particularly feminine nature:

> As if she said, 'I know there's something wrong;
> I know I have not ground you down enough
> To flatten and bake you to a wholesome crust
> For household uses and proprieties,
> Before the rain has got into my barn
> And set the grains a-sprouting. What, you're green
> With outdoor impudence? you almost grow?'[57]

In fact, as she rejects marriage, Aurora regrets that she, as an artist, is gendered:

> Poets needs must be
> Or men or women – more's the pity.[58]

Unlike Armgart's argument for the specific importance of women's voices, Aurora employs a musical metaphor that measures women's abilities against men's, saying that

> she is going to London to live her life
> straight out, vocally, in books;
> Harmoniously for others, if indeed
> A woman's soul, like man's, be wide enough
> To carry the whole octave (that's to prove).[59]

In contrast, when Eliot reviewed *Aurora Leigh*, she emphasised the importance both of its writer's gender and of how Barrett Browning is capable of masculinity as well as femininity:

> Mrs Browning is, perhaps, the first woman who has produced a work which exhibits all the peculiar powers without the negations of her sex; which superadds to masculine vigour, breadth, and culture, feminine subtlety of perception, feminine quickness of sensibility, and feminine tenderness. It is difficult to point to a woman of genius who is not either too little feminine, or too exclusively so. But in this her longest and greatest poem, Mrs Browning has shown herself all the greater poet because she is intensely a poetess.[60]

In choosing to marry Romney, Aurora ultimately embraces a feminine art:

> Passioned to exalt
> The artist's instinct in me at the cost
> Of putting down the woman's, I forgot
> No perfect artist is developed here
> From any imperfect woman.[61]

In assuming the feminine role of wife, however, Aurora domesticates her art, whereas Armgart emphasises the entry of women into the public sphere. In Armgart, Eliot created a female artist whose art is essentially feminine even as she wields the public power traditionally coded as masculine.

In order to assume a position of authority in the public world, Armgart must engage in a negotiation of power between audience and performer like that explored by Charles Dickens in his 1850 essay 'The Amusements of the People'. Discussing the Victorian spectacular theatre designed to enchant a working-class public that does not have the patience to read, Dickens argues that theatre is dependent on the audience and, thus, controlled and created by the audience's taste – the very control that Aurora sees as a corruption of art. Dickens, however, challenges the audience not only by observing them and turning them into a spectacle but also by urging that the spectacle of the theatre be used for educational ends.[62] Exhibiting a confidence in the possibility of morally influencing an audience that, Janice Carlisle claims, pervaded the mid-century novel, Dickens underscores the theatre's potential as a form of social control.[63] Moreover, Dickens suggests that spectacle does not only comprise the entertainment of the working classes but also pervades the operas of the 'polite society' that shunned early and mid-Victorian theatre. The opera singer Armgart is indeed subject to the controlling gaze of the audience yet, as Rutherford points out: 'the female singers of [the Victorian] era ... inhabited an operatic marketplace ... in which the boundaries for challenge to received opinion were fluid and mutable'.[64] When Armgart argues that she was right to add a trill to her performance that neither the composer nor her mentor Leo sanctioned, her comment that the audience

> was held
> As if a storm were listening with delight,
> And hushed its thunder[65]

suggests the audience's ability to overwhelm the performer. Leo responds by explaining that playing to the audience's desires will only debase art and her own stature. He urges Armgart:

> lift your audience
> To see your vision, not trick forth a show
> To please the grossest taste of grossest numbers.[66]

Armgart agrees that she must not allow the audience to control her, indicating that the public opinion of which Mill and Aurora Leigh were wary particularly commodifies women. She describes the audience's response when, in the role of Gluck's Orpheus, she first appeared on stage before singing:

> The women whispered, 'Not a pretty face!'
> The men, 'Well, well, a goodly length of limb:
> She bears the chiton.' – It were all the same
> Were I the Virgin Mother, and my stage
> The opening heavens at the Judgment-day:
> Gossips would peep, jog elbows, rate the price
> Of such a woman in the social mart.[67]

The chiton, a form of tunic, was among the cross-dressing costumes, including the notorious 'breeches', that sexualised Victorian actresses by revealing more of their bodies than would have been considered proper off stage. This physical display provides an excellent example of Gail Marshall's argument that, despite the distinctions drawn between the legitimate theatre and burlesque, 'there is a tangible continuity of interest, audience, and function which links actresses of the burlesque and legitimate stages and which . . . is effected in part by precisely that Classical drapery which is ostensibly a primary signifier of the respectable theatre'.[68] In her examination of how various prima donnas negotiated the gendered implications of such costumes, either playing up or concealing their sexuality, Rutherford particularly discusses Pauline Viardot, whom Eliot and George Henry Lewes knew personally. Rutherford argues that Viardot influenced the figure of Armgart, pointing out that a photo of Viardot as Orpheus reveals how her costume 'acknowledges Greek classical male dress but does not make especial capital out of her own sexuality'.[69]

The complexity of Armgart's views about the power of the theatre audience and her negotiation with it crystallise a complexity in Eliot's view of theatricality, and this complexity accounts for differences in recent Eliot criticism. While Kurnick views Eliot's theatricality (albeit not in *Armgart*) as a nostalgic longing for a communal art form that is no longer available, Nancy Henry notes that over the course of her writing career 'Eliot grew more disdainful of the mass reading public.'[70] Yet while these positions appear, on the surface, to be in opposition to each other, *Armgart* reveals how Eliot held both positions simultaneously, engaging in the sort of negotiation between public and private that McCormack and Bernstein have explored.

The attention that Armgart's audience pays to her body reflects Eliot's uneasiness with the physical nature of drama, which may account for Eliot's use of the paradoxical genre of closet drama. Gail Marshall has pointed out that Eliot felt that the statue-like qualities of the actress's physical presence detract from a drama's narrative, and that Eliot's descriptions of actresses as statues echo reviews of Victorian actresses and demonstrate the isolating and objectifying effect that theatrical performance has on the actress.[71] Litvak argues that *Daniel Deronda*, mirroring Lewes's criticism of the actor Salvini in *On Actors and the Art of Acting* (1875), creates a hierarchy in which poetry is placed higher than concrete dramatic representation in order to criticise sensationalism. Salvini fails because he relies on the physical, which Lewes conflates with a feminisation of the (foreign) actor.[72] In support of his assertion that Eliot views theatricality as dangerous, Litvak analyses how, in a passage from *Middlemarch* that 'illustrates a tendency of Victorian novels to make spectacularization and feminization virtually synonymous, and to invest both with the apparently contradictory attributes of danger and weakness', Tertius Lydgate is feminised by theatricality.[73] In *Armgart*, the heroine's vocal talent allows her to transcend the audience's sexualisation of her as a physical spectacle and to inhabit a masculine role both in the sense of playing a role on stage and in the sense that she assumes the power of a man in the public sphere.

When she sings, Armgart triumphs over her audience and transforms herself into the male role of Orpheus. Contemplating Armgart's cross-gender performances, Hudd argues that Armgart 'denigrates the specifically feminine, incapable of doing what George Eliot believed that Barrett Browning had done with *Aurora Leigh*, and truly expressing her sex through her art'.[74] This analysis neglects Armgart's point about opera's need for female voices, which, according to Pope, the role of Orpheus situates in a specific moment in music history when women were first used instead of male castrati. Moreover, Rutherford points out that the historical moment in which *Armgart* is set is one in which 'opera articulated women's experience in a manner that undeniably privileged the display of female vocal and histrionic talents, and that secured for the prima donna . . . the most consistently powerful position in the box office'.[75] Hudd also neglects the specific mechanism through which Armgart inhabits a male role. Leo describes the sequence of events:

> Well! tones came clearly, firmly forth. . . .
> The house was breathing gently, heads were still;
> Parrot opinion was struck meekly mute,
> And human hearts were swelling. Armgart stood
> As if she had been new-created there,
> And found her voice which found a melody. . . .
> Orpheus was Armgart, Armgart Orpheus.
> Well, well, all through the *scena* I could feel
> The silence tremble now, now poise itself
> With added weight of feeling, till at last
> Delight o'er toppled it. The final note
> Had happy drowning in the unloosed roar
> That surged and ebbed and ever surged again,
> Till expectation kept it pent awhile
> Ere Orpheus returned.[76]

Whereas earlier, '[s]he walked *like* Orpheus in his solitude', now Armgart's female voice fuses her with her male role.[77] Her voice first stilled the audience, suggesting that she is able to assume a masculine role because she has controlled the audience that had previously sexualised her and subjected her to feminine social roles. Armgart's success with her audience echoes the plot of the opera she is performing. On 9 January 1855, in a letter to Sara Sophie Hennell about seeing Johanna Jachmann Wagner, Richard Wagner's niece, perform Orpheus in Berlin, Eliot remarks on the power of the soprano and Gluck's use of women's voices. Most notably, however, she describes the scene in which the lyric poet charms the shades of Tartarus, referring to the soprano as 'die Wagner' – using the feminine article to suggest a female performer appropriating and supplanting the power of male authorship – and calling her 'a fine actress and a fine singer':

> The scene in which Orpheus (Johanna Wagner) enters Tartarus, is met by the awful shades, and charms them into ecstatic admiration till they make way for him to pass on, is very fine. The voices – except in the choruses – are all women's voices, and there are only three characters – Orpheus, Amor, and Euridice. One wonders that Pluto does not come as a Basso, and one would prefer Mercury as a tenor to Amor in the shape of an ugly German soprano – but Gluck willed it otherwise and the music is delightful. The scene in Elysium is immensely absurd – Ballet girls dance in the foreground and in the background are Greek shades looking like butchers in *chemises*. But the worst of it is, that instead of letting it be a tragedy, Euridice is brought to life again and we end with another Ballet girl scene before Amor's temple.[78]

While Eliot praises the auditory qualities of the opera, she takes particular exception to the physical display of the female dancers and to an ending that evokes a conventional marriage plot. Meanwhile, the masculinity of Armgart commanding power in the public sphere through her voice is further emphasised by the role that she unsuccessfully attempts in rehearsal when she loses her voice and her ability to perform. On the evening that Eliot wrote to Hennell about *Orpheus*, she had just returned from seeing *Fidelio*, and Armgart's failure in the title role of Beethoven's opera – a woman who assumes a male disguise in order to aid her imprisoned husband – underscores her lost ability to enter the masculine public world.

Public v. Private Performance: Exceptional and Unexceptional Women

Eliot's exceptionally talented performers, Armgart among them, achieve power and self-determination that elude women whose talents are limited to drawing-room entertainment and who are able to exercise little control over their social audiences and only fulfil their audiences' demands. One of the most notable examples of such social performers is Gwendolen, in *Daniel Deronda*, whose 'belief that to present herself in public on the stage must produce an effect such as she had been used to feel certain of in private life' is dashed by the professional musician Klesmer.[79] She continues her theatricality as she maintains a social façade in a domestic world of terror. David Marshall, who demonstrates how Gwendolen's social life is an ongoing theatrical performance, notes that Gwendolen 'is not always in control of what makes her theatrical; this is especially evident after she assumes her most dramatic role: Mrs Grandcourt' and points out that, as Grandcourt's wife, 'she finds herself imprisoned in a role, forced to act out a scenario controlled by a theatrical master of appearances'.[80] While she expects to rule her husband, she is ultimately controlled by his watchful gaze.

Another example of a social performer who fulfils her audience's demands is Rosamond Vincy, in *Middlemarch*. Rosamond's theatricality is presaged by the previous entanglement that her husband, Tertius Lydgate, had with an actress. After Tertius discovers that the French actress he loved, Madame Laure, used her acting to commit murder, actually killing her husband by feigning an accident in a scene in which she was supposed to stage a murder, he 'believ[ed] that illusions were at an end for him. . . . [H]e had more reason than ever for trusting his judgment, now that it was so experienced.'[81] Unlike Edward Rochester in *Jane Eyre*, however, Tertius does not marry a plain Jane. Eliot's description of his facile confidence in his improved ability to read appearances foreshadows his failure to discern Rosamond's performances and their consequent disastrous marriage. To Tertius, Rosamond appears to be Madame Laure's 'very opposite', but she is actually a virtuoso social performer.[82] Eliot underscores Rosamond's theatricality by contrasting her to Dorothea Brooke, whom she meets for the first time in Chapter 43. The chapter's epigraph describes the difference between two figurines of women. The first is carved in ivory with

> Nought modish in it, pure and noble lines
> Of generous womanhood that fits all time.
> The second is a piece of majolica,
> a table ornament
> To suit the richest mounting.[83]

The chapter develops Dorothea's likeness to ivory, a valuable, natural, solid substance, and Rosamond's likeness to majolica, a manufactured, glazed earthenware that has no inherent value but only superficial craftsmanship. When Dorothea enters the room, her lack of self-consciousness about an audience's scrutiny is augmented by her nearsightedness as she admires Rosamond but can only see that there is a gentleman in the room and does not realise that the second, riveted, spectator of her arrival is Will Ladislaw. While Dorothea does not realise that she is being observed, Rosamond is delighted by Dorothea's visit because she sees Dorothea as the perfect, genteel audience to appreciate her own finishing-school charms. In contrast to Dorothea, famously described in the novel's opening sentence as possessing 'that kind of beauty which seems to be thrown into relief by poor dress', Rosamond has an elaborate hairstyle, fashionable dress, abundant jewelry, and 'that controlled self-consciousness of manner which is the expensive substitute for simplicity'.[84] Beer describes Rosamond as 'a tragic satire on the ideal woman as described in much Victorian writing; in particular, on what constitutes "women's work" and "women's influence"'.[85] Rosamond is a satire of what Armgart characterises as the woman who seeks to influence the world by influencing her own husband:

> What, leave the opera with my part ill-sung,
> While I was warbling in a drawing-room?
> Sing in the chimney corner to inspire
> My husband reading news?
> Let the world hear
> My music only in his morning speech
> Less stammering than most honorable men's? No![86]

Rosamond's attempts to control her husband have disastrous consequences for both of them as they sink into debt.

The difference in power between Eliot's professional and social performers is a difference not only in talent but also in training. When Gwendolen consults Klesmer about her qualifications for the stage, she says that she would like 'to be an actress – to go on the stage' and, because she 'should like to take a high position', she asks about being a 'singer' since 'to sing and act too, like Grisi, is a much higher position'.[87] Gwendolen's omission of a first name for this diva means that her role model could be one of the sister opera singers Giuditta or Giulia Grisi, or their cousin, the dancer-singer Carlotta Grisi. On the one hand, Giulia was known for her strength in both singing and acting, and Rutherford notes that she was particularly liberated 'from bourgeois notions of female decorum'.[88] On the other hand, the fact that Carlotta retired from the stage in her prime when she became pregnant by Prince Léon Radziwill provides a subtext suggestive of the commodification of women's bodies and the limitations that the female body places on women's talent. Gwendolen, who needs to support herself or marry, sees acting as 'easier than the dead level of being a governess', suggesting that a gentlewoman's talents equip her for either position.[89] Indeed, Newey cites Fanny Kemble's correspondence, in which she describes how the education that her successful theatre family provided allowed her the choice of becoming either a governess or an actress, and Rutherford describes how, after 1850, 'middle- and upper-class women' who began as 'domestic' singers were able to parlay their amateur experience into professional careers, thereby achieving 'a measure of financial independence'.[90] Nevertheless, when Gwendolen, reflecting on her physical attractions and class background, says, 'in Paris I am sure I saw two actresses playing important ladies' parts who were not at all ladies and quite ugly. I suppose I have no particular talent, but I *must* think it is an advantage, even on the stage, to be a lady and not a perfect fright', Klesmer responds that only through true art can the artist overcome objectification by the audience:

> I was speaking of what you would have to get through if you aimed at becoming a real artist – if you took music and the drama as a higher vocation in which you would strive after excellence. . . . But – there are certainly other ideas, other dispositions with which a young lady may take up an art that will bring her before the public. She may rely on the unquestioned power of her beauty as a passport. She may desire to exhibit herself to an admiration which dispenses with skill. This goes a certain way on the stage: not in music: but on the stage, beauty is taken when there is nothing more commanding to be had. Not without some drilling, however: as I have said before, technicalities have in any case to be mastered. But these excepted, we have here nothing to do with art. The woman who takes up this career is not an artist: she is usually one who thinks of entering on a luxurious life by a short and easy road – perhaps by marriage – that is her most brilliant chance, and the rarest. Still, her career will not be luxurious to begin with: she can hardly earn her own poor bread independently at once, and the indignities she will be liable to are such as I will not speak of.[91]

Klesmer describes how the actress who does not possess an art that transcends the power of the audience but instead lives by pleasing the audience will be subject to unspeakable degradations. That even this, however, requires training, challenges Wilkie Collins's depiction of Magdalen, in *No Name*, as a 'born actress'.[92] Klesmer tells Gwendolen that there is much that one of the actresses that Gwendolen scorns could teach her: 'For example, she can pitch her voice so as to be heard: ten to one you could not do it till after many trials. Merely to stand and move on the stage is an art – requires practice.'[93] According to Klesmer, it is only through striving for excellence that one will be able to control public audiences:

> You have exercised your talents – you recite – you sing – from the drawing-room *standpunkt*. My dear Fräulein, you must unlearn all that. You have not yet conceived what excellence is: you must unlearn your mistaken admirations. You must know what you have to strive for, and then you must subdue your mind and body to unbroken discipline. Your mind, I say. For you must not be thinking of celebrity: – put that candle out of your eyes, and look only at excellence.[94]

Klesmer's rejection of Gwendolen's amateur talents echoes Diderot's speaker in *The Paradox of Acting*, who emphasises the difference between a 'fireside tone' and 'the open-mouthed emphasis fit for the boards'.[95] George Henry Lewes, in his introduction to his collection of theatre criticism, *On Actors and the Art of Acting*, echoes Diderot and anticipates, or perhaps serves as a model for, Klesmer. Lewes attacks the

> general misconception that there is no special physique nor any special training necessary to make an actor. Almost every young person imagines he could act, if he tried. . . . [Acting does] not come by nature. Nor is it any argument that Private Theatricals . . . often reveals a certain amount of histrionic aptitude in people who have never been trained. . . . In the next place, amateur acting bears the same relation to the art of the stage as drawing-room singing bears to the opera. We often listen with pleasure to a singer in private whom we should mercilessly hiss from the concert-room or stage.[96]

Where Robertson asserted the actress's respectability by demonstrating how the actress possessed genuine emotions, the fictional Klesmer, building on Diderot's and Lewes's emphasis on the craft of acting, promotes her respectability by establishing her professionalism. Klesmer's position is representative of Eliot's larger movement away from melodrama's moment of spectacular emotional appeal as a vehicle for making connections between characters and between audience and characters.

Klesmer's plea for art, however, goes one step further by professionalising acting and music while at the same time removing it from the world of commerce. Recently betrothed to an heiress who is prepared to sacrifice her social class standing for art, Klesmer believes that great artists serve art rather than use it as a tool to gain wealth and status. He responds to Gwendolen's desire for financial self-sufficiency by telling her: 'the honour comes from the inward vocation and the hard-won achievement: there is no honour in donning the life as a livery'.[97] In stating that true artists pursue their calling for reasons other than financial need, Klesmer responds to Diderot's assertion that

> The stage is a resource, never a choice. Never did actor become so from love of virtue, from desire to be useful in the world, or to serve his country or family; never from any of the honourable motives which might incline a right mind, a feeling heart, a sensitive soul, to so fine a profession.[98]

Klesmer seeks not only to prevent the debasement of Gwendolen through the 'indignities' to which some actresses are exposed, but also the debasement of the performer's profession by women such as Gwendolen, who do not choose it but employ it merely as a last resort in order to earn money.

Klesmer deems Mirah 'a musician', or a true artist, because she is dedicated to her art.[99] She shrinks from audiences. Even before Mirah's father effects a shift from acting to prostitution by trying to sell Mirah to an admirer whose 'eyes were always on' her but who had 'scorn for the Jewess and the actress', Mirah dislikes being looked at:

> it was painful that he boasted of me, and set me to sing for show at any minute, as if I had been a musical box. . . . [T]he clapping and all the sounds of the theatre were hateful to me; and I never liked the praise I had, because it seemed all very hard and unloving: I missed the love and the trust I had been born into.[100]

Mirah's antitheatricality takes the form of seeking familial and particularly maternal origins. Mirah's decision to marry Daniel and become his helpmate in working to found a new Jewish state echoes Aurora's decision to marry Romney, just as her dedication to art apart from public performance is similar to Aurora's views. Furthermore, Mirah appears to support Litvak's argument that *Daniel Deronda* 'associat[es] music and song with (an always implicitly and essentially *lyric*) poetry, rather than with performance'.[101]

Yet when the title character Daniel seeks his own familial and maternal origins, we discover that at the core of this novel is a woman who, like Armgart and in stark contrast to the family-centred works that we saw in Chapter 2, chose the public world over a domestic life. The Alcharisi, Daniel's mother and the diva of *Daniel Deronda*, abandoned her son to pursue her stage career, and it is she who, when considered in light of Gwendolen's plight, reveals the value of performing for a public audience. The difference between the lives of exceptional and unexceptional women is dramatised in *Daniel Deronda* by the Alcharisi and Gwendolen. It is the life of the Alcharisi, who has a 'thoroughly Rachelesque style', that Gwendolen covets when she contemplates 'whether she should become an actress like Rachel'.[102] Mirah, Klesmer, the Alcharisi and Rachel all share a Jewish heritage, and in *Daniel Deronda* the artistic world is reserved for those who stand outside mainstream English society. Gwendolen's 'questioning... whether she need take a husband at all – whether she could not achieve substantiality for herself and know gratified ambition without bondage' reveals that her ambition to perform on stage is motivated by the same desire for freedom from 'bondage' that the Alcharisi voices.[103] The social roles that acting enables Daniel's mother to assume are reflected by the names that she bears at various stages in her life. Born Leonora Charisi, she retains that name even when she marries, because her husband is also a Charisi. She begins to assume new names and new identities only when she acts, becoming the Alcharisi on stage and then the Princess Halm-Eberstein when she marries royalty as a result of her fame. Despite its association with prostitution, she sees professional acting as a form of liberation. Leonora's father is the utter opposite of Mirah's father and the Alcharisi's way of thinking about the theatre is entirely different from Mirah's. The Alcharisi says that her father 'hated that Jewish women should be thought of by the Christian world as a sort of ware to make public singers and actresses of. As if we were not the more enviable for that! That is a chance of escaping from bondage.'[104] She describes how pursuing a career as an actress allowed her to escape a confining domestic sphere and participate in the public world, and she tells Daniel: 'I cared for the wide world, and all that I could represent in it.'[105]

In contrast to the Alcharisi's 'wide world', Eliot's passing reference to Gwendolen's agoraphobia – 'Why she should suddenly determine not to part with the necklace was not much clearer to her than why she should sometimes have been frightened to find herself in the fields alone' – is ultimately thematised in the novel as Gwendolen's helplessness in a world wider than her own narrow experience.[106] Gwendolen's small, isolated world stands in juxtaposition with the larger world of which she has at last become aware. When Daniel explains to her the public role that he is assuming as he dedicates himself to the 'duty' of 'restoring a political existence' to Jews by 'awaken[ing] a movement in other minds',

> The world seemed getting larger round poor Gwendolen, and she more solitary and helpless in the midst. The thought that he might come back after going to the East, sank before the bewildering vision of these wide-stretching purposes in which she felt herself reduced to a mere speck. There comes a terrible moment to many souls when the great movements of the world, the larger destinies of mankind, which have lain aloof in newspapers and other neglected reading, enter like an earthquake into their own lives. . . .
>
> That was the sort of crisis which was at this moment beginning in Gwendolen's small life: she was for the first time feeling the pressure of a vast mysterious movement, for the first time being dislodged from her supremacy in her own world, and getting a sense that her horizon was but a dipping onward of an existence with which her own was revolving. All the troubles of her wifehood and widowhood had still left her with the implicit impression which had accompanied her from childhood, that whatever surrounded her was somehow specially for her. . . . But here had come a shock which went deeper than personal jealousy – something spiritual and vaguely tremendous that thrust her away, and yet quelled all anger into self-humiliation.[107]

Gwendolen's experiences as a wife and widow have not challenged the narrow horizons of her world. The smallness of her worldview echoes a characterisation of women that is found in both Mill's *The Subjection of Women* and *Aurora Leigh*. Careful to explain that differences between the genders cannot be ascribed to nature, Mill states, 'A woman seldom runs wild after an abstraction. The habitual direction of her mind [is] to dealing with things as individuals rather than in groups.'[108] Similarly, Romney tells the young, aspiring Aurora that women

> . . . generalise
> Oh, nothing – not even grief! Your quick-breathed hearts,
> So sympathetic to the personal pang,
> Close on each separate knife-stroke, yielding up
> A whole life at each wound, incapable
> Of deepening, widening a large lap of life
> To hold the world-full woe. The human race
> To you means, such a child, or such a man,

> You saw one morning waiting in the cold,
> Beside that gate, perhaps. You gather up
> A few such cases, and when strong sometimes
> Will write of factories and of slaves, as if
> Your father were a negro, and your son
> A spinner in the mills. All's yours and you,
> All, coloured with your blood, or otherwise
> Just nothing to you. Why, I call you hard
> To general suffering. . . .
> . . . does one of you
> Stand still from dancing, stop from stringing pearls
> And pine and die because of the great sum
> Of universal anguish? – Show me a tear
> Wet as Cordelia's, in eyes bright as yours,
> Because the world is mad. You cannot count,
> That you should weep for this account, not you!
> You weep for what you know. A red-haired child
> Sick in a fever, if you touch him once,
> Though but so little as with a finger-tip,
> Will set you weeping; but a million sick . . .
> You could as soon weep for the rule of three
> Or compound fractions.[109]

After characterising women as capable of sympathising with individuals but incapable of understanding the problems of the world on a larger scale, Romney asserts:

> Therefore, this same world
> Uncomprehended by you, must remain
> Uninfluenced by you. – Women as you are,
> Mere women, personal and passionate,
> You give us doting mothers, and perfect wives,
> Sublime Madonnas, and enduring saints!
> We'll get no Christ from you – and verily
> We shall not get a poet, in my mind.[110]

Conversely, Barrett Browning, who herself wrote poems 'of factories and slaves' that focus on individual examples such as Romney describes, notably 'The Cry of the Children' (1844) and 'The Runaway Slave at Pilgrim's Point' (1850), is critical of Romney's application of abstract principles without regard for individuals.

Armgart, however, does not live life within a small circumference. She is guilty of Romney's rather than Aurora's fault. As a public artist, she is unable to understand the individual lives that comprise her audience.

As long as she possesses her voice, the exceptional Armgart fails to form a sympathetic bond with others. Walpurga angrily points out that the everyday performances of unexceptional women, including herself, went unnoticed by the exceptional Armgart until she lost her talent:

> Ay, such a mask
> As the few born like you to easy joy,
> Cradled in privilege, take for natural
> On all the lowly faces that must look
> Upward to you! What revelation now
> Shows you the mask or gives presentiment
> Of sadness hidden? You who every day
> These five years saw me limp to wait on you,
> And thought the order perfect which gave *me*,
> The girl without pretension to be aught,
> A splendid cousin for my happiness.[111]

Walpurga explains, however, that her own mask was one of love, not patience, and that she prefers her own concealed misery to Armgart's inability to see beyond masks and sympathise with the thousands of individuals who were her audience. Illustrating Rae Greiner's point that 'because seeing others does not guarantee our sympathy (and instead frequently prevents it), reflection becomes an indispensible activity in which potential sympathizers engage', Walpurga demands that Armgart, who has failed to sympathise with what she has seen, do the imaginative work to understand the sufferings of others.[112] In this way, the connection among women that *Armgart* establishes is founded in a different mechanism than the melodramatic affective moments that we have seen between Peg and Sybil in *Masks and Faces*, Magdalen and Louisa in *No Name*, and the audience and Esther in *Caste*. Eliot's closet drama eschews the moralistic and spectacular logic of melodrama, and adopts what Greiner has called 'sympathetic realism' or, for our purposes, realistic sympathy.

Such bonds between a talented woman and a woman lacking talent and power are an example of how, according to Beer, 'Eliot turned to the difficulty of the exceptional woman and of women seeking to be exceptional. "Exceptionalness" was a moral and a technical problem for her.'[113] While Rutherford points out that prima donnas' views of their own exceptionality complicated the relationship between the professional singer and the women's suffrage movement, Hudd and Beer suggest that Eliot is critical of both the talented Armgart and the aspiring Gwendolen for lacking a 'sense of community with other women'.[114] Although women of talent are exceptional because of the public power that their abilities afford them, even with her limited talents Gwendolen looks askance at contemporary women's rights movements, thinking of herself as exceptional even as she is incapable of being an unconventional woman:

> Gwendolen was as inwardly rebellious against the restraints of family conditions, and as ready to look through obligations into her own fundamental want of feeling for them, as if she had been sustained by the boldest speculations; but she really had no such speculations, and should at once have marked herself off from any sort of theoretical or practically reforming women by satirising them. She rejoiced to feel herself exceptional; but her horizon was that of the genteel romance where the heroine's soul poured out in her journal is full of vague power, originality, and general rebellion, while her life moves strictly in the sphere of fashion; and if she wanders into a swamp, the pathos lies partly, so to speak, in her having on her satin shoes.[115]

The continuation of Eliot's passage emphasises how Gwendolen, lacking talent that would justify her belief that she is exceptional, falls back on such conventional figurations because she cannot overcome the power of public opinion: 'Poor Gwendolen had both too much and too little mental power and dignity to make herself exceptional. No wonder that Deronda now marked some hardening in a look and manner which were schooled daily to the suppression of feeling.'[116] Gwendolen's theatricality responds to social demands.

Readings of Eliot's works, however, have overstated Eliot's criticism of Armgart and the Alcharisi, underestimating Eliot's argument for the broadening of women's lives and the importance of participating in the public sphere. Litvak, for example, argues that in *Daniel Deronda*, 'Just as the narrative inserts the theater inside poetry, so Daniel sets up a domestic frame to contain Mirah's theatrical frame.'[117] While this aligns Mirah with T. W. Robertson's containment of his heroine's theatricality by domesticity, *Daniel Deronda* also demonstrates that the theatricality of Gwendolen's domestic life is worse than the liberating theatricality that the Alcharisi achieved on stage. Even as Litvak correctly recognises the feminist implications of the Alcharisi, saying that she 'articulates the novel's strongest feminist refusal of the poetic therapy of patriarchal Jewishness', he, among other critics, also emphasises how Eliot 'punish[es] her', claiming for himself the transgressive role of writing 'in the name of the "bad" [theatrical] Jewishness that Eliot's novel, among other more or less well-intentioned agents of Western ideology, punishes so grandly'.[118] In contrast to Litvak, Beer recognises the sympathy that Eliot had for the Alcharisi:

She never permitted to any of the women in her fiction such radical acts as she herself took, except perhaps to . . . the great singer Alcharisi, who has given away her child to devote herself to the freedom of her career. The plot of *Daniel Deronda* turns on the need to mortify herself, to knit up again the unyielding continuities of descent and culture, but not, let it be noted, to renege on her choice.[119]

Rather than domesticating theatricality, Eliot employs professional performing women as an alternative to and criticism of the domestic sphere that Collins and Robertson privilege. Through talent and dedication, Eliot's performing women are able to transcend mere social performances, gaining social power as they control their audiences. Following Klesmer's formula that the professional artist succeeds only through devotion to her art, Armgart identifies the audience's attention as service to the art that she worships. She states that she was not 'glad' with 'vanity' but that her

> only self
> Was consciousness of glory wide-diffuse,
> Music, life, power – I moving in the midst
> With a sublime necessity of good.[120]

Leo states that he saw a '*prima donna*' who was proud of the flowers and jewels delivered from royalty – a woman who was conscious of the personal prestige she had achieved in society and of the material gains her art provided.[121] Where Aurora Leigh rejects such attentions, Armgart is pleased by such gifts because they signify her effect on the audience:

> I sing to living men, and my effect
> Is like the summer's sun, that ripens corn
> Or now or never. If the world brings me gifts,
> Gold, incense, myrrh – 'twill be the needful sign
> That I have stirred it as the high year stirs
> Before I sink to winter.[122]

In addition to likening herself to a Messianic figure in her reference to the gifts that the Magi brought to Jesus, Armgart explains that she seeks celebrity in order to have wide influence in the world:

> Shall I turn aside
> From splendours which flash out the glow I make,
> And live to make, in all the chosen breasts
> Of half a Continent? No, may it come,

> That splendour! . . . .
> Shall I lie?
> Pretend to seek obscurity – to sing
> In hope of disregard? A vile pretence!
> A blasphemy besides. For what is fame
> But the benignant strength of One, transformed
> To joy of Many? Tributes, plaudits come
> As necessary breathing of such joy;
> And may they come to me![123]

Armgart's exultant description of fame underscores how her voice does not merely enable her to express her passions.[124] Rather, Armgart's voice enables her to play a role in the public sphere by influencing many people.

In a letter to John Blackwood on 8 August 1874, in which Eliot explicitly identifies with Armgart, Eliot voices her gratification about how 'the sale of Middlemarch' which 'is wonderful out of all whooping . . . considered as manifesting the impression made by the book, is more valuable than any amount of immediate distribution'.[125] Like Armgart, Eliot values tangible tributes as evidence of her influence. She continues:

> As to confidence in the work to be done I am somewhat in the condition suggested to Armgart, 'How will you bear the poise of eminence, With dread of falling?' And the other day . . . I did what I have sometimes done before at intervals of five or six years – looked into three or four novels to see what the world was reading. The effect was paralyzing, and certainly justified me in [my] abstinence from novel-reading. . . .
>
> To be delivered from all doubts as to one's justification in writing at this stage of the world, one should either have plentiful faith in one's own exceptionalness or plentiful lack of money. . . . To write indifferently after having written well – that is, from a true, individual store which makes a special contribution – is like an eminent clergymen's spoiling his reputation by lapses and neutralising all the good he did before.[126]

For Eliot, writing is a way of participating in the world, but she believes that the privilege of exercising this influence requires an exceptional talent that provides one with an authentic, original contribution to make to the world.

Therefore, in retiring her divas, Armgart and the Alcharisi, Eliot conveys a sense of regret for their loss of public influence. After she has lost her voice forever, Armgart 'sits like a helpless image', reduced to the physical, visual presence that, in Eliot's view, objectified women.[127] Describing her new life as a prison, she bewails how she has become impotent like multitudes of women whom she had not understood before:

> I can do nought
> Better than what a million women do –
> Must drudge among the crowd, and feel my life
> Beating upon the world without response,
> Beating with passion through an insect's horn
> That moves a millet-seed laboriously.
> If I *would* do it![128]

Like the educated women Eliot feared would spurn commonplace duties, having known greatness Armgart cannot bear to perform humble tasks. Armgart's insect metaphor appears again in the epigraph to the chapter in *Daniel Deronda* in which Daniel meets his mother, the Alcharisi, now beyond her theatrical career, married, and ill. Drawn from an unpublished poem by Eliot about Erinna, 'a young woman poet in Ancient Greece, who was chained by her mother to the spinning-wheel and died thus, imprisoned',[129] the epigraph captures the frustration of the Alcharisi's lost fame and power, describing how

> Erinna sat
> Gazing with a sad surprise
> At surging visions of her destiny –
> To spin the byssus drearily
> In insect-labour, while the throng
> Of gods and men wrought deeds
> that poets wrought in song.[130]

The bleakness with which Eliot characterises the diminished lives of Armgart and the Alcharisi contrasts with Aurora's description, at the end of Barrett Browning's poem, of the humble work in which all people – women as well as men – can take satisfaction:

> Be sure, no earnest work
> Of any honest creature, howbeit weak,
> Imperfect, ill-adapted, fails so much,
> Is not gathered as the grain of sand
> To enlarge the sum of human action used
> For carrying out God's end. No creature works
> So ill, observe, that therefore he's cashiered.

> The honest earnest man must stand and work,
> The woman also – otherwise she drops
> At once below the dignity of man,
> Accepting serfdom. Free men freely work.
> Whoever fears God, fears to sit at ease.[131]

Aurora ultimately resolves:

> Art is much, but love is more.
> Oh Art, my Art, thou'rt much, but Love is more!
> Art symbolizes heaven, but Love is God
> And makes heaven. I, Aurora, fell from mine.
> I would not be a woman like the rest,
> A simple woman who believes in love
> And owns the right of love because she loves,
> And, hearing she's beloved, is satisfied
> With what contents God: I must analyze,
> Confront, and question.[132]

Unlike the religious Aurora, Armgart cannot be content as 'a woman like the rest'. Aurora's retreat to solitude in Italy with the fallen Marian Erle, and her subsequent marriage to Romney, are not imbued with the combined regret and resignation that Armgart expresses when, with few choices because even her suitor Dornberg has abandoned her, she decides to go to Freiburg with Walpurga and teach music, replacing her influence over many with influence over few.[133]

In planning how she would face Dornberg, were he to return to her, Armgart eschews theatricality:

> I shall behave
> Like what I am, a common personage
> Who looks for nothing but civility.
> I shall not play the fallen heroine,
> Assume a tragic part, and throw out cues
> For a beseeching lover.[134]

Yet she also recognises the theatricality involved in women's everyday lives. At the same time that she says she will not play a role for Dornberg, she, according to a stage direction, 'assum[es] calmness'.[135] She says that she would rather die 'than bear the yoke of thwarted life', which requires her to perform

> basely feigned content, the placid mask
> Of women's misery.[136]

Like the contrast of Gwendolen and the Alcharisi, Armgart's fall from stardom demonstrates that performance in the home does not grant power like public performance. Her metaphor of the mask for the life of an average woman participates in the Victorian cultural association of death, acting and artifice that Chapter 1 of this book traced. Eliot emphasises the deadening aspect of acting when the compensating benefits of performing for a broad audience have passed, for the Alcharisi and Armgart, or are never gained, by Gwendolen. When the Alcharisi is dying, her 'sincere acting ... in which all feeling ... immediately become matter of conscious representation' is described as 'the excitement or spiritual intoxication which at once exalts and deadens'.[137] Gwendolen's startled scream, when playing the role of Hermione in a drawing-room tableau, is an awakening to unacted life and is a moment of extreme embarrassment for her that reveals her normal state as one of careful self-representation – a theatricality that the reference to *The Winter's Tale* scene underscores as death-like. Additionally, Eliot comments that Grandcourt's mistress's appearance in a social venue, to which Gwendolen responds with a passionate 'rage' that she does not express, is a 'Medusa-apparition' – in other words, an apparition that turns Gwendolen to statue-like stone and thus underscores the deadening theatricality of her everyday life.[138] This incident follows shortly after a description of how Gwendolen treats all social interactions as she would the opera. She continued

> presenting herself as she was expected to do in the accustomed scenes, with the accustomed grace, beauty, and costume; from church at one end of the week, through all the scale of desirable receptions, to the opera at the other. Church was not markedly distinguished in her mind from the other forms of self-presentation.[139]

As Eliot dramatises Armgart's reversion to the life of an average woman, she gives voice to Walpurga, the domestic woman, allowing her momentarily to take centre stage.[140] This, however, remains in tension with the performative charisma of the lead character, Armgart, who commands the stage. Although Kurnick has argued that closet drama forestalls such effects of live performance, McCormack's views of George Eliot's Sunday receptions at her home provide evidence from Eliot's circle of dramatic verse as contiguous with performed drama.[141] McCormack chronicles a Sunday on which Robert Browning read from *The Ring and the Book* and told the actress Helen Faucit, a regular visitor to Eliot's Sundays, of his desire for her to act the character of Pompilia.[142] McCormack also points out that, while public readings are 'rarely associated if ever associated with Eliot', Eliot read to her guests from her novels and, on 28 February 1869, read *Armgart* aloud.[143] Moreover, examining Eliot's manuscript of *Armgart* in contrast with its first publication in *MacMillan's Magazine* (1871) and its publication in the Cabinet Edition reveals the earlier text's greater performativity. For example, in addition to changes of syntax and punctuation throughout that shift the drama from more colloquial, naturalistic dialogue in the manuscript to more formal, poetic sentences in its published versions, Eliot clearly imagined *Armgart* in its manuscript form as embodied performance, writing in the margin to insert a stage direction mid-sentence at the beginning of scene 5: '*Walp*. Armgart, dear Armgart, *(kneeling & taking her hands)* only speak to me.'[144] Immediately after this line, the next stage direction appears to have the word Act, in a circle, written in the left-hand margin next to a bracket around a lengthy stage direction that was somewhat truncated in the published versions: '(*Armgart* looks at her an instant, then draws away her hands &, turning aside, buries her face against the back of the chair. *Walpurga* rising & standing near her in mute sorrow for a moment, is moving towards Leo, when the door opens & the Doctor enters.)'[145] Thus, in the manuscript, Eliot employs not only dialogue, but the imagined physical positioning of bodies.

While in the drama, the unexceptional Walpurga must compete with her stage-worthy cousin Armgart, Eliot's novels focus on women who are thwarted in their attempts to participate in public life. The novel's tendency to depict unexceptional women is emphasised by Armgart's statement, after she has lost her talent:

> I read my lot
> As soberly as if it were a tale
> Writ by a creeping feuilletonist and called
> 'The Woman's Lot: a Tale of Everyday':
> A middling woman's, to impress the world
> With high superfluousness; her thoughts a crop
> Of chick-weed errors or of pot-herb facts,
> Smiled at like some child's drawing on a slate.
> '. . . Well, she can somewhat eke her narrow gains
> By writing, just to furnish her with gloves
> And droschkies in the rain. They print her things
> Often for charity.'[146]

This is consistent with Henry's point that Eliot believed 'that fiction should tell the stories of unexceptional, ordinary people', yet it complicates Henry's related assertion that Eliot 'never modeled a female author/character on herself' and felt 'that the author's experiences should not be confused with his writing'.[147] Armgart's elision of figures – she moves from being reader of the tale to a character within it, and she finally identifies with its mediocre author – underscores how the performing woman served as a figure for the writer's participation in the public world. This blurring of distinctions also represents the accomplishment of sympathy, as it models the type of parallel alignment that Greiner, citing Harry E. Shaw, describes as 'an experience of mental sharing – between reader, character, and narrator'.[148] Lacking the quotation marks around the world's view of the mediocre novelist, the original manuscript text further blurred these identities.[149]

The author that Armgart describes is powerless because she has no talent. Eliot's depictions of professional theatrical women, in contrast, demonstrate that talented women can exercise power in the public world. Although the professional is subject to the audience's gaze and gossip, if she is talented she can gain influence and self-determination that is unavailable to the domestic, socially performing woman. The fact that this power vanishes with the loss of the heroine's gift further underscores the difference between the creative woman and the domestic woman. The talented writer, thus, has public influence that is unavailable to most women. Although Kathryn Hughes points out that Eliot believed that '"[t]he highest work" – the creative work which she did – must always be reserved for the special few', in *Armgart* Eliot develops a sense of community between the exceptional woman who participates in the public sphere and the ordinary woman.[150]

Eliot herself, in her novels, used her exceptional talents to examine and represent the lives of women who, as Eliot famously concludes *Middlemarch*, 'lived faithfully a hidden life, and rest in unvisited tombs'.[151] In its treatment of the talented professional performer, her public audience and her relationship to other women, *Armgart* provides a view into Eliot's concept of authorship. In *Armgart*, Eliot explores both the challenges and the ethical and political responsibilities of a woman who is talented enough to participate in the public sphere. In this regard, in its theme of the power one can gain from public performance, and in its use of the drama to present and draw sympathy for otherwise silenced voices, *Armgart* is a precursor of suffrage theatre.

Gail Marshall has pointed out how Leslie Stephen's 1880 obituary for Eliot elevated her to exceptional status, 'a position of temporal isolation, notably one which does not allow of the possibility of a sustained influence, of successors', and points out that 'this curtailment of Eliot was symptomatic of aspects of the treatment of women in the coming decade, which was one of tremendous gender-anxiety, generated by . . . the implications of women entering into new professional arenas'.[152] Indeed, Elaine Showalter and Sandra Gilbert and Susan Gubar have demonstrated how New Woman novelists writing in the decade after Eliot's death did not feel liberated by Eliot's example, but rather resentful of what Gilbert and Gubar have characterised as an overwhelming 'literary matrilineage'.[153] While Chapter 4 will examine some of these hostilities and reservations about George Eliot, Chapter 5 will ultimately demonstrate how the suffrage playwright Elizabeth Robins and the broader suffrage movement revisited the issues presented by Eliot as they drew on the class-transcending abilities of the actress to foster a sense of solidarity, claiming places in the public sphere not only for the exceptional woman but also for her long-silenced sisters. In consciously and deliberately using individual stories for a political purpose, Robins's work echoes Eliot's assertion that the female artist can participate in and understand the public world but must maintain an ability to sympathise with individuals. Moreover, in using theatre for a political cause, suffrage theatre would employ the visual, affective strategies of melodrama, but it would also employ the realistic sympathy of Eliot in order to forge communities of women united in a political cause.

Notes

1. McCormack, *George Eliot in Society*, passim; Bernstein, *Roomscape*, p. 115.
2. See, for example, Leonardi, 'To Have a Voice: The Politics of the Diva'; Pope, 'The Diva Doesn't Die'; Beer, *George Eliot*; and Rutherford, *The Prima Donna and Opera, 1815–1930*.
3. Eliot, *Armgart*, p. 130. Unless otherwise noted, all citations are to *The Works of George Eliot*, Cabinet Edition.
4. Katherine Newey, *Women's Theatre Writing in Victorian Britain*, asserts that Eliot's dramatic writings, even though they were not created for the stage, are part of 'a tradition of women's performance writing which, like the work of [Felicia] Hemans and [Mary Russell] Mitford, was grounded in sympathetic presentation of rebellion' (p. 110).
5. Beer, *George Eliot*, p. 202. Additionally, Rosemarie Bodenheimer in 'Ambition and Its Audiences' and Nina Auerbach in *Romantic Imprisonment* have read Eliot's female performers as explorations of her sense of public stature.
6. My analysis of Eliot's writing is, thus, consistent with David Kurnick's argument that 'the novel of interiority is a record not only of relentless

intensifications of interiority but of the desire to escape from it'. Kurnick's argument, however, is not inflected by gender, as mine is, and it is worth noting that Eliot's performers are women and their performances are significant because they allow women to play public roles (*Empty Houses*, p. 4).
7. Hudd, 'The Politics of a Feminist Poetics', p. 68. Similarly, Beer points out that 'in her poems, particularly *The Spanish Gypsy* and "Armgart", and in *Daniel Deronda*, George Eliot turned to the problem of the exceptional woman and of women seeking to be exceptional. Exceptionalness was a moral and a technical problem for her' (*George Eliot*, p. 200).
8. On Aurora's exceptionality, see also Corbett, *Representing Femininity*, p. 65.
9. Beer, *George Eliot*, pp. 51, 179.
10. Eliot, review of *Aurora Leigh*, pp. 306–7.
11. Litvak, *Caught in the Act*.
12. Eliot, review of *Aurora Leigh*, p. 306.
13. Ibid. pp. 306–7.
14. Kurnick has analysed 'the collectivist technology of the theatrical imagination' in Eliot's *The Spanish Gypsy* (*Empty Houses*, p. 73). As I have noted elsewhere, I depart from Kurnick in my emphasis on how the public and collective was of particular significance for women, and it is for this reason that the actress embodied the theatre in such powerful and troubling ways.
15. Barrett Browning, *Aurora Leigh*, p. 30.
16. Ibid. p. 154.
17. Ibid. pp. 154–5.
18. Ibid. p. 45.
19. Ibid. p. 56.
20. Brontë, *Jane Eyre*, p. 130.
21. Ibid. p. 136.
22. Ibid. pp. 134–5, 256.
23. Ibid. p. 136.
24. Litvak, *Caught in the Act*, p. 149.
25. Corbett, *Representing Femininity*, p. 58.
26. Eliot, review of *Aurora Leigh*, p. 306.
27. Litvak, *Caught in the Act*, pp. 27, 33.
28. Ibid. p. 41.
29. Barrett Browning, *Aurora Leigh*, p. 173.
30. Litvak, *Caught in the Act*, p. 45.
31. Gilbert and Gubar, *The Madwoman in the Attic*; Bodenheimer, 'Ambition and Its Audiences'.
32. Rutherford, *The Prima Donna and Opera, 1815–1930*, p. 58.
33. Litvak, *Caught in the Act*, p. 38.
34. Ibid. p. 43. Litvak borrows this term from Fried, *Absorption and Theatricality*.

35. Litvak, *Caught in the Act*, p. 51.
36. Quoted in Gertrude Himmelfarb's 'Editor's Introduction' to John Stuart Mill, *On Liberty*, p. 23.
37. Barrett Browning, *Aurora Leigh*, p. 322.
38. Mill, *On Liberty*, pp. 72–3.
39. Ibid. p. 136.
40. Ibid. pp. 137–8.
41. Hudd, 'The Politics of a Feminist Poetics', p. 80.
42. *The George Eliot Letters*, vol. 4, p. 196.
43. For a history of Mill's involvement with the women's suffrage movement, see Kent, *Sex and Suffrage in Britain, 1860–1914*, p. 187.
44. Barrett Browning, *Aurora Leigh*, p. 148.
45. Ibid. p. 149.
46. Emily Davies, Letter to Annie Crow, 24 September 1876, in *The Papers of Emily Davies and Barbara Bodichon*, ED 5/16, p. 3. Also published in *The George Eliot Letters*, vol. 8, p. 469.
47. Bodenheimer, 'Ambition and Its Audiences', p. 25.
48. McCormack, *George Eliot in Society*, p. 67.
49. Eliot, *Armgart*, p. 73.
50. Ibid. p. 95.
51. Ibid. p. 73.
52. Ibid. p. 87.
53. Ibid. p. 105.
54. Ibid. pp. 95–6.
55. Ibid. p. 98.
56. Hudd, 'The Politics of a Feminist Poetics', p. 74; Mill, *The Subjection of Women*, p. 194.
57. Barrett Browning, *Aurora Leigh*, pp. 34–5.
58. Ibid. p. 40.
59. Ibid. p. 73.
60. Eliot, review of *Aurora Leigh*, p. 306.
61. Barrett Browning, *Aurora Leigh*, p. 316.
62. Dickens, 'The Amusements of the People', pp. 13–15, 57–60.
63. Carlisle, *The Sense of an Audience*.
64. Rutherford, *The Prima Donna and Opera, 1815–1930*, p. 22.
65. Eliot, *Armgart*, p. 78.
66. Ibid. p. 78.
67. Ibid. p. 80.
68. Gail Marshall, *Actresses on the Victorian Stage*, p. 113.
69. Rutherford, *The Prima Donna and Opera, 1815–1930*, pp. 59, 62, 248.
70. Henry, *The Life of George Eliot*, p. 9.
71. Gail Marshall, *Actresses on the Victorian Stage*, p. 3. See also Chapter 1 of this book for an examination of the association of artifice, actresses, statues and death.

72. According to Litvak, 'sensationalism reveals the sex-gender system and the text-genre system as being closely and profoundly intertwined. . . . Lewes's strategy, like Eliot's, though on a much smaller scale, is to divide the latter against the former, abstracting from a hideously theatricalized narrative an apparently autonomous poetics with which to rule and, ultimately, to reform it. . . . Lewes's theoretical comments about Salvini's acting . . . function as condensed versions of what happens so grandly in *Daniel Deronda*, where the criticism of theatricality gives way to the masterful discourse of "poetry"' (*Caught in the Act*, pp. 156–8).
73. Ibid. p. 150.
74. Hudd, 'The Politics of a Feminist Poetics', p. 72.
75. Rutherford, *The Prima Donna and Opera, 1815–1930*, p. 15.
76. Eliot, *Armgart*, p. 82.
77. Ibid. p. 80; emphasis added.
78. *The George Eliot Letters*, vol. 2, p. 191.
79. Eliot, *Daniel Deronda*, p. 229.
80. David Marshall, *The Figure of Theater*, pp. 196–8, 205, 207.
81. Eliot, *Middlemarch*, p. 183.
82. Ibid. p. 188.
83. Ibid. p. 469.
84. Ibid. pp. 29, 471.
85. Beer, *George Eliot*, p. 153.
86. Eliot, *Armgart*, p. 97.
87. Eliot, *Daniel Deronda*, pp. 226–7. Rutherford provides a context that suggests that the status of a performer who could 'sing and act in equal measure' became particularly elevated in the nineteenth century, and notes Giulia Grisi as a stand-out in this regard (*The Prima Donna and Opera, 1815–1930*, p. 205).
88. Rutherford, *The Prima Donna and Opera, 1815–1930*, p. 15.
89. Eliot, *Daniel Deronda*, p. 229.
90. Newey, *Women's Theatre Writing in Victorian Britain*, p. 23; Rutherford, *The Prima Donna and Opera, 1815–1930*, p. 73.
91. Eliot, *Daniel Deronda*, p. 233.
92. Collins, *No Name*, p. 43.
93. Eliot, *Daniel Deronda*, p. 232.
94. Ibid. pp. 229–30.
95. Elsewhere, Diderot emphasises the difference in scale between the drawing room and the stage (*The Paradox of Acting*, pp. 19, 81).
96. Lewes, *On Actors and the Art of Acting*, pp. ix–x.
97. Eliot, *Daniel Deronda*, p. 229.
98. Diderot, *The Paradox of Acting*, pp. 63–4.
99. Eliot, *Daniel Deronda*, p. 439.
100. Ibid. pp. 194, 190.

101. Litvak, *Caught in the Act*, p. 177.
102. Stokes, 'Rachel's "Terrible Beauty"', pp. 771–93; Eliot, *Daniel Deronda*, p. 45.
103. Eliot, *Daniel Deronda*, p. 226.
104. Ibid. p. 576.
105. Ibid. p. 575.
106. Ibid. p. 248.
107. Ibid. pp. 734–5.
108. Mill, *The Subjection of Women*, p. 192.
109. Barrett Browning, *Aurora Leigh*, pp. 43–4.
110. Ibid. p. 44.
111. Eliot, *Armgart*, p. 128.
112. Greiner, *Sympathetic Realism*, p. 8.
113. Beer, *George Eliot*, p. 200.
114. Rutherford, *The Prima Donna and Opera, 1815–1930*, pp. 85–6; Beer, *George Eliot*, p. 219.
115. Eliot, *Daniel Deronda*, pp. 44–5.
116. Ibid. p. 550.
117. Litvak, *Caught in the Act*, p. 188.
118. Ibid. pp. 189, 194. Hudd also emphasises Eliot's criticism of the Alcharisi's individualism in favour of Mirah's participation in a collectivity.
119. Beer, *George Eliot*, p. 24.
120. Eliot, *Armgart*, pp. 85–6.
121. Ibid. p. 86.
122. Ibid. pp. 86–7.
123. Ibid. pp. 87–8.
124. See Brown, 'Determined Heroines', for an argument about the self-expression that Armgart's voice provides her.
125. *The George Eliot Letters*, vol. 6, p. 75.
126. Ibid. pp. 75–6.
127. Eliot, *Armgart*, p. 110.
128. Ibid. p. 127.
129. Beer, *George Eliot*, p. 207.
130. Eliot, *Daniel Deronda*, p. 569.
131. Barrett Browning, *Aurora Leigh*, p. 282.
132. Ibid. p. 316.
133. Eliot, *Armgart*, p. 139.
134. Ibid. p. 121.
135. Ibid. p. 121.
136. Ibid. p. 128.
137. Eliot, *Daniel Deronda*, p. 574.
138. Ibid. pp. 550–1.
139. Ibid. p. 550.
140. Hudd points out that 'George Eliot restores subjectivity and importance to the ordinary woman, and in doing so broadens the base of Barrett Browning's feminist aims.' Hudd also contrasts *Aurora Leigh*'s

'one controlling narrative voice, Aurora's' to '[t]he poetic form chosen by George Eliot [that] offers the sort of interdependent unity which forms the basis of a political ideology which stresses that the collective need outweighs the ambition of the individual' ('The Politics of a Feminist Poetics', p. 79). David Marshall's reading of *Daniel Deronda* as a theatrical novel further suggests that Eliot's use of theatre urges the reader to understand 'multiple subjectivities and points of view' and to '*read* characters in order to know them' (*The Figure of Theater*, p. 238).

141. In his analysis of *The Spanish Gypsy*, Kurnick points out that 'in an actual staging, the democratic tropism implicit in the collectivity of the theatrical "cast" would be affected by the semiotics of stage management: certain characters are designated to stay in the spotlight, just as others will remain subordinated by the mis-en-scène. But in the textual realm, this democracy reigns as a typographical fact, and as an injunction' (*Empty Houses*, p. 89).
142. McCormack, *George Eliot in Society*, p. 62.
143. Ibid. p. 64.
144. Eliot, *Armgart*, British Library Add MS 34038, p. 106.
145. Ibid. pp. 106–7; Eliot, *Armgart*, *MacMillan's Magazine* 24 (1871): p. 176.
146. Eliot, *Armgart*, pp. 124–5.
147. Henry, *The Life of George Eliot*, pp. 12–13.
148. Greiner, *Sympathetic Realism*, p. 26.
149. Eliot, *Armgart*, British Library Add MS 34038, p. 111.
150. Hughes, *George Eliot*, p. 283. Henry characterises Eliot's later work as being concerned with 'the opposition between the great and the ordinary' (*The Life of George Eliot*, p. 15).
151. Eliot, *Middlemarch*, p. 896.
152. Gail Marshall, *Actresses on the Victorian Stage*, p. 92.
153. Showalter, *A Literature of Their Own*, p. 108; Gilbert and Gubar, *No Man's Land, Volume 1: The War of the Words*, p. 167.

Chapter 4

Novelistic Naturalism: 'The Ideal Mother Cannot Be the Great Artist'

In the 1880s, George Moore's unabashedly antitheatrical use of the actress served a number of purposes for him as he positioned himself quite consciously – and in some cases explicitly – in opposition to works that we have traced in the previous chapters. As he claimed a new form of naturalism for the novel, like Robertson he employed the domestic to signal the realism of his work over the artifice that he used the actress's performance to embody. Yet while both Robertson and Moore curbed the actress's performative powers, Robertson did so by claiming a home for the actress, while Moore did so by denying it. In *A Mummer's Wife* (1885), widely considered the first naturalist British novel, Moore used an actress's deadly neglect of her child to challenge the theatre's realism, respectability and encroachment on the domestic sphere while asserting the superior naturalism of his own novel. In contrast to Eliot's performing women, the central character's desire to act provides her initially with freedom from a suffocating domestic life and seems to give her the ability to become anything she wants, but ultimately her alcoholism and failure to fulfil her role as a mother demonstrate that the actress's power to play various roles easily becomes the horrific problem of the complete dissolution of a stable identity. Additionally, while Eliot employed the actress as a figure for considering the female artist's relationship to audiences, Moore's essay 'Sex in Art' mobilises antitheatricality to argue that women are incapable of being true artists as he declares, 'It is only in the inferior art – the art of acting – that women approach men. In that art it is not certain that they do not stand even higher.'[1] Moore proceeds to criticise George Eliot, and particularly *Romola* and *Daniel Deronda*, because her work is not 'feminine', identifying the feminine realm as that of 'boudoirs and fans'.[2]

A central element of Moore's antitheatricality has to do with popular audiences. In his essay 'Why I Don't Write Plays' in the *Pall Mall*

Gazette, George Moore defines bad drama as that which is written to please its audience:

> the taste of the public lies wholly with the bad play – not the play that is bad because it is written by a writer without talent, or the play that is written in an unfortunate inspiration by a writer with talent, but the crude, shapeless, brainless composition, written with deliberation and strict knowledge of 'the sort of thing the public wants'.[3]

A leading proponent of the 'Independent Theatre', J. T. Grein's subscription organisation founded in 1891 to be free from commercial interests, Moore argued against the taste of 'the general public', saying:

> if there should be three thousand people in London who like a good play, if there should be two thousand people – if there should be a thousand people in London who like a good play sufficiently to subscribe five or six pounds each for eight of nine performances a year the art of dramatic writing may be preserved.[4]

Nevertheless, he also maintained the novel's superior ability to communicate with a large audience:

> Some collaboration on the part of the multitude is necessary to enable the artist to produce art that is vital, and so it seems to me that those who would interpret the life of their time do well to choose the novel, rather than the play, as a means of expression. The success of 'Anna Karenina' proves that the narrative form permits the novelist to put his best thoughts and his most accomplished art into his work and still be read, whereas the failure of the plays I have named and the success of plays which I shall not name prove that the dramatic form of to-day is disregard for every kind of moral sequence and the violent dislocation of the inevitable course of human action.[5]

Emily Allen has examined how novelists who made avant-garde claims to literary distinction use the figure of theatre as they 'posit cultural capital and literary value over and against abjected competitors for the very market from which the novel must at the same time distinguish itself'.[6] Allen's point that the '*retreat* from market forces in their construction of private, emotional space and privatized family values' in the novel 'depends upon' the theatre as a public foil partly explains why the Robertsonian theatre's claim to the domestic sphere impelled a response from novelist Moore.[7] This chapter argues that Moore's use of the figure of the theatre and the actress were a response to developments in the theatre itself.

Through understanding Moore's reactivity, this chapter demonstrates that the theatre's gain in respectability in the 1860s and following decades contributed to a change in the form of the novel as novelists attempted to attract an intellectual rather than a popular readership to create an audience distinct from the one that attended the theatre. This chapter traces Moore's response to the drama's earlier claims to realism and respectability through their depictions of the actress's domesticity, and his rejection of the theatre's appeal to popular audiences. It thus demonstrates the as-yet-unexplored role of the theatre in what Garrett Stewart has called the novel's 'decline of reader address in that wholesale modernist recoil from communalistic literary rhetoric', as novels moved away from seeking the ties to popular readership, as we saw in the introduction, that were so evident in *Vanity Fair* (1847–8).[8] In addition to reading Moore's *A Mummer's Wife* in the context of his non-fiction essays on the theatre in order to understand Moore's novel as a reaction against the cultural, literary and theatre history we have studied thus far, this chapter also examines a further reaction against Moore himself. Elizabeth Robins's satirical novel *George Mandeville's Husband* (1894) represents a feminist actress's objections to Moore.

The Actress's Dissolution in *A Mummer's Wife*

From 1888 to 1890 George Moore frequently wrote about the theatre and called for a national 'subventioned theater' that would 'allow us to say what we have to say, and in the form which is natural and peculiar to us'.[9] His emphasis on innovation and national character echoed the terms used to praise *Caste*. Yet even as Moore called for more 'natural' drama, his tendency to find fault with the movement towards increased dramatic realism suggests that his dramatic criticism was a defensive response to the threat that he perceived in the theatre. In 'Our Dramatists and Their Literature', Moore identified drama and the novel as competitors when he wrote that 'the real cause for the decline of dramatic literature is cheap books'.[10] In his essay 'Mummer-Worship' Moore derides a theatrical realism that allows an actor to be 'applauded not for what he does, but for what he is' and an actress with 'no previous experience' to succeed on the stage.[11] In plays like Robertson's, middle-class women began to perform characters of their own class. Tracy C. Davis explains that the restriction of women's education to the 'feminine' accomplishments of music, modern languages, fine needlecrafts, and the cultivation of beauty and genteel manners prepared only a specific class of women for the theatrical world where such frivolities could be easily adapted from the drawing rooms of middle-class society to the box sets of the 1860s and after.[12]

Moore also ridicules the new respectability of performers that resulted from the theatre's improved stature. In contrast to the life of the roving actor who existed 'on the outskirts of society' in 'those times when Shakespeare and Jonson lived', Moore describes how, 'about twenty years ago' – in other words, in Robertson's time –

> a great and drastic change came.... [A]nd now, in full fig, that is to say in a villa, in a silk hat, and with the cards of the parson and his wife in their hands, they lay claim to our sympathies and demand our household affections. Their women assure us that they are excellent mothers and have not known the joys of lovers; the men invite us to their club, and speak of aristocratic connections. So the mummer has changed his garb and name; he is now the actor, and wears a silk hat. Can the leopard change his spots or the Ethiopian his skin? The modern mummer sits on the lawn outside his villa in St John's Wood; his boys play beneath the leafage; his wife, a portly lady on the verge of forty-five and society, tells you of the many acts of Christian charity she is performing and of the luncheon parties to which she has been asked.[13]

Opposing Robertson's criticism of the caste system, Moore argues that 'mummers' – a term that emphasises the marginal social position and itinerant lifestyle of the travelling actor, rather than the professionalism that enabled successful actors to achieve respectability – should remain excluded from polite society. He particularly scoffs at actresses and their pretensions to the domestic sphere: 'Five years have not passed since we heard for the first time that a favourite actress nursed her children, read prayers, and gave tea and tracts to naughty chorus girls.'[14] Furthermore, Moore's approbation for the fact that 'an eighteenth-century *salon*' would never have received mummers may be a direct response to Henry Irving's description, in his response to Diderot, of how the actor is no longer the classless being of the previous century.[15] Moore thus underscores the particularly mid-Victorian mindset of Taylor and Reade's attempt to reclaim the previous century's Peg Woffington through friendship with a genteel woman.

Attacking the theatre's new-found respectability by focusing on the actress, Moore argues that although such posturing has provided actresses with social acceptance, actresses are neither respectable nor domestic:

> To-day the stage is as moral as it was a hundred years ago – as much so and not one jot more. The alliance between church and stage is a subject wherewith the hypocritical may trade on the eternal credulity of mankind; the dramatic profession has been, is, and always must be, a profession for those to whom social restraints are irksome, and who would lead the life their instinct dictates. The ideal mother cannot be the great artist. The ancients knew this well, and did not waste time in striving to unite the cradle and the *chef-d'oeuvre*. And since, in the eternal wisdom of things, we must find a place for vice as well as for virtue, for the Bohemian as well as the housewife, I believe that little will be gained by emptying the *coulisse* [backstage] into the drawing-room, and the drawing-room into the *coulisse*. We have no belief in the amalgamation of classes, and still hold by the old distinctions.[16]

Accordingly, Moore's essays recount the seamy unseen lives of actresses, rather than their wholesome family lives. In addition to revealing the promiscuity, divorce and alcoholism of three middle-class sisters raised for the stage, he displays the actress's negligence of maternal duties.[17] While she and her colleagues 'read plays after breakfast, after lunch, and after dinner, and the readings are only interrupted by fashionable men who come from the clubs and make up parties to go to the theatre', '[t]he poor husband sits on the stairs with his only child on his knees; the child says, "When will mother come home, father?"'[18]

In *A Mummer's Wife* Moore uses the actress to demonstrate the incompatibility between domestic life and imaginations shaped by sentimental and melodramatic plays and novels – and it is with domestic life as its touchstone that his novel establishes its own realism. The central character, Kate Ede, is dissatisfied with her seamstress job, her invalid shopkeeper husband and her prosaic home. Lured by the attractions of the theatre and by her romanticisation of a travelling actor-manager, she becomes not only a mummer's wife but an actress herself. But such a life – a disastrous combination, Allen points out, of acting and the respectable, middle-class domesticity that she carries over into her new life – leads to Kate's disintegration.[19] She becomes an alcoholic, causes the death of her own child and ultimately drinks herself to death.

Moore's attraction to unromanticised portrayals of the domestic plainness behind the actress's glamour is evident in his 'An Actress of the Eighteenth Century'. Praising Edmond de Goncourt's biography of Mlle Clairon because it 'reconstruct[s] the character of the illustrious *tragédienne* and pseudo-German Princess in all its crude reality, and the material routine of her existence', Moore delights in quotidian details: 'We learn that her sprained arm is better, and that her cook has left her'.[20] *A Mummer's Wife* adopts the naturalism of not only Goncourt but also of Zola, whom Moore identified as an influence.[21] Unlike Robertson's realism, naturalism violated Victorian codes of respectability. Moore's publisher, Henry Vizetelly, was imprisoned for obscenity when, at Moore's urging, he published Zola's works in England, and reviews of *A Mummer's Wife* criticised the fundamental tenets of naturalism. A famous attack on the novel in the *Saturday Review* focused on the subject matter so central to Moore's naturalism, 'the pitiful drab whom he has chosen for his heroine, and the grimy and unwholesome experiences he has chosen to believe the essentials of art'.[22] An equally severe review in the *Spectator* homed in on Moore's espousal not only of a new, 'unsavoury' and 'revolting' material, but also of a new, 'vivid' mode of representation that, 'both in matter and manner, reminds us very strongly of the work of M. Emile Zola'. It was precisely because of Moore's rendering of the concrete details of a life stripped of illusion that the reviewer condemned the novel: 'As the objects portrayed by the new school of realists are admittedly unpleasant in themselves, a representation of them must needs be also unpleasant in proportion to its veracity and realisableness.'[23] The novel's most famous episodes include its accounts of childbirth and of Kate's decline into alcoholism, complete with a graphically rendered scene in which she vomits in a cab. Another scene, 'described with sickeningly realistic minuteness', depicts one of Ralph Ede's wrenching asthmatic attacks.[24] Moore contrasts such scenes with the illusions of sentimental literature and drama. Before Kate's vision is corrupted by these influences, when she can still experience genuine affect from the real domestic world in which she lives, her husband's recoveries

> always seemed to her like miracles, and she watched the long pallid face crushed under a shock of dark matted hair, lifting him beyond the pale of loving or loathing, investing and clothing him in the pity of tragic things. The room, too, seemed transfigured. The bare wide floor, the gaunt bed, the poor walls plastered with religious prints cut from journals, even

the ordinary washhandstand with the common delf [sic] ewer, the chest of drawers that might have been bought for thirty shillings – lost their coarseness; their triviality disappeared, until nothing was seen or felt but this one suffering man.[25]

In this description Moore implies that the mundane details of Kate's domestic life are the subject of true art. Her reimmersion into romantic literature and melodrama, however, obliterates the significance of her daily life.

In *A Mummer's Wife* Moore represents the stage at its most melodramatic so that the theatre can be bested by his own form of realism.[26] He must do so, because his own naturalistic technique of studying how characters are shaped by their environments, in laying out the details of the domestic world, somewhat resembles the Robertsonian stage realism that he rejects. Robertson's stage sets, after all, anticipate Zola's call, in the 1870s, for greater naturalism in drama:

> The environment must determine the character. When . . ., as the curtain rises, one catches the first glimpse of the characters, their personalities and behaviour, if only to see the actual locale in which they move, the importance of exact reproduction in the decor will be appreciated.[27]

In his dramatic criticism, however, Moore derides the 'practicable' stage sets that Robertson employed:

> Stage realism corrupts our intelligence by easy satisfactions instead of stimulating the imagination, which should create all from the words of the poet. . . . I look back to those times when theatrical audiences did not require *real* fountains and *real* trees, believing that they who did not require these realities were gifted with a sense that is wanting in us.[28]

Moore does not privilege a fanciful imagination but self-interestedly, as a novelist, advocates textual naturalism over naturalism performed in the theatre.

Moore thought that melodramatic theatrical conventions resulted from audience demand. Although he argues that poor theatrical fare is not solely a consequence of audience taste, he states that

> it is difficult to find a test more just and more conclusive of the state of the popular mind than the open and spontaneous verdict expressed in a theatre. The poet and the novelist may sacrifice the present, but in

the case of the dramatist such a sacrifice is not possible, for his work hardly exists off the stage, and depends upon the temper of the public mind.[29]

In his view of the audience's power to degrade drama – a view that places the theatre firmly in the category of popular entertainment – Moore concurs with other Victorian writers, several of whom were discussed in the introduction to this book. But Moore was less ambivalent than earlier novelists such as Charles Dickens and Wilkie Collins, who were attracted to popular audiences. Anthony Farrow describes Moore's belief that the writer's art suffers if it 'operates on terms dictated by the demands of his market'.[30] Allen adds that *A Mummer's Wife* aims to 'stake out a cultural position high above the middle-class mainstream' and to 'transcend the materiality of middle-class consumption by positioning itself against the mass market it thematised as a matter of vulgar, vested interests'.[31] Moore's competition with the theatre, therefore, complicates the idea that the novel and the theatre competed for market share.[32] Moore sought to avoid a theatrical relationship to a popular audience. His desire for freedom from one market structure that he believed corrupted art, the circulating library, shaped the form of *A Mummer's Wife*. The circulating libraries' monopoly, which enabled them to censor novels, was grounded in the publication of three-volume novels priced for purchase by the libraries rather than by readers. After Moore's *A Modern Lover* (1883) had been banned by the circulating libraries Smith's and Mudie's, he wrote *A Mummer's Wife* as a one-volume novel, which could be sold directly to the consumer.[33] Although this marketing strategy meant a more direct appeal to the reading audience, it was mainly an attempt to gain acceptance for a work that did not conform to popular taste as defined by the circulating libraries, and therefore it signalled a movement towards attracting a more avant-garde readership. Although Moore's strategy took a different form, it followed on a similar challenge to the circulating libraries in Eliot's *Middlemarch*. Kathleen McCormack writes of how 'Lewes's innovative plan of publishing *Middlemarch* in its own volumes issued serially during 1871 and 1872 as a revolutionary and pivotal publishing strategy that helped weaken the dominance of the officious lending libraries', was accompanied by his 'marketing' campaign waged in his and Eliot's weekly salon.[34] This technique of using a select audience to generate interest in the novel would also have generated a more high-brow audience.

In *A Mummer's Wife* Moore aligns the conventional, false art forms of the theatre and sentimental fiction with the artifice of the actress and contrasts them with the domestic, which he takes as his real subject. At the novel's opening Kate eschews the stories of her childhood for everyday life, which Moore describes in prosaic detail:

> On the corner of the table lay a book, a well-worn volume in a faded red paper cover. It was a novel she used to read with delight when she was a girl, but it had somehow failed to interest her, and after a few pages she had laid it aside, preferring for distraction her accustomed sewing. She was now well awake, and, as she worked, her thoughts turned on things concerning the daily routine of her life. She thought of the time when her husband would be well; of the pillow she was making; of how nice it would look in the green armchair; of the much greater likelihood of letting their rooms if they were better furnished; of their new lodger; and of the probability of a quarrel between him and her mother-in-law, Mrs Ede.[35]

The new lodger is the actor Dick. He disrupts Kate's home by reawakening her romantic imagination, which is fed by the literary and theatrical works to which she increasingly turns. Kate insists on her 'right to look through her books and poetry' – her right not only to peruse them but also to view the world through them.[36] They provide a 'luminous mist of sentiment' that Moore contends distorts the truth.[37] He provides a detailed history of the texts that shape Kate's imagination. After giving up fairytales for romances, she has made an easy transition from fantasy literature to works that are only superficially 'realistic', 'from the authors who deal exclusively with knights, princesses, and kings to those who interest themselves in the love fortunes of doctors and curates'.[38] Moore characterises Kate's favourite book as 'a grotesque mixture of prose and poetry, both equally false'.[39] This novel 'enchant[ed]' her 'and she always fancied that had she been the heroine of the book she would have acted in the same way' – a tautological statement that reveals how apt an actress Kate will be, because she steps easily into roles.[40] In her imagination Kate 'became the heroine of the absurd fiction, substituting herself for the lady who used to read Byron and Shelley to the gentleman who went to India in despair', and later she loses herself further when the composer Montgomery refers to her elopement as 'such a romantic story'.[41] Kate replies that 'the story of her life ... would, were it taken down, make the most wonderful story-book ever written', and takes licence with the details of her marriage to Ralph in order to shape her narrative.[42]

For Kate, the stage provides a spectacular realisation of escapist novels; her first visit to the theatre 'seduce[s] [her] like a sensual dream'.[43] She herself elides sentimental novels and stage representation when she explains to her seducer, Dick, that her attraction to him was the result of her literature-scripted fantasies:

> You were so different from all the other men I've seen – so much more like what I imagined a man should be, so much more like the heroes in the novels. You know in the books there's always a tenor who comes and sings under the window in the moonlight, and sends the lady he loves roses.[44]

As a child and young woman, in the bleak industrial landscape Moore describes realistically, Kate looks to the hills beyond the town, 'the theatre of all [her] travels before life's struggles began', and envisions a world filled first with 'the palaces of the kings and queens who would wave their wands and vanish' and later with 'the lovers with whom she sympathize[s] in the pages of her novels'.[45] Dick, in turn, likens the hills to 'the gallery of a theatre', puts himself and Kate 'on the stage, the footlights run around here', and suggests her transformation into a woman who plays the sentimental roles that have made her dissatisfied with the 'hard reality' of her life: 'The valley is the pit; and there are plenty of pits in it.'[46] Kate again imagines the realistic industrial landscape of Moore's novel as a dreamscape on the eve of going away with Dick:

> The tall stems of the factory chimneys, the bottle-shaped pottery ovens, the intricate shafts of the collieries were hidden in the mist, and the furnace fires flashing through the mist enhanced the likeness of the Hanley Valley to a sea of stars; like stars these furnaces flamed, now here, now there, over the lower slopes of the hills, till at last one blazed into existence high amid the hills, so high that it must have been on the very lowest verge. It seemed to Kate like a hearth of pleasure and comfort awaiting her in some distant country, and all her fancies were centred in this distant light, till another light breaking suddenly higher up in the hills attracted her, and she deemed that it would be in or about this light that she would find happiness. She must ascend from one light to the next, but the light on which her eyes were fixed was not a furnace light, but a star. Would she never find happiness, then, in this world? she asked. Was Dick going to desert her? And without telling him that she had mistaken an earthly for a heavenly light, she threw her arms about him.[47]

Kate is fashioning her 'hearth of pleasure' out of an illusion, and leaving her actual hearth to do so.

Disruptions of theatrical illusion, such as the behind-the-scenes viewpoint of her assistant Hender, who is familiar with Dick's acting company, mar Kate's enjoyment of performances. However, it is precisely this viewpoint, which she continually rejects, that Moore adopts in the novel. Kate witnesses and Moore describes, for example, how the actress playing the bride Clairette takes care not to stain her costume while drinking because 'beer plays the devil with white satin'.[48] Similarly, when Kate sees the chorus of women off stage, 'She remembered their appearance from Thursday, but she had not seen their vulgar, everyday eyes, nor heard until now their coarse, everyday laughs and jokes.'[49] Moore neatly aligns domesticity with the ability to penetrate performance and see reality clearly: Hender marries Kate's ex-husband and lives in Kate's home.

The death of Kate's child is Moore's most striking demonstration of the conflict between the illusion of sentimental fiction and drama, on the one hand, and the reality of the domestic world, on the other, and it expresses the vehemence with which Moore denied the realism and respectability of these literary forms and asserted the realism of his own work. The theatre's threat to motherhood is foreshadowed when Dick first visits Kate's shop, 'filled with babies' frocks, hoods, and many pairs of little woollen shoes': 'It was a very tiny corner, and, like a Samson, Mr Lennox [Dick] looked as if he would only have to extend his arms to pull the whole place down upon his shoulders.'[50] Conversely, motherhood provides a slight brake to the temptations of a theatrical lifestyle. Drawn to examine Dick's personal effects in his room, Kate checks herself when she remembers the 'little girls' who serve as her two apprentices, about whom she catches herself 'wishing suddenly that they were her own children'.[51] But Kate is incapable of being a satisfactory mother, because she is lost in a world of artifice, defined by escapism in the mutually reinforcing forms of bad literature, the theatre and alcohol. Like Esther's father's shiftiness and alcoholism in *Caste*, Kate's alcoholic dissolution is linked to her ability to play theatrical roles. Merely attending a performance has the same effect as alcohol and leads to 'an absence of her own proper individuality', even to self-destructiveness, as she is overwhelmed and intoxicated by the play:

> All her musical sensibilities rushed to her head like wine; it was only by a violent effort, full of acute pain, that she saved herself from raising her voice with those of the singers, and dreading a giddiness that might precipitate her into the pit, she remained staring blindly at the stage.[52]

Her response to being on stage, 'her thoughts fizzing like champagne', prefigures her drunkenness.[53] In fact, 'drinking to the night's success' with two other actresses is what introduces Kate to alcohol.[54] For a time, her ability to act goes hand in hand with her drinking, as alcohol makes it all the easier for her to enter a world of illusion. Later, alcohol increasingly becomes Kate's mode of escape from the real world after her child's death, as she drinks 'enough to blend and soften the lines of a too hard reality to a long sensation of tickling, in which no idea was precise'.[55]

Although Kate does not return to the theatre after her child is born, and in fact becomes quite domestic, she returns to the literature that her acting has supplanted: 'A story in a copy of *The Family Herald* ... took hold of Kate's imagination, and when she raised her eyes a tear of joy fell upon the page, and in the effusion of these sensations she would take her little girl and press it almost wildly to her breast.'[56] The dream world of Kate's reading jeopardises her child. A story's religious tone only contributes to its escapist effect on Kate:

> The christening [of her daughter] had awakened in her many forgotten emotions, and now that she was an honest woman, she did not see why she should not resume her old church-going ways. The story she was reading was full of allusions to the vanity of this world and the durability of the next; and, her feet on the fender, penetrated with the dreamy warmth of the fire, she abandoned herself to the seduction of her reveries. Everything conspired against her. Being still very weak the doctor had ordered her to keep up her strength with stimulants; a tablespoonful of brandy and water taken now and then was what was required. This was the ordinance, but the drinks in the dressing-rooms had taught her the comforts of such medicines, and during the day several glasses were consumed. Without getting absolutely drunk, she rapidly sank into sensations of numbness, in which all distinctions were blurred, and thoughts trickled and slipped away like the soothing singing of a brook. It was like an amorous tickling, and as her dreams balanced between a tender declaration of love and the austere language of the Testament, the crying of the sick child was unheeded.[57]

This reference to Kate's 'seduction' by alcohol and narrative emphasises that the process by which she imaginatively aspires to church-going respectability as a mother is the same by which she assumed a romanticised life in eloping with Dick. The impressionability that makes her a performer leaves her unable to grip reality. Surrendering to her imagination and an actress's habit of drinking, Kate fails to warm her daughter's milk properly and on schedule, and she sleeps through the cries of the cold, dying child. The night her baby dies Kate sees the moon as 'a sort of pantomime light', and 'it seem[s] to her very like a fairy tale' – again Moore employs both the theatre and fantastic literature to describe the world of illusion in which Kate, disastrously, lives.[58] Shortly before her own death Kate runs into her former husband Ralph, who provides the novel's most poignant and ironic statement: 'I shouldn't have minded your being an actress, and I should have gone to fetch you home every evening.'[59] Although Ralph suggests that Kate could have had it all, Moore indicates that the successful actress, by virtue of her ability to assume roles, is incapable of the authenticity demanded by the home.

The significant difference between Boucicault's, Robertson's, and Taylor and Reade's claiming authenticity for their theatrical heroines and Moore's view that the actress is incapable of authenticity is crystallised in Kate's tears. While Taylor and Reade, as demonstrated in Chapter 1, and Boucicault and Robertson, as discussed in Chapter 2, use spontaneous emotional outbursts, including crying, to signify authenticity, Kate's tears are caused by reading the sentimental texts of her adolescence. In order to placate the craving for romance that Dick has reawakened, she examines 'old books' that she had stored in a box: 'Scenes, heroes, and heroines long forgotten came back to her, and in what minuteness, and how vividly! It appeared to her that she could not go on fast enough; her emotion gained upon her until she became quite hysterical.' When she comes across a dried flower, 'Tears started to her eyes. . . . and unable to restrain herself any longer, she burst into a tumultuous storm of sobs.'[60] Although 'Kate had learnt that there is life within us deeper and more intense than the life without us', this life within has been shaped by romantic, unrealistic texts.[61] Her return to a previous self is not a return, by any means, to an authentic self:

> By well-known ways the dog comes back to his kennel, the sheep to the fold, the horse to the stable, and even so did Kate return to her sentimental self. One day she was turning over the local paper, and suddenly, as if obeying a long-forgotten instinct, her eyes wandered to the poetry column, and again, just as in old time, she was caught by the same simple sentiments of sadness and longing.[62]

In its use of an actress's infanticide to attack the theatre and to contrast its own realism with that of the stage and other literature, *A Mummer's Wife* is similar to another work of the period, Olive Schreiner's *The Story of an African Farm* (1883), a novel that Rachel Blau DuPlessis views as distinctly modern because it 'originated the critique of narrative characteristic of twentieth-century writing by women'.[63] Schreiner's novel also broke from the convention of the three-volume Victorian novel, defined itself in opposition to drama, and repudiated the theatre's responsiveness to audiences' conventional tastes. Its preface rejects the 'stage method' of representation in favour of 'the method of life we all lead', which will be more authentic but less satisfying, because less predictable, for audiences.[64] The novel's epigraph, from Alexis de Tocqueville, reveals that *The Story of an African Farm*, like *A Mummer's Wife*, aims to be a study in naturalism:

> We must see the first images which the external world casts upon the dark mirror of his [a man's] mind; or must hear the first words which awaken the sleeping powers of thought, and stand by his earliest efforts, if we would understand the prejudices, the habits, and the passions that will rule his life. The entire man is, so to speak, to be found in the cradle of the child.[65]

Schreiner sympathises with the struggles of her New Woman heroine, Lyndall, and depicts her ambition to be an actress not as the irresponsible escapism of Moore's Kate Ede but as the pursuit of one of the few vocations available to women that make use of the talents that Lyndall possesses. Her desire to act in order to give her life purpose and herself independence, however, is associated with her rebellion against social forms, her refusal to marry and, in turn, the death of her child.[66] Like Moore, Schreiner uses a dead baby to emphasise the irrelevance of contemporary theatre. When Lyndall attempts to read dramatic literature after the child's death, she gives up and asks her nurse to throw the 'foolish' book out the window.[67]

Entr'acte: The Female Playwright in Moore and Robins

In contrast to the actress Kate, Laura, a female playwright in Moore's novel, is able to maintain control in a theatrical environment and even nurses Kate on her deathbed. As she is dying, Kate elides all of the various roles of her own life:

> The most diverse scenes were heaped together in the complex confusion of Kate's nightmare; the most opposed ideas were intermingled. At one moment she told the little girls, Annie and Lizzie, of the immorality of the conversations in the dressing-rooms of theatres; at another she

stopped the rehearsal of an *opéra bouffe* to preach to the mummers – in phrases that were remembrances of the extemporaneous prayers in the Wesleyan Church – of the advantages of an earnest, working, religious life. It was like a costume ball, where chastity grinned from behind a mask that vice was looking for, while vice hid his nakedness in some of the robes that chastity had let fall. Thus up and down, like dice thrown by demon players, were rattled the two lives, the double life that this weak woman had lived, and a point was reached where the two became one, when she began to sing her famous song: 'Look at me here, look at me there', alternately with the Wesleyan hymns. Sometimes in her delirium she even fitted the words of one on to the tune of the other.[68]

Kate's illusionary dream worlds have become a 'nightmare'. The actress, in attempting to move between many roles, is unable to hold a single one. Dick observes that Laura is also a very theatrical woman, 'more mummer than myself or Kate'.[69] In fact, the narrator notes, 'Her soul seemed to pass back and forwards easily, and Dick did not feel sure which was the real woman and which the fictitious.' Dick comments that '[s]he doesn't know herself.'[70] Unlike the actress Kate, however, who loses herself amidst pre-scripted roles, the playwright writes her own scripts and lives an unconventional and even eccentric life. Moore characterises Laura as sexually frank, the Mother Superior of the Yarmouth Convent, and an independent woman who lectures on 'the necessity of man worship' for women who 'have turned from men and are occupied now with their own aspirations'.[71] Although Laura is full of contradictions, she exercises a control over her life that Kate cannot muster. In Laura, Moore caricatures the self-importance of the female writer. Yet the power that she wields prefigures the satire that the suffragette actress, novelist and playwright Elizabeth Robins would offer, in apparent response to Moore, in *George Mandeville's Husband*.

George Mandeville's Husband has been read as a rejoinder to George Eliot, rather than George Moore. Elaine Showalter points out that Robins 'throws some light on the jealousies, animosities, and ambitions that underlay women novelists' response to George Eliot'.[72] Robins was a 'lifelong devotee' of Eliot and called her 'my idol', while 'Shaw dubbed [Robins] the American George Eliot'.[73] Yet in 'The Suffrage Camp Re-Visited', a lecture that Robins delivered in 1908, she describes how the myth of the 'Exceptional Woman' had hindered the cause of women's rights, and specifically names, among other women, 'that great spirit, George Eliot . . . preaching subservience to others and herself practising the largest liberty – each one fancied herself not in her gift alone, but in her fundamental needs, to be an Exceptional Woman'.[74] Levelling against Eliot the same criticism that Eliot herself levelled against Armgart, Robins reveals at once the suffragettes' indebtedness to Eliot and their unwillingness to acknowledge this debt precisely because Eliot's exceptional status had eclipsed her own interest in overcoming exceptionality. Robins also illustrates a key problem for the suffragettes, who, in plays such as Hamilton's 'A Pageant of Great Women' and street processions, used the accomplishments of other exceptional women such as Joan of Arc as justification for the vote and as inspiration for their own efforts even as they recognised how exceptionality had been used to oppose women's rights and even as they aimed to achieve enfranchisement for the many, rather than the few.

But the fact that *George Mandeville's Husband* echoes the title of *A Mummer's Wife* (1885) while inverting the hierarchy of genders suggests that Robins's novel was meant as an attack on Moore. Robins knew Moore personally and, in 1893, he had aggressively pursued her as an actress for his play, produced by the Independent Theatre Society, *The Strike at Arlingford*.[75] Robins's short story 'A Lucky Sixpence' (1894), which is included in her book of sketches about domestic servants, *Below the Salt* (1896), was criticised for its realism and when it first appeared under her pseudonym, C. E. Raimond, was attributed to Moore.[76] Most importantly, Robins was 'stirred . . . to indignation' by Moore's 'attack on the stage' in his essay 'Mummer-Worship'.[77] *George Mandeville's Husband* reworks Moore's attack on the theatre and his consequent assertion that performing for an audience is incompatible with motherhood. It defends both the theatre and the public woman by exposing the commercialism of the market for novels and by satirising criticism of the performing woman. The novelist George Mandeville neglects her daughter, Rosina, while devoting herself to the staging of her first drama. Robins pointedly follows Moore's *A Mummer's Wife* in naming her heroine's husband Ralph, and Robins reveals that Rosina dies not because of her mother's theatricality but because her father, Ralph Wilbraham, denies her the ability to participate in the public sphere.

Building on Eliot's metaphor of public performance for artistic creation, *George Mandeville's Husband* considers the relationship between writer and audience for both novelists and playwrights. In doing so, it rehearses concerns that would be key to the use of the theatre for the suffrage movement, in particular, how best to interact with an audience. Ultimately, by revealing that the theatricality that many nineteenth-century writers eschewed and scapegoated actually pervades the literary marketplace, Robins challenges what Jonas Barish has called the 'antitheatrical prejudice'. Barish, citing George Bernard Shaw's theatre criticism as an example of the nineteenth-century antitheatrical prejudice, writes: 'The very nature of the theater, one would conclude, brings out the worst in its votaries, and turns its aesthetic triumphs into human defeats, or a least into human disabilities. It does so by licensing, and hence nurturing, our penchant for self-display.'[78] This book has demonstrated how Victorian writers such as Elizabeth Barrett Browning, Dickens, Eliot and Moore believed that this 'penchant for self-display' could lead to art that merely panders to an audience's demands. This fear led some writers, including Barrett Browning and Moore, to define their work in poetry or the novel as less audience-centred than the theatre. Robins, who was a close friend of Shaw as well, challenges this hierarchy of genres in her depiction of George Mandeville writing novels and plays.

According to Robins, the literary scene encourages self-display in the novelist while, in contrast, such egotism on the part of the playwright is incompatible with effective theatre. George Mandeville's personality is showcased in her 'at homes', in which she theatrically stages public appearances within a controlled setting. These echo accounts of George Eliot's carefully crafted appearances, summarised by Nina Auerbach: 'Descriptions of the artist and sibyl receiving audiences at the Priory exude theatricality.'[79] One of Auerbach's sources, Matilda Betham-Edwards, writes of Eliot: 'There in the centre of the room, as if enthroned, sat the Diva; at her feet in a semicircle gathered philosophers, scientists, men of letters, poets, artists – in fine, the leading spirits of the great Victorian age.'[80] Similarly, Robins refers to George Mandeville's royal status and catalogues the talents represented in her adoring circle, with a disparaging twist:

> Once a week the former studio, now 'drawing room', was filled to suffocation with the fine flower of literary mediocrity. Mrs Wilbraham sat like a queen among her courtiers, or laboriously squeezed her way from admiring group to group. . . . People contended for her cards of invitation; not mere nobodies either, but people who 'had written things', as well as singers, actors, musicians, even a few obscure politicians and still fewer painters.[81]

Robins pokes fun at the author's personality taking precedence over the texts that she produces. One year after George Mandeville insists on relocating from Paris to London in order to become a fixture of the literary scene, she tells her husband, 'She was "getting to be known."' When he replies, 'you mean your stories, I suppose', she provides her view of the literary marketplace, 'No, no, no. I mean myself, my personality. It's everything these days. My work attracts too much attention to make it possible to preserve an incognito. All the world knows now who George Mandeville is. It's unavoidable.' She continues, arguing that an author's written works are of secondary importance: 'Yes, the personal note is the great thing nowadays. . . . It's not so much the story that matters, as what *you* say and think. You must be known, and then people read you.'[82] George Mandeville does not misunderstand the milieu in which she writes. Auerbach, describing Eliot, argues: 'Like her magnetic contemporary Ellen Terry, "the Diva" triumphs over her age almost as much, it seems, by artful self-placement as by the painstaking and essentially solitary perfection of her art.'[83] Mary Jean Corbett has traced how literary autobiography, as a form of authorial display, was an important aspect of the professionalisation of authorship, and how women writers often struggled with the Romantic, male tradition of literary autobiography.[84] Robins herself was pressured by the publisher of her early novels, William Heinemann, to parlay her theatrical fame into book sales by writing under her own name, rather than her non-gendered pen name C. E. Raimond.[85] Robins's criticism, therefore, is not of George Mandeville alone, but of the literary scene that Robins represents in the character of George Mandeville's close friend and amanuensis, the fawning Mrs Harley, and in the drawing room of enthusiastic admirers.

In contrast to George Mandeville's use of a pen name, Robins's own fiercely defended anonymity functioned as a mask and led readers to misunderstand the thrust of her satire:

> Because she did not reveal that the novel was actually a woman's reading of how a man might project his fears about female success, contemporaries were unable to appreciate her intentions and the nature of her parody. . . . Even modern assessments have fallen into this trap, portraying the book as a satire on pseudo-intellectual novelists especially George Eliot.[86]

I hold, however, that Robins's 'intentions' were more ambivalent. Contemporary feminist critics disagree about Robins's attitude towards George Mandeville. While Gates argues, 'Robins's indictment of Wilbraham for insisting that his daughter lead a sheltered life is as strong as her burlesque of a presumptuous literary woman',

Showalter suggests that the novel is more critical of Wilbraham than of George Mandeville: 'Robins seems to empathize with George Mandeville's ambitions, and she hints that Wilbraham's suffocating love, rather than the mother's neglect, destroys the daughter.'[87] The distinction that Robins draws between Mandeville and Eliot is tinged with resentment towards a female role model who sets an impossibly high standard:

> Don't tell us there was no element of courage and of steadfast strength in the woman who year in, year out, sat chained to her writing table, ceaselessly commemorating the futile and inept – leaving behind her day by day upon that sacrificial altar some fragment of youth and health, some shred of hope, some dead illusion. To sit down daily to the task of being George Eliot and to rise up 'the average lady novelist' to the end must, even if only dimly comprehended, be a soul-tragedy of no mean proportion.[88]

George Mandeville is not only writing about unexceptional women, as Eliot did; Mandeville is herself unexceptional and in this passage Robins writes sympathetically of her plight. At the very least, the literary marketplace that allows a successful self-promoter such as George Mandeville to achieve renown even though she lacks the literary accomplishments of George Eliot allows the unexceptional woman to play a public role.

Robins simultaneously criticises attention to an authorial personality and arguments that are based on the exceptional woman. When Wilbraham and Rosina mock George Eliot, they fall into the same trap of focusing on personality rather than artistic production that Wilbraham perceives as George Mandeville's mistake. Wilbraham states that '[t]here's never been a woman who deserved the name "great"', and Rosina responds, 'Mother says George Eliot –'. Rosina proceeds to deride Eliot's appearance and Wilbraham launches into one of his typical tirades against women artists, arguing that George Eliot

> was abnormal.... Read her letters and diaries when you grow up, study her life – not as it was commonly reported, but as it *was*. She was a poor borderland creature, fitter to be pitied than be blazoned abroad as an example and excuse. But all that has nothing to do with the real question. One unique mind proves nothing. The fact is that in the few cases where women *have* competed successfully with men – never in the highest grades, of course – but where they have held their own at all in art, they've done so at the price of their health or their womanliness; and for the very small change they get in return it's a precious bad bargain.[89]

Wilbraham and Rosina's focus on George Eliot, the person, rather than Eliot's works is another example of Robins's critique of the literary marketplace. Wilbraham is not Robins's mouthpiece but, as the book's title suggests, the subject of her satire. His emphasis on George Eliot as an exceptional woman, however, represents the real quandary that women faced in claiming Eliot's accomplishments for the suffragette cause. The suffragettes sought to appropriate the accomplishments of foremothers such as Eliot but also sought to avoid the division of women along lines of class, talent or profession. The problem that Eliot explores in *Armgart* – that the exceptional woman enters public life at the expense of her connection to her less talented sisters – remained a problem for the suffragettes.

Because the narrator follows the point of view of George Mandeville's husband, Robins does not commit herself to a criticism of the unexceptional George Mandeville even as she provides a satiric view of the literary scene. Rachel Brownstein points out that a celebrity takes shape and can only be known through the eyes of her audience, and Corbett has examined the self-fashioning conducted by Robins in her memoirs.[90] In her biography of Elizabeth Robins, Angela V. John pays particular attention to the ways in which Robins carefully constructed herself for her audience and how her audience attempted to construct her in return. By providing the reader with a view of George Mandeville through her resentful husband's eyes, filtering even the praise of her fans through his self-interested narrative, Robins suggests that the artist, despite her own self-fashioning, is indeed at the mercy of her audience. Gates argues that the non-gendered narrator's 'affinity with the husband helped readers to empathize with a presumably masculine viewpoint' that protected Robins's anonymity.[91] In Wilbraham, however, Robins suggests that misogynists who loathe strong, independent women do so because they themselves are milquetoast husbands, resentful because they are dominated by their wives. Wilbraham experiences increasing revulsion as his wife pursues a career and achieves the fame that has eluded him. Robins's depiction of Wilbraham satirises male responses to women's literary success, and participates in what Gilbert and Gubar have described as a 'battle of the sexes' over the public sphere in the twentieth century.[92]

Thus, even though George Mandeville's ambitions involve the self-display in the public marketplace that Robins derides, the novel criticises Wilbraham's desire to keep women out of the public sphere. In trying to mould his daughter, Rosina, Wilbraham cautions again and again against women's desire for self-display and the female artist's vanity. When Rosina says that amateur dabbling is innocuous, Wilbraham responds, 'No. No woman will ever see the harm of corrupting taste and lowering standards. Just so a woman may air her vanity she is content, and art is lost in a deluge of amateurism.'[93] Echoing Herr Klesmer's emphasis on art for art's sake in Eliot's *Daniel Deronda* (1876), but with a misogynist twist, Wilbraham argues that women's art is motivated solely by self-interest:

> No woman understands the patient, inexhaustible joy of work for the sake of the work. That's *masculine*, my child. The woman nature asks at every step, 'What shall I get for it?' It 'pleases' them? Not a whit – till they've translated it into gold or gush.[94]

Robins's satiric view of George Mandeville's self-representation suggests her partial agreement with Wilbraham – she clearly derides the vanity of authors. But Robins criticises Wilbraham's belief that restriction to the domestic sphere is the only alternative to the public self-display of his wife: 'Was he selfish about Rosina? Was it the old barbarian in men that made them want to keep their women to themselves, instead of putting them up for inspection in the market-place? Perhaps – perhaps!'[95] While George Mandeville is producing a stage adaptation of one of her novels, Wilbraham describes all women's activity in the public sphere as 'spectacle':

> 'But the generations pass', he told himself, 'and the new woman, if she has come to stay, will bear new men, who will sit in the chimney-corner, while the girls go forth to war.' A good deal of that sort of thing went on even now. There was Mrs Wilbraham round the corner making war on the scene-shifter and wading through indignities to glory. In every quarter of this vast London were hordes of toiling, struggling women, waging the great economic war, to the peril of their bodies and their souls. Gods! What a spectacle when one thinks of it![96]

Wilbraham conflates women entering the public sphere with the showy vanity of his wife. His understanding of women and theatricality is based on an 'antitheatrical prejudice' that neglects an alternative view of actresses such as that provided by Florence Nightingale, who explained that young women envy actresses 'not for the sake of the admiration, not for the sake of the fame', but because its round of 'stud[y]' and performance enables an 'exercise of faculty'.[97] Wilbraham denies his daughter the exercise of her faculties.

Rosina appears to suffer because of her mother's theatrical ambitions. In a burlesque of actresses such as Marie Wilton and Madge Kendal attaining the status of 'respectable public professional women' by 'asserting their ties to the privacy of the middle-class drawing room', George Mandeville completely transforms her private life into public spectacle during the staging of her drama, performing the role of a good mother only superficially for the image that it will enable her to project.[98] Her role-playing of motherhood thus echoes Moore's Kate Ede. Although Wilbraham is the more attentive and affectionate parent, while Rosina is dying he is sent to handle the 'at home' – his wife's salon – because, as George Mandeville says, 'I can't be expected to see visitors when Rosina's so ill.'[99] Her motivation, however, is the construction of her public persona. In the salon, George Mandeville's friend

> Mrs Harley drew a spirited picture for her own circle of the lady dramatist worn out with anxiety and rehearsals – watching with devotion at the bedside of her sick child. Everybody was loud in sympathy and admiration for this model of domestic virtue – this heroine of the hearth today and of the theatre tomorrow.[100]

Robins, however, differs from Moore in that she does not employ the dead child to suggest that the private 'hearth' and public 'theatre' are incompatible. Quite the opposite: she reveals that Rosina is incapable of survival because her father denies her the ability to participate in the public sphere and enforces her unhealthy dependence on him. Rosina raises a question that her father does not consider, namely, how she would support herself if she outlived him. In fact, this question is so disturbing to her that she hopes that she will predecease her father.[101] Wilbraham's cloistering of Rosina leads to her helplessness and, ultimately, her death. At his wife's bidding, Wilbraham leaves the ailing Rosina at the dress rehearsal of George Mandeville's play. He is late in returning to the theatre because he is absorbed in thinking about what his daughter should and should not be. When Rosina feels herself to be abandoned by the father who sheltered her – 'he had never "deserted her" before; never till to-day had she had the experience of "waiting for him" in vain' – she falls ill and dies.[102]

Although Robins tempers her advocacy of women's participation in the world beyond the home by noting, albeit through Ralph Wilbraham, the dangers of seeking the attention of a public audience, Robins ultimately defends drama. George Mandeville's approach to staging her play is as ego-driven as her approach to authorship, and her self-display leads to her failure as a playwright. The narrator describes how, incapable of allowing the play to take centre stage independent of its author, she ruins the production by meddling incessantly:

> George Mandeville's frequent excursions into their midst to readjust and admonish – a stout, frowsy, blowsy vision – did not add to the aesthetic, if it did to the dramatic, effect of the scene. Her presence certainly did not seem to increase the amiability of the company. Wilbraham felt there was a storm brewing; if she tortured her hero much more he foresaw a scene not set down in the prompt-book.[103]

While success as a novelist may call for a theatrical author, the theatre requires playwrights to be eclipsed by their own creations. Robins thus inverts the antitheatrical prejudice that the theatre is the province of self-display while legitimising women's participation in the public sphere and addressing the problem of exceptionalism. As a work of fiction, *George Mandeville's Husband* was, therefore, an important prelude for Robins's political activity as she herself, as we shall see in Chapter 5, made the transition from actress to playwright.

Notes

1. Moore, 'Sex in Art', in *Modern Painting*, p. 229.
2. Ibid. pp. 226, 227.
3. Moore, 'Why I Don't Write Plays', *Pall Mall Gazette*, 7 September 1892, p. 3.
4. Ibid. p. 3.
5. Ibid. p. 3.
6. Allen, *Theater Figures*, p. 3.
7. Ibid. pp. 3–4.
8. Stewart, *Dear Reader*, p. 150.
9. Moore, 'Théâtre Libre', in *Impressions and Opinions*, pp. 227–9. See also Moore, 'Our Dramatists and Their Literature', 'Note on "Ghosts"' and 'On the Necessity of an English Théâtre Libre', in *Impressions and Opinions*, pp. 181–214, 215–26, 238–48. These essays originally appeared under different titles in periodicals. For details about the original publication of these essays see Gilcher, *A Bibliography of George Moore*.
10. Moore, 'Our Dramatists and Their Literature', in *Impressions and Opinions*, p. 209.
11. Moore, 'Mummer-Worship', in *Impressions and Opinions*, pp. 164–5.

12. Tracy C. Davis, *Actresses as Working Women*, p. 13.
13. Moore, 'Mummer-Worship', in *Impressions and Opinions*, pp. 154–5. Gail Marshall cites T. H. S. Escott's similar characterisation of actresses mingling with titled nobility but points out that 'Escott goes on to suggest that such social advances were not in fact facilitated by the actress's increased respectability, but rather by society's being "in a sense, stage-struck"' ([T. H. S. Escott], 'A Foreign Resident', in *Society in London* [London: Chatto & Windus, 1885], pp. 295–6, cited in Marshall's *Actresses on the Victorian Stage*, p. 96. Elizabeth Robins, in *Both Sides of the Curtain*, suggested that St John's Wood signalled only superficial respectability for actresses. She describes how Genevieve Ward 'now lived in that part of London called St John's Wood. I had already heard the lovely name spoken with a slight hesitation or a covert smile. There was a good deal of obvious wealth there judging by the fine horses and carriages to be seen in the streets and, standing among trees and gardens, the many attractive houses. Too often these were said to be inhabited by the *declassee*. As for the others, I was told that only persons of the most unchallengeable position in the public mind dared live in St John's Wood. It was quite in order that Miss Ward was one of these' (p. 109). Furthermore, Robins describes her own crisis of facing a suitor who proposed a 'happy ending (happy Never-Ending) . . . in the guise of a charming villa with a garden where I should be out of the conflict, under protection'. The villa was in St John's Wood, and Robins explains: 'I knew that not only some of my most respected acquaintances lived in that haunt of the subtly-mingled name, at once rural and apostolic; I knew that character it had come to have – as far from woodland as from St John.' Robins intimates that being 'kept in a house in St John's Wood' was potentially cause for 'outraged dignity' and that it spurred her to commit to her independence (p. 243).
14. Moore, 'Mummer-Worship', in *Impressions and Opinions*, p. 156.
15. Ibid. p. 159. 'Mummer-Worship' was originally published in the *Universal Review* on 15 September 1888, five years after the publication of Irving's Preface to Diderot's *The Paradox of Acting*.
16. Moore, 'Mummer-Worship', in *Impressions and Opinions*, p. 178.
17. Ibid. p. 175.
18. Ibid. p. 161.
19. Allen, *Theater Figures*, p. 179.
20. Moore, 'An Actress of the Eighteenth Century', in *Impressions and Opinions*, pp. 141, 147.
21. Mitchell, 'A New Perspective', p. 20.
22. 'Two Novels', review of *A Mummer's Wife*, by George Moore, *Saturday Review* 59 (1885): pp. 214–15.
23. [Noble], 'An English Disciple of Zola', pp. 83–5.
24. Ibid. p. 84.
25. Moore, *A Mummer's Wife*, pp. 6–7.

26. My understanding of Moore's criticism of melodrama and sensation fiction and of Kate's impressionability has been shaped by Allen and by Masters, '"A Great Part to Play"'.
27. Zola, 'From *Naturalism in the Theatre*', p. 873.
28. Moore, 'Our Dramatists and Their Literature', in *Impressions and Opinions*, p. 207.
29. Ibid. p. 187.
30. Farrow, *George Moore*, p. 33.
31. Allen, *Theater Figures*, p. 171.
32. See J. Jeffrey Franklin's analysis of the commercial competition between the novel and the drama in *Serious Play*.
33. Mitchell, 'A New Perspective', p. 20.
34. McCormack, *George Eliot in Society*, p. 75.
35. Moore, *A Mummer's Wife*, p. 2.
36. Ibid. p. 106.
37. Ibid. p. 8.
38. Ibid. p. 38.
39. Ibid. p. 39. Mitchell, who identifies this novel as a sensation novel, explains that Kate's book is more similar to Mary Elizabeth Braddon's *The Doctor's Wife* than to Flaubert's *Madame Bovary* (p. 21). Mitchell cites Christopher Haywood, 'Flaubert, Miss Braddon, and George Moore', *Comparative Literature* 12 (1960): 151–8.
40. Moore, *A Mummer's Wife*, p. 39.
41. Ibid. pp. 99, 198.
42. Ibid. pp. 203–4.
43. Ibid. p. 124.
44. Ibid. pp. 147–8.
45. Ibid. pp. 58–9.
46. Ibid. p. 60.
47. Ibid. p. 146.
48. Ibid. p. 138.
49. Ibid. p. 139.
50. Ibid. p. 26.
51. Ibid. pp. 84, 78.
52. Ibid. p. 124.
53. Ibid. p. 228.
54. Ibid. p. 231.
55. Ibid. p. 318.
56. Ibid. p. 303.
57. Ibid. p. 304.
58. Ibid. p. 306.
59. Ibid. p. 416.
60. Ibid. pp. 101–2.
61. Ibid. p. 96.
62. Ibid. p. 98.
63. DuPlessis, *Writing Beyond the Ending*, p. 30.

64. Schreiner, *The Story of an African Farm*, p. 27.
65. Ibid. p. iv.
66. DuPlessis suggests that Lyndall's 'dead child should be read as a sign of her self-division between thralldom and independence' (*Writing Beyond the Ending*, p. 27).
67. Schreiner, *The Story of an African Farm*, pp. 210–11. She does not, however, respond in the same way to Shakespeare.
68. Moore, *A Mummer's Wife*, p. 429.
69. Ibid. p. 424.
70. Ibid. p. 424.
71. Ibid. pp. 342, 335.
72. Showalter, *A Literature of Their Own*, p. 108.
73. John, *Elizabeth Robins*, p. 109; Robins, *Both Sides of the Curtain*, p. 283; John, *Elizabeth Robins*, p. 120. Born in Kentucky and reared in Ohio, Robins began her acting career in the United States and relocated to London in 1888 after the suicide of her husband, Gordon Parks, who tied himself to a suit of theatrical armor and drowned himself in Boston's Charles River. Accounts by Gates, *Elizabeth Robins*; John, *Elizabeth Robins*; and Kerry Powell, *Women and Victorian Theatre* suggest that Robins's independence and self-display as an actress contributed to turbulence in their marriage and to Parks's emotional state.
74. Robins, 'The Suffrage Camp Re-Visited', 1908, in *Way Stations*, pp. 53, 72. Newey discusses Robins and the suffragettes' rejection of the concept of exceptionality in favour of the collective (*Women's Theater Writing in Victorian Britain*, p. 156).
75. Correspondence from Moore to Robins to this effect is in the Elizabeth Robins Papers, Fales Library, New York University.
76. John, *Elizabeth Robins*, p. 116.
77. Robins repeatedly complains about Moore in her memoir *Both Sides of the Curtain*, pp. 67, 70, 73–4, 89. She does, however, admit that 'he deserved acknowledgment on two counts: his faithful and merciless exhibition of the mean part allotted to most women in the Theatre, and his one beautiful sensitive phrase which I must needs italicize here . . . : "The young lady who, wild with love of adventure and masquerade . . . beats her wings against the plate glass window of her prison and *looks to the dark doorway as the lark to the bright sky*, will possibly fight her way to the front. Nature has chosen her for the battle of the footlights"' (p. 256).
78. Barish, *The Antitheatrical Prejudice*, p. 348.
79. Auerbach, *Romantic Imprisonment*, p. 254.
80. Betham-Edwards, *Mid-Victorian Memories*, p. 42. McCormack supports this view of Eliot's salons by characterising 'the literary self-promotion George Eliot – and even more actively, Lewes – engaged in Sunday after Sunday', but she challenges Betham-Edwards's accuracy on matters such as Eliot's physical stature and the lack of pets at the Priory (*George Eliot in Society*, pp. 3, 32).

81. C. E. Raimond [Elizabeth Robins], *George Mandeville's Husband*, pp. 22–3.
82. Ibid. p. 12.
83. Auerbach, *Romantic Imprisonment*, p. 254.
84. Corbett, *Representing Femininity*, p. 11.
85. John, *Elizabeth Robins*, p. 107.
86. For a description of Robins's struggle to maintain anonymity, see Gates, *Elizabeth Robins*; John, *Elizabeth Robins*, p. 109.
87. Gates, *Elizabeth Robins*, p. 76; Showalter, *A Literature of Their Own*, p. 109.
88. C. E. Raimond [Elizabeth Robins], *George Mandeville's Husband*, p. 88.
89. Ibid. p. 81.
90. Brownstein, *Tragic Muse*; Corbett, 'Performing Identities'.
91. Gates, *Elizabeth Robins*, p. 72.
92. Gilbert and Gubar, *No Man's Land, Volume 1: The War of the Words*, p. 4.
93. C. E. Raimond [Elizabeth Robins], *George Mandeville's Husband*, p. 82.
94. Ibid. p. 82.
95. Ibid. p. 157.
96. Ibid. p. 157.
97. Nightingale, *Cassandra*, p. 41.
98. On Wilton and Kendal, see Corbett, 'Performing Identities', p. 129.
99. C. E. Raimond [Elizabeth Robins], *George Mandeville's Husband*, p. 207.
100. Ibid. p. 208.
101. Ibid. pp. 84–6.
102. Ibid. p. 166.
103. Ibid. p. 148.

Chapter 5

From Playing Parts to Rewriting Roles: Actresses and the Political Stage

The actress played scripted roles that were usually, given the preponderance of male playwrights and actor-managers in the production of Victorian drama, written and shaped by men. The tension inherent between actress and male playwright is the subject of Henry James's short story 'Nona Vincent', published in the *Illustrated English Magazine* in February/March 1892. As in many of the novelists' views of the theatre that the introduction of this book explored, the playwright Wayworth is attracted to the drama but has qualms about how his vision might be realised by flesh-and-blood actors in a concrete production:

> The scenic idea was magnificent when once you had embraced it – the dramatic form had a purity which made some others look ingloriously rough. It had the high dignity of the exact sciences, it was mathematical and architectural.... There was a fearful amount of concession in it, but what you kept had a rare intensity.[1]

He views getting the play staged as 'a totally different part of the business, and altogether secondary' to the rigour of writing the drama. When his intellectual patron and friend Mrs Alsager asks him if he wants his play acted, he responds, 'Of course I do – but it's a sudden descent. I want to intensely, but I'm sorry I want to.'[2] Mrs Alsager observes that the 'difficulties' that arise in production are 'not inspiring ... they're discouraging, because they're vulgar. The other problem, the working out of the thing itself, is pure art.'[3] Of critical importance to the play's success is whether its lead actress, Violet Grey, will succeed in bringing the heroine to life. Although she and Wayworth work together so closely that they become romantically involved, Violet is fraught with anxiety and fails on opening night. Before her second performance, however, Wayworth has a mystical vision of his dramatic character. He later learns that he experienced this vivid dream at the very moment that Violet was visited by Mrs Alsager, who likely was the author's inspiration and who instils in Violet the proper concept of the role. After succeeding in the role, Violet retires from the stage to marry Wayworth – which itself speaks to the tenuous position of actresses as professionals. Notably, Violet is able to inhabit the male-written script only through a connection to a 'real' woman within the pages of James's short story.

This chapter will examine how this figure of the actress playing her part was challenged in various ways in the final years of the nineteenth century and the beginning of the twentieth century: through alterations to modes of theatrical production and to theatrical conventions, but also through engagements with the larger cultural history that this book has studied. This history, shaped by the interrelated development of the novel and the drama, composed a script that defined the place of the actress in the theatre and in society, and in turn, through her as a metaphor for women's public performance, the place of women in the public sphere. This chapter begins by examining the actress at the heart of Henry James's *The Tragic Muse* (1890). Miriam Rooth is an embodiment of the rich cultural history that *The Victorian Actress* has examined, and she stands both in juxtaposition and as a threat to the political world. This chapter then turns to the work of James's friend, the actress Elizabeth Robins. As an essayist, novelist and playwright and in her activity in the women's suffrage movement as vice president of the Actresses' Franchise League and president of the Women Writers' Suffrage League, Robins in her own person brings to fruition the political potential of the actress that had been cultivated and remained implicit in the cultural history that this book has traced. Moreover, Robins builds on that cultural history in order to use the theatre for the purpose of arguing for women's participation in the public sphere.

Two Figures for Public Women in *The Tragic Muse*

Henry James was a novelist who was a keen observer of and essayist on the theatre, and who himself was a famously failed playwright.[4] In Miriam Rooth, the actress character at the centre of *The Tragic Muse,* James recapitulates many of the themes about the actress and the stage in Victorian England that this book has explored in its earlier chapters, and Miriam embodies many of the points that James made in his periodical essays on the theatre from 1872 to 1901 that were collected in *The Scenic Art*. Indeed, the concrete details of Miriam's professional aspirations are composed of a collection of elements we have seen in earlier novels and plays. One of her contemplated stage names, 'Gladys Vane', echoes the name of Mabel Vane in Charles Reade and Tom Taylor's *Masks and Faces* and *Peg Woffington*, and, like Ernest Vane, Miriam's impresario and potential lover Peter Sherringham has a 'fond[ness]' for the green room.[5] Sherringham's very interest that promises to launch Miriam's career also imperils her respectability, as in *Masks and Faces*, both versions of *Peg Woffington*, and *The Life of an Actress*, and, as we have seen in George Eliot's *Armgart* and *Daniel Deronda*, her pursuit of her profession. Miriam is 'more than half Jewess', her mother having married her music teacher, as Catherine Arrowpoint in *Deronda* marries the Jewish Julius Klesmer, and Miriam's Jewishness leads to comparisons to Rachel Félix, whom we have also seen as an influence in *Daniel Deronda*.[6] Like Magdalen in Wilkie Collins's *No Name*, Miriam seeks to become an actress to escape becoming a governess because her family has come down in the world.[7]

The Tragic Muse also recapitulates Victorian critical assessments of the nineteenth-century English theatre as a popular form. Miriam's ability to succeed is dependent on conditions characterised by the aesthete Gabriel Nash as 'the essentially brutal nature of the modern audience':

> the *omnium gatherum* of the population of a big commercial city, at the hour of the day when their taste is at its lowest, flocking out of hideous hotels and restaurants, gorged with food, stultified with buying and selling and with all the other sordid speculations of the day, squeezed in their seats, timing the author, timing the actor, wishing to get their money back on the spot, before eleven o'clock. Fancy putting the exquisite before such a tribunal as that! There's not even a question of it. The dramatist couldn't if he would. He has to make the basest concessions. One of his principal canons is that he must enable his spectators to catch the suburban trains, which stop at 11.30. What would you think of any other artist – the painter or the novelist – whose governing forces should be the dinner and the suburban trains? The old dramatists didn't defer to them (not so much, at least), and that's why they are less and less actable.... What can you do with a character, with an idea, with a feeling, between dinner and the suburban trains? ... What crudity compared with what the novelist does![8]

Miriam tires of her first successful venture in London because of the play's lack of substance and because of the long run that had become a staple of the theatre in the interest of profitability:

> when she thought it would probably run a month or two more she was in the humour to curse the odious conditions of artistic production in such an age. The play was a simplified version of a new French piece, a thing that had taken in Paris, at a third-rate theatre, and had now, in London, proved itself good enough for houses made up of ten-shilling stalls.[9]

While her first play is a stereotypical translation from the French, her second play is another iteration of how the Victorian theatre reputedly failed to produce original drama: 'a romantic drama of thirty years before, covered, from infinite queer handling, with a sort of dirty glaze'.[10] Peter faults 'the want of life in the critical sense of the public, which was ignobly docile', as the source of such 'rubbish' on stage, and his view of the sort of theatre that would 'give the girl's talent a superior, glorious stage' echoes those that we have seen by George Moore and William Archer of a national theatre unfettered by the need for profit and drawing a more sophisticated audience:

> a great academic, artistic theatre, subsidized and unburdened with money-getting, rich in its repertory, rich in the high quality and the wide array of its servants, and above all in the authority of an impossible administrator – a manager personally disinterested, not an actor with an eye to the main chance, pouring forth a continuity of tradition, striving for perfection, laying a splendid literature under contribution.[11]

In *The Scenic Art*, James attributes the weakness of the stage in part to the blurring of the line between the theatre and society:

> Plays and actors are perpetually talked about, private theatricals are incessant, and members of the dramatic profession are 'received' without restriction. They appear in society, and the people of society appear on the stage; it is as if the great gate which formerly divided the theatre from the world had been lifted off its hinges. There is, at any rate, such a passing to and fro as has never before been known; the stage has become amateurish and society has become professional. . . . It is part of a great change which has come over English manners – of the confusion of many things which forty years ago were kept very distinct. The world is being steadily democratized and vulgarized, and literature and art give their testimony to the fact.[12]

In contrast to this amateurisation of the stage in England, in France 'the actor's art, like the ancient arts and trades, is still something of a "mystery" – a thing of technical secrets, of special knowledge'.[13] This position is echoed by Peter in *The Tragic Muse*, who also characterises the erosion of the boundaries between 'actresses' and 'society' as a problem particular to London, and, using terms similar to those we saw in Moore, tells his rival Basil Dashwood that in the time of Garrick actors did not mingle with 'society', 'and it was better all round'.[14] *The Tragic Muse* also expands on French stage professionalism. While Miriam shares Magdalen's talent for mimicry, in Paris the first professional judge of her talent echoes Klesmer in *Daniel Deronda* in holding that it is 'work, unremitting and ferocious work' that comprises an actress. Although beauty may allow an actress to 'succeed' through marrying well, it is only through rigorous professional training that an actress can rise above the degrading commodification of her body.[15] Miriam's training with this ageing French actress provides her with 'a ferocious analysis[,] an intelligence of the business and a special vocabulary'.[16]

James's representation of Miriam's professionalism is informed by both George Henry Lewes's and William Archer's views on acting, which this book explored in Chapter 1, and puts aside the melodramatic convention of emotional authenticity that we saw in Peg Woffington, Violet, Magdalen Vanstone and Esther. Miriam recognises that the occasional impression she makes is not sufficient, but rather she must train in order to perform with predictability.[17] Peter echoes Lewes on the importance of 'reflection': 'The talent, the desire, the energy are an instinct; but by the time these things become a performance they are an instinct put in its place.'[18] In fact, Miriam's 'plastic quality' echoes Lewes's language:

> When an actor feels a vivid sympathy with the passion or humour, he is representing, he *personates, i.e.* speaks through the *persona* or character; and for the moment *is* what he *represents*. He can do this only in proportion to the vividness of his sympathy, and the plasticity of his organization, which enables him to give *expression* to what he feels; . . . But within the limits which are assigned by nature to every artist, the success of the personation will depend upon the vividness of the actor's sympathy, and his honest reliance on the truth of his own individual expression in preference to the conventional expressions which may be accepted on the stage. This is the great actor, the creative artist.[19]

Epitomising Lewes's theory of acting, Miriam is successful because, as Peter discovers, she has no authentic identity:

> far from there being any question of her having the histrionic nature, she simply had it in such perfection that she was always acting; that her existence was a series of parts assumed for the moment, each changed

for the next, before the perpetual mirror of some curiosity or admiration or wonder – some spectatorship that she perceived or imagined in the people about her. . . . It struck him abruptly that a woman whose only being was to 'make believe', to make believe that she had any and every being that you liked, that would serve a purpose, produce a certain effect, and whose identity resided in the continuity of her personations, so that she had no moral privacy, as he phrased it to himself, but lived in a high wind of exhibition, of figuration – such a woman was a kind of monster, in whom of necessity there would be nothing to like, because there would be nothing to take hold of.[20]

John Stokes traces how Miriam's French mentor was based on the actress Madame Arnould Plessy, whose 'coquette' style of acting, in contrast to the 'nerveuse' actress Sarah Bernhardt, was marked by emotional distance.[21] In his theatre criticism, James responded to charges that Plessy was 'too artificial': 'She is brilliant, she is cold; and I cannot imagine her touching the source of tears. But she is in the highest degree accomplished; she gives an impression of intelligence and intellect.'[22] Indeed, James does not use emotional moments of tears or the blush in order to signify Miriam's emotional authenticity. In *The Tragic Muse* Peter is aware that Miriam's blush is not the spontaneous, involuntary expression of emotion that we saw in Peg Woffington's blush or Magdalen's tear:

> Miriam flushed a little, but he immediately discovered that she had no personal emotion in seeing him again; the cold passion of art had perched on her banner and she listened to herself with an ear as vigilant as if she had been a Paganini drawing a fiddle-bow.[23]

Even in blushing, Miriam is a spectator of herself, viewing herself with a critical detachment that Archer theorised as 'dual consciousness'.[24] As her talent blossoms, Sherringham understands her accomplishment in the context of the emotionalist debate, as he perceives

> the perfect presence of mind, unconfused, unhurried by emotion, that any artistic performance requires . . . ; the application, in other words, clear and calculated, crystal-firm as it were, of the idea conceived in the glow of experience, of suffering, of joy. Sherringham afterwards often talked of this with Miriam, who however was not able to present him with a neat theory of the subject. She had no knowledge that it was publicly discussed; she was just practically on the side of those who hold that at the moment of production the artist cannot have his wits too much

about him. When Peter told her there were people who maintained that in such a crisis he must lose himself in the flurry she stared with surprise and then broke out: 'Ah, the idiots!'[25]

The performance that results conceals the self-awareness that creates it. When Sherringham tells Miriam, 'I wish you could see yourself', she responds: 'My dear fellow, I do. What do you take me for? I didn't miss a vibration of my voice, a fold of my robe.' When Sherringham notes, 'I didn't see you looking', Miriam rejoins, 'No one ever will. Do you think I would show it?'[26]

At one point, Miriam makes a claim to authenticity that echoes Peg Woffington's plea, in Reade's novel:

> And what have we to do with homes, or hearts, or firesides? Have we not the play-house, its paste diamonds, its paste feelings, and the loud applause of fops and sots – hearts? – beneath loads of tinsel and paint? Nonsense! The love that can go with souls to Heaven – such love for us?[27]

Miriam says: 'I'm not such a low creature. I'm capable of gratitude. I'm capable of affection. One may live in paint and tinsel, but one isn't absolutely without a soul. Yes, I've got one . . . though I do paint my face and practice my intonations.'[28] Unlike *Peg Woffington*, however, *The Tragic Muse* provides no authentication for Miriam's claim. In fact, Peter is unconvinced by it: 'the old impression was with him again; the sense that if she was sincere it was sincerity of execution, if she was genuine it was the genuineness of doing it well'.[29] Unlike previous actresses we have seen – youthful Margaret, Magdalen Vanstone, Peg Woffington – neither home nor family serve to anchor Miriam to an authentic identity:

> Her character was simply to hold you by the particular spell; any other – the good-nature of home, the relation of her mother, her friends, her lovers, her debts, the practice of virtues or industries or vices – was not worth speaking of. These things were the fictions and shadows; the representation was the deep substance'.[30]

Whatever feeling Miriam does possess becomes a role that she plays: 'the expression of this was . . . a strange bedevilment: she began to listen to herself, to speak dramatically, to represent. She uttered the things she felt as if they were snatches of old play-books, and really felt them the more because they sounded so well.'[31] It is by being absorbed in this role-playing that Miriam blushes and sheds tears as

Peter is leaving her: 'she was ... moved – the pure colour that had risen to her face showed it.... She was moved even to the glimmer of tears.'[32] Peter reflects on her success in her second play in London:

> Miriam had never been more present to him than at this hour; but she was inextricably transmuted – present essentially as the romantic heroine she represented.... Miriam was a beautiful, actual, fictive, impossible young woman, of a past age and undiscoverable country, who spoke in blank verse and overflowed with metaphor, who was exalted and heroic beyond all human convenience, and who yet was irresistibly real and related to one's own affairs. But that reality was a part of her spectator's joy, and she was not changed back to the common by his perception of the magnificent trick of art with which it was connected.[33]

This appreciation of the actress's mutability was echoed by Oscar Wilde's *The Picture of Dorian Gray* (1890), which began its serial publication just months after the serialisation of *The Tragic Muse* concluded. The close parallels between these two novels are well documented. J. Hillis Miller suggests that Wilde was influenced by James, who had based the character of Gabriel Nash on Wilde.[34] Indeed, while Peter betrays some ambivalence that Miriam has 'a hundred' characters rather than a single, stable character, Dorian rapturously catalogues Sybil Vane's multitude of Shakespearean roles, concluding,

> I have seen her in every age and in every costume. Ordinary women never appeal to one's imagination. They are limited to their century. No glamour ever transfigures them.... But an actress! How different an actress is! Harry! Why didn't you tell me that the only thing worth loving is an actress!'[35]

Dorian also echoes the protagonist Vivian in 'The Decay of Lying' (1889), who is interested in 'the mask' worn by individuals, 'not the reality that lies behind the mask', and who describes the changeability of a friend: 'what interested me most in her was not her beauty, but her character, her entire vagueness of character. She seemed to have no personality at all, but simply the possibility of many types. ... In fact, she was a kind of Proteus.'[36] Sybil loses Dorian because she loses all talent for acting once she has experienced true love and, mirroring how her love kills her art, she poisons herself with what Dorian's aesthetic mentor, Lord Henry Wotton, describes as 'some dreadful thing they use at theatres'.[37] One of the two substances that

From Playing Parts to Rewriting Roles 181

Lord Henry names is white lead, which, according to John Scoffern, a chemist who wrote a series of articles in Mary Elizabeth Braddon's *Belgravia* magazine in 1867–8, is a highly toxic substance 'used to impart whiteness to the skin'.[38] In fact, the death of cosmetic purveyor Madame Rachel, mentioned in Mary Elizabeth Braddon's *Lady Audley's Secret,* who was herself associated with the theatre through the prostitution ring of actresses that she ran, was attributed to the lead used in her 'enamelling' process.[39] The fatal qualities of cosmetics are also apparent in Aubrey Beardsley's 1894 illustrations for Wilde's *Salomé*, which use the process of being made-up as an elaboration on the theme of a woman who converts her body into a seductive spectacle and represent cosmetics as ultimately fatal to the woman. The final illustration for the play (Fig. 5.1) depicts Salomé's interment in a giant powder box. Sybil's death by cosmetics similarly functions as a metaphor for the incompatibility between lived feeling and dramatic performance.[40] Although Beerbohm's 'The Pervasion of Rouge', published the same year as Beardsley's illustrations, states that science has eradicated toxins from cosmetics, it repeatedly comments on the toxic

Salome:
Tailpiece.

Figure 5.1 *Salomé*, Tailpiece, Aubrey Beardsley (Mary Evans Picture Library)

qualities of earlier cosmetics and on the ability of contemporary cosmetics to kill the New Woman and women's suffrage movements.[41] The use of cosmetics will defeat activist women because it will occupy all of their time and: 'Artifice's first command to them is that they should repose. With bodily activity their powder will fly, their enamel crack.'[42] Cosmetics and, by extension, performance, according to Beerbohm, impose a statue-like inactivity on women.

While Sybil Vane's theatrical energies are contained by proving fatal to herself, James depicts Miriam as a powerful but uncontrollable inspiration. Joseph Litvak points out that both *The Picture of Dorian Gray* and *The Tragic Muse* contain a portrait invested with significance in a relationship between two men, 'both novels present the configuration of three men and an actress', and '*Dorian Gray*, no less than *The Tragic Muse*, could be read as an allegory of how a male-identified "art of the novel" (and of literary criticism) responds to the peculiar disturbance represented by a female-identified theatricality.'[43] To the painter Nick's 'inner vision, Miriam became a magnificent result, drawing a hundred formative instincts out of their troubled sleep, defying him where he privately felt strongest and imposing herself triumphantly in her own strength'.[44] Miriam provides Nick the sensation of a loss of control: 'his quick attempt was as exciting as a sudden gallop – it was almost the sense of riding a runaway horse'.[45] As we saw in Thackeray's *Vanity Fair*, actress characters, paradoxically, can be written in such a way that they appear to defy their authors. Litvak argues that Miriam plays such a role in *The Tragic Muse*: 'Here is a center that wanders from its assigned post, pervading and disfiguring the text that tries to master it.'[46] Analogously, Miriam directly confronts the Victorian antitheatrical prejudice, identifying theatre as that which gets abjected, but the attraction of which is too strong to repudiate:

> You say to-day that you hate the theatre; and do you know what has made you do it? The fact that it has too large a place in your mind to let you repudiate it and throw it over with a good conscience. It has a deep fascination for you, and yet you're not strong enough to make the concession of taking up with it publicly, in my person. You're ashamed of yourself for that, as all your constant high claims for it are on record; so you blaspheme against it.[47]

The novel's lack of control over its actress character is evinced by what James himself, in his 1908 retrospective preface to the novel, characterises as its 'dramatic, or at least . . . scenic conditions': 'we have no direct exhibition of [Miriam's consciousness] whatever,

[but] we get at it all inferentially and inductively, seeing it only through a more or less bewildered interpretation of it by others'.[48] Just as Peter believes that Miriam has no authentic self, but rather a series of performances, the narrator does not provide a sense of her interiority. The narrator, for example, does not explain why Miriam chooses to sit for Nick Dormer: 'that mystery would be cleared up only if it were open to us to regard this young lady through some other medium than the mind of her friends. We have chosen . . . for some of the advantages it carries with it, the indirect vision.'[49]

While Miriam's professionalism as an actress involves radical emotional control of dual consciousness and a consequent lack of a stable, unperformed identity, another element of her acting technique that James viewed as lost to the amateurism of the English stage was elocution, and it is this technique that gives Miriam the potential to be a powerful figure in English national culture. In *The Scenic Art* James writes that for 'old actors',

> the touchstone of accomplishment was the art of delivering the great Shakespearean speeches. That way of considering the matter has lost credit, and the clever people on the London stage to-day aim at a line of effect in which their being 'amateurs' is almost a positive advantage. Small, realistic comedy is their chosen field, and the art of acting as little as possible has – doubtless with good results in some ways – taken the place of the art of acting as much.[50]

We have seen how T. W. Robertson's *Caste* was viewed, in its own time, as a harbinger of a new English theatre. James, however, sees the plays of Robertson as an example of such 'small' realism:

> The Prince of Wales is a little theatre, and the pieces produced there dealt mainly in little things – presupposing a great many chairs and tables, carpets, curtains, and knickknacks, and an audience placed close to the stage. They might, for the most part, have been written by a cleverish visitor at a country-house, and acted in the drawing-room by his fellow-inmates. The comedies of the late Mr Robertson were of this number, and these certainly are among the most diminutive experiments ever attempted in the drama.[51]

James's theatre criticism expounds on the inadequacy of the state of English theatre, and he specifically identifies Robertson's *Caste*, in an essay written in 1879, as from 'the primitive stage of dramatic literature': 'It is the infancy of art; it might have been written by a clever under-teacher for representation at a boarding-school.'[52] James's linkage between the decline of elocution and the predominance of small and underdeveloped realistic drama on the Victorian stage is amplified by Peter's emphasis on Miriam's speech as central to his vision of how she can save the indigenous English drama. Peter sees Miriam as someone who will raise the 'standard' of the '[p]urity of speech' on the English stage: 'Everyone speaks as he likes, and audiences never notice. . . . The place is given up to abominable dialects and individual tricks, any vulgarity flourishes, and on top of it all the Americans, with every conceivable crudity, come in to make confusion worse confounded.'[53] The emphasis here is on a national theatre, and the decline in speech serves as a synecdoche for the larger problems of the English stage. Sherringham deplores the state of the English theatre in terms that are familiar to us from those who called for an English *Théâtre Libre*. He believes 'that the personal art *is* at an end, and that henceforth we shall have only the arts . . . of the stage carpenter and the costumer. In London the drama is already smothered in scenery; the interpretation scrambles off as it can.'[54] That Sherringham is arguing for the importance of a national drama is evident when Miriam assures him that she 'can act just like an Italian', and he responds: 'I would rather you acted like an Englishwoman, if an Englishwoman would only act.'[55] The source of such a national drama, in Peter's view, is the literary drama. Peter urges Miriam to learn 'passages of Milton, passages of Wordsworth', even if they did not write plays, because it will give her 'authority'.[56]

This focus on the English theatre is thematised in the novel's setting, which begins in France but moves to England as it is on the English stage that Miriam decides to succeed as an actress. It is further underscored by Peter's internationalism as a diplomat. In the novel's opening chapters, all of its central characters are in Paris, and the narrator frequently calls attention to how out of place the English women are in France. At the same time that Miriam travels to London, Peter's sister, the widow Julia Dallow, is called back to England by the necessity of her involvement in a Parliamentary election for her borough. In fact, Peter's faith in Miriam's ability to initiate a 'new era' for the English theatre as playwrights will write for her parallels Julia's appeal to Nick's sense of service to his country.[57] J. Hillis Miller identifies the two plots of the novel as focused on Peter and Nick and their conflicts as they are each drawn to the aesthetic world in contrast with their careers in national diplomacy and politics.[58] Yet these two narrative threads must also be read as being motivated by Miriam and Julia, the respective love interests of the two men, who pull them in the respective directions of art and politics.

The Tragic Muse thus puts the actress in juxtaposition and context with a woman who wields power on the national political stage. While Miriam's own public acting (in both senses of the word) is central to the English theatre, Julia Dallow is, in Nick's words, 'a real English lady, and at the same time she's a very political woman'.[59] Although Miriam is powerful by-and-large through fulfilling the feminine scripts of men, she nevertheless refuses to give up this power in the public world in order to exercise power through 'indirect influence' as the respectable wife of a diplomat, refusing Peter's proposal as Armgart, as we saw in Chapter 3, refuses Graf Dornberg's. Julia Dallow, in contrast, is an avowedly 'political' woman who wields power indirectly through scripting the lives of others.[60] Regarding the election in her borough, she says with confidence: 'They'll have the person I want them to have, I dare say.'[61] Metaphorically, her method of control is also expressed in her role in charades, in which she directs from off stage: 'Nick of course was in the charades and in everything, but Julia was not; she only invented, directed, led the applause.'[62] James emphasises Julia's dependence on Nick to fulfil her own ambitions: 'the cause of her interest in him was partly the vision of his helping her to the particular emotion that she did desire – the emotion of great affairs and of public action'.[63] Like the playwright in 'Nona Vincent', Julia must have a performer, and she seeks both to marry Nick and to have him elected to Parliament, following in the career of his deceased father and abandoning his own artistic aspirations as a painter. She finds herself frustrated by his lack of political interest, and she tells him: 'I can do a good deal, but I can't do everything. If you work I'll work with you; but if you are going into it with your hands in your pockets I'll have nothing to do with you.'[64] Julia and Miriam, as distinctly different figures for women's relationship to the public sphere, are put in direct conflict with each other when Nick, after being elected, returns to his studio to paint, and Julia is shocked to find the actress Miriam serving as his model.

The political sphere is characterised as involving the same sort of publicity and public exhibition as the stage. The aesthete Gabriel Nash suggests that the worlds of Miriam and Julia are two competing theatres when he urges Nick Dormer to see Miriam perform: 'your engagement at your own theatre keeps you from going to others. Learn then . . . that you have a great competitor and that you are distinctly not . . . *the* rising comedian. The Tragic Muse is the great modern personage.'[65] Although Julia must exercise power indirectly, Nick's mother describes her as 'fascinating, she was a sort of leading woman', and Nick also identifies Julia's politics as theatre: 'You must have so many things, so many people, so much *mise-en-scène* and such a perpetual spectacle to live.'[66]

Agnes, Nick's sister, underscores how Julia's power on such a public stage is dependent on her domestic life, on her marriage to a 'public man' for whom 'she would be the ideal companion'. Agnes further highlights the paradox of Julia's position of public power and dependency: she is 'made for public life; she's made to shine, to be concerned in great things, to occupy a high position and to help him on'.[67] As in Thackeray's *The History of Pendennis*, in which Blanche Amory's husband will serve as the borough's member of parliament, against a theatrical backdrop a domestic woman wields political power. Julia Dallow, however, has a self-conscious and sophisticated awareness of her role on the national stage. In a characterisation of what Julia, as the landed gentility, does for the borough of Harsh, Nick also provides an image that characterises Julia's indirect influence and the ways in which a woman in the home can nevertheless exercise political power:

> Julia says the wants of Harsh are simply the national wants – rather a pretty phrase for Julia. She means *she* does everything for the place; *she's* really their member, and this house in which we stand is their legislative chamber. Therefore the *lacunae* that I have undertaken to fill up are the national wants.... I represent the ideas of my party.[68]

It is for this reason that Nick's position in Julia's home as her husband and in the nation as a member of parliament go hand in hand. Yet Nick also observes that such an elision between the domestic and the political leads Julia, like Miriam, to lack privacy and interiority, as she is always dining with guests in her home: 'Must you *always* live in public, Julia?'[69] Thus *The Tragic Muse* maintains two distinct models of women participating in the public sphere – the theatrical woman and the political woman – even as the parallels and overlaps between them seem to deconstruct the differences between them.

Roles for Women: *Alan's Wife* and the Independent Theatre

While James maintains the actress and the political woman as distinct albeit interrelated figures, in the early twentieth century actresses became involved in politics as they became key participants in the women's suffrage movement. They thereby combined the modes of public power represented by Miriam and Julia, using the theatre as the political platform for their politics. The other art form that figures in *The Tragic Muse*, painting, occupied a different relation to the suffragettes. In fact, on opening day of the Royal Academy exhibition in 1914, as part of a rash of suffragette acts of violence against painting, suffragette Mary Wood slashed John Singer Sargent's portrait of Henry James. Although it is tempting to try to read this incident as the 'founding moment of feminist critique of Henry James's fiction', Thomas J. Otten points out that the moment does not occupy such a position in James scholarship, as Wood provided no explanation for why she chose this work as her target.[70] Otten himself analyses Wood's act as consistent with and explained by both *The Tragic Muse* and Dorian stabbing his own portrait in *The Picture of Dorian Gray* to argue that at the 'turn of the century',

> painting is regarded as an image which is itself part of a larger economy; its material making and subsequent exhibition shape the socio-economics of the world beyond its frame. Further, painting's images exert a social force because they have the capacity to make themselves real, the capacity to do something to their viewers, to bridge the distance which observation entails.[71]

He further argues that 'political stability turns out to have a wholly fictive basis, turns out to be based on the endless cultivation of convention, the perpetual shaping power which late-century aesthetics finds exemplified in the act of viewing a painting'.[72] Yet while this provides the aesthetic and political context that explains Wood's attack on a painting, the theatre occupied a central role in the suffrage movement precisely because it too shaped 'the world beyond its frame'. Because theatre does not have a permanent, static physical form, its conventions invited the less violent intervention of reworking. Elizabeth Robins, one of the most prominent of the actress-suffragettes, was a friend of James. Having met her fellow American expatriate in January 1891, the year after *The Tragic Muse* was published, Elizabeth performed in his own adaptation of his novel *The American*, and he became a great supporter of her career as an actress of Ibsen.[73] Angela V. John describes James's 'Nona Vincent' as 'thinly disguised Jamesian representations of Florence [Bell] and Elizabeth [Robins]', which makes Robins the young actress struggling to please a playwright.[74] Indeed, Robins's friendships with both Wilde and James helped to sustain her as a newly arrived actress in London, frustrated with the roles available to her. *Theatre and Friendship*, a collection of letters from James to Robins, documents what she describes as a 'friendship [that] made itself at home . . . in the haunts of Adelphi melodrama' and 'made [James] welcome with an ardour that astonishe[d] even [Robins] a play devoted to justification of Militant Woman-Suffrage'.[75] In other words, the sustained connection between James and Robins traces the transition from Robins as an actress struggling to play roles in the Victorian theatre – both literally as an actress playing a part on stage and figuratively as an actress with a rich cultural legacy scripting her place in society – to Robins as a playwright who reworks both theatrical conventions and the ways in which actresses and women participated in the public sphere. Robins thus embodies Miriam's unfulfilled speculation, in complaining that the contemporary stage does not create roles that capture the lives of people she sees in London, of what she might do 'if *she* only had a pen'.[76]

James viewed Ibsen as a vital influence on the English theatre. Departing from calls for a nativist drama that embodies English sensibilities, as we saw in the praise of *Caste* and in Moore's calls for a national theatre, James identifies the highly critical views of Ibsen's works as 'emotion [that] is conspicuously and exclusively moral, one of those cries of outraged purity which have so often and so pathetically resounded through the Anglo-Saxon world'.[77] On Robins's 1891 production of *Hedda Gabler* James wrote that Ibsen 'is destined to be adored by "the profession"' –

> the actor and actress. He cuts them out work to which the artistic nature in them joyously responds – work difficult and interesting, full of stuff and opportunity. The opportunity that he gives them is almost always to do the deep and delicate thing – the sort of chance that, in proportion as they are intelligent, they are most on the look out for. He asks them to paint with a fine brush; for the subject that he gives them is ever our plastic humanity.[78]

Robins similarly believed that Ibsen's power was in creating new theatrical roles for actresses, stating in her lecture *Ibsen and the Actress*:

> Ibsen had taught us something we were never to unlearn. The lesson had nothing to do with the New Woman; it had everything to do with our particular business – with the art of acting. Events, after Hedda, emphasised for us the kind of life that stretched in front of the women condemned to the 'hack-work' of the stage. That was what we called playing even the best parts in plays selected by the actor-manager.[79]

After forming a joint management company in 1891 with fellow actress Marion Lea to bring Ibsen's *Hedda Gabler* to the London stage with Robins in the title role and Lea in the role of Thea, other Ibsen roles became part of Robins's repertoire. Ibsen was a critical transitional step for Robins, who credits the stage with having given Ibsen a platform, but also credits Ibsen with having changed theatre: 'without the help of the stage the world would not have had an Ibsen to celebrate; and without Ibsen the world would not have had the stage as it became after his plays were acted'.[80] She describes the London production of *A Doll's House* in 1889 as 'an event that was to change lives and literatures', and the importance to her own 'self-respect' of playing the role of Mrs Linde in a later production.[81] According to Robins, 'Ibsen was justifying what some of us, with very little encouragement, had blindly believed about the profession of acting.'[82] Ibsen provided an illustrative example of something that Robins would herself develop in her political drama; in Robins's view the domestic drama of *Hedda Gabler* has a significance that transcends the particular: 'Ibsen not only knew better; he saw further than the special instance. He saw what we at that time did not; I mean the general bearing of Hedda's story.'[83] Hedda epitomises the claustrophobia of women confined to the domestic sphere, and Robins had earlier, despite her desperation for work upon first settling in London, turned down the role of Mabel Vane, whose domesticity is juxtaposed with Peg Woffington's life as an actress in Taylor and Reade's *Masks and Faces* (1852).[84] According to Robins, 'no dramatist has ever meant so much to the women of the stage as Henrik Ibsen', not only for the roles that he created, but for the roles that his writing made possible.[85] Robins herself would develop a realistic theatre that moved beyond the domestic confines of the box set.

In part through Robins herself, but also through her companion, the prominent theatre critic and Ibsen translator William Archer, Ibsen's plays would serve as foundational and touchstone productions for J. T. Grein's Independent Theatre Society, a 'private subscription theater' that was, as George Bernard Shaw described it, 'independent of commercial success'.[86] The Independent Theatre Society sought to redress what, as we have already seen, critics identified as the commercial and, in turn, artistic, limitations of the theatre. George Moore was among its supporters, and Archer described how, inspired by the Théâtre Libre that Moore extolled, the Independent Theatre was founded on 'the principle that what is novel and daring in dramatic art must be directly subsidized for their behoof and benefit by the few who have the wit to care for it', because 'what is newest, subtlest and most truly alive in art will never appeal to the crowd, and therefore cannot have "money in it."'[87] Free 'from the trammels of commercialism', it provided a venue for 'progressive, experimental, unconventional drama'.[88] Between its founding in 1891 and its demise in 1897, the Independent Theatre Society staged Ibsen's *Ghosts* (13 March 1891, 26 January 1893, 24 June 1897), *The Wild Duck* (4 May 1894, 17 May 1897), *Rosmersholm* (25 March 1895), *The Master Builder* (27 March 1895) and *A Doll's House* (10 May 1897). According to Archer, although Grein's role in the English theatre is similar to that of Robertson because it marks a new era in English theatre, it is set apart because of his heavy reliance on foreign plays, including those of Ibsen and Zola: 'The movement, it cannot be denied, comes from without, not from within. It is not, like the Robertsonian movement of the 'sixties, . . . a thing of native growth. The impulse which seems to dominate the 'nineties is a foreign one.'[89] Robins's first attempt at playwriting – a drama produced by the Independent Theatre Society – itself had a continental influence. *Alan's Wife*, which she wrote with Florence Bell, was based on Elin Ameen's Swedish story 'Befriad'.

In a pivotal moment in her career, Robins surrendered the part of the title role in Arthur Wing Pinero's *The Second Mrs Tanqueray* to Stella Campbell, Pinero's first choice for the role, who had arranged to be released from another contract.[90] The role of a courtesan who kills herself because she cannot conceal her sexual fallenness despite having married into respectable and genteel society, Paula Tanqueray made the fame of Campbell after the play opened on 27 May 1893 at the St James Theatre. According to Mary Jean Corbett, although Campbell herself chafed against Pinero's plays, which 'retain the moral framework of melodrama', she 'was no political "woman agitator". While she participated in some of the activities of the Actresses' Franchise League, . . . she never became a member.'[91] Robins, in contrast, took on initiatives developing roles for women that broke the mould of the society drama and the fallen woman. Instead of acting the role of Stella Campbell, she engaged in a project that would build on Ibsen's representation of women's experience within society and would continue to move her towards becoming a key figure in the Actresses' Franchise League. In *Alan's Wife* she herself would perform the path-breaking female part when it was produced on the afternoon of 28 April and the evening of 2 May 1893 at Terry's Theatre, even as she and Bell kept their authorship a secret.

Alan's Wife was Robins's first attempt to consciously rewrite dramatic conventions and the tropes of and about the late-Victorian stage in order to engage in political action and social criticism, redefining women's social and theatrical roles. Unlike Moore's Kate Ede, whose baby dies of neglect, the title character, Jean, intentionally kills her baby. When her husband dies in a factory accident during her pregnancy and her baby is born deformed, Jean fears for its ability to fend for itself in a society that shows no mercy for the weak. Jean's infanticide is 'intricately connected with her decision to marry Alan, whom she describes as if he were a member of a master race. Ultimately, she is asserting that the life of a crippled child . . . is inferior to that of a physically beautiful, natural leader of men.'[92] This poses a problem for viewers who want to sympathise with Jean, but it is the crux of the play: Jean perceives the society in which she lives as one in which masculine strength is necessary for survival. This explains the title of the play, which 'denoted possession'.[93] Jean is in the grip of a society in which she sees herself and her child as wielding little power.

Jean adopts extreme measures in order to exercise her own agency. Her denial of being under the influence of puerperal insanity (known today as postnatal depression) leads the authorities to sentence her to death, but it also 'provides [her] with absolute responsibility for her actions'.[94] Jean thereby prevents a clinical explanation from masking the conditions endured by wives and mothers, as legal and medical reports about infanticide at that time did.[95] But rather than explain the circumstances that prompted her crime, as she is urged to do in the final scene, Jean keeps her silence to indict a legal system that cannot do justice to her experience. Her dramatic power lies in her silence, which underscores her plight – an illustration of Jean-François Lyotard's 'differend', which he defines as a 'case' in which 'the "regulation" of the conflict that opposes [two parties] is done in the idiom of one of the parties while the wrong suffered by the other is not signified in that idiom'.[96] Jean's silence bespeaks the problems of representing her experience within the oppressive social idiom that the play portrays and within the theatrical idiom that the play employs. John suggests that the scene in which Jean refuses to speak is about 'emotions apparently "speaking" for themselves, Jean's feelings transcending everyday speech and theatrical conventions'.[97] On the one hand, this legal scene, in which Jean refuses to detail the extenuating circumstances that might save her from execution, revises the traditional trial scenes of Victorian melodrama. Carolyn Williams has noted that 'melodrama's obsession with social recognition often takes the form of the trial scene', which often fails to provide justice, leading therefore to 'the last-minute revelation or rescue – one great hallmark of melodrama – [that closes] the gap that has dangerously opened up between Justice and human law'.[98] Unlike melodrama, in which the trial or the revelation that follows visibly enacts justice, *Alan's Wife* employs this silent trial scene to criticise a society in which justice is impossible for Jean's experience. On the other hand, as it rejects stage dialogue, Bell and Robins draw on and develop the melodramatic convention, explored in Chapter 1 of this book, of the physical expression of emotion standing for authenticity. A *tour de force* for the actress, who must communicate non-verbally, the scene relies on the effect that Jean will be viewed as authentic because emotional gestures are truer than spoken words.

The play represents the society in which Jean lives as incapable of understanding her motivation. Even when Jean finally speaks, there is an unbridgeable distance between her and her on-stage audience, which consists of her mother and the law. When the colonel describes Jean's infanticide as a 'crime', performed 'in cold blood . . . because [she] hadn't the courage to bear the sight of [the child's] misfortunes', Jean finally speaks: 'Crime! . . . I hadn't courage? I've had courage just once in my life – just once in my life I've been strong and kind and it was the night I killed my child!'[99] By dramatising the impossibility of representing Jean's experience to her audience within the play in speech, *Alan's Wife* demonstrates an uncertainty about women's ability to gain a voice in the public world at the same time that it attempts a public theatrical representation of a crisis in a woman's life. Echoing criticism of the naturalistic subjects and mode of representation of *A Mummer's Wife* and Ibsen's *Ghosts*, a review of the play in the *Illustrated Sporting and Dramatic News* argued that *Alan's Wife* 'deals with matters wholly unsuited to the traffic of the stage, that in its dramatic methods it is crude, and even barbaric, and that it is wholly lacking in the taste and the instinct needed for the accomplishment of all sound artistic work'.[100] The review even took issue with 'Jean's hopeful talk with her mother about her unborn child – a kind of conversation which the average playgoer feels it indiscreet to hear'. Late-Victorian theatre audiences were not prepared to accept Bell and Robins's theatrical representation of Jean. *Alan's Wife* thus delineates a challenge that suffrage drama would strive to overcome: the need to speak women's experience within the theatre and society.

From Silence to Speaking Out: Political Theatre of the Actresses' Franchise League

As public women, actresses were logical supporters of women's suffrage, and the theatre was an apt structure for depicting women who perform in the public sphere. Holledge notes a variety of additional specific factors that led actresses to become politically active. As working women, they faced discrimination within their profession. Their wages lagged far behind those of actors and, as we have seen in James's and Robins's criticisms of the theatre, the actor-manager system privileged male roles and male perspectives over the interests of actresses.[101] Furthermore, actresses' professional experiences provided them with a view of what poorer women suffered, a view that allowed for the bond between women of divergent classes and abilities that Taylor and Reade, Collins and Eliot had imagined: 'Touring the industrial cities of the North of England and Glasgow made a lasting impression on many young actresses, who had never seen slums or the effects of poverty before.'[102] Audiences' perceptions of the sexual availability of female performers also provided actresses with a view of relationships between men and women that middle-class domestic women did not possess.[103] Because of these particular experiences, many actresses battled for women's suffrage, motivated both to improve the conditions of their profession and to better the lives of women who did not enjoy the freedoms that actresses possessed as working women. Their efforts were part of a larger movement of militant, spectacular political tactics used by the suffragettes in the early twentieth century: 'stone throwing, window breaking, newspaper selling, public speaking – [strategies that] created performances of protest, designed for both effect and affect in public spaces'.[104]

Katherine Newey argues that,

> However much the suffragette movement in its public activism consciously rejected the previous forty years of constitutionalists' battles for the female suffrage, the 'spectacular activism' of suffragette protest was not wholly cut off from the past struggles of the Victorian woman writer or artist. Suffragette activism, and the range of performances it encompassed, dramatised in striking terms women's negotiations with the constraints of gendered ideology of the nineteenth century.[105]

The previous chapters of this book reveal how the actress, as an emblem of women in the public sphere, had accrued a rich cultural history. The themes that the Victorian cultural imagination associated with the actress provide another reason for the alliance between actresses and suffragettes: the blurring of class distinctions, the social and aesthetic significance of domesticity, the power of public opinion and the problem that the exceptional woman posed for arguments in favour of enfranchising women collectively were all critical issues for the suffrage movement. The suffragettes, and actress-suffragettes more particularly, employed theatre and theatricality strategically and symbolically in order to engage with these issues for the cause of women's political rights.

Elizabeth Robins wrote her suffrage drama *Votes for Women* under the auspices of a group that would become the Actresses' Franchise

League (AFL), a multi-hundred-member organisation that developed its own Play Department, as actresses such as Cicely Hamilton, Inez Bensusan and Gertrude Jennings turned their hands to playwriting in order to use the theatre for the suffrage movement. It was one of a cluster of arts organisations that were founded to support women's suffrage in what Lisa Tickner has called 'the first highly organized mass movement of cultural and ideological struggle for political ends'.[106] Critically, Tickner points out that 'the use of a new kind of political spectacle' was the critical link in the alliance between the constitutionalist and the militant wings of the suffrage movement, and we will see how suffrage drama effectively hailed conservative tastes even as it advocated for political, social and aesthetic change.[107]

Barbara Green argues that conditions of production are not merely a context but rather 'a network of associations that give a text its meaning', and that

> [f]or suffrage texts, those associations would be the feminist meetings that gave readers the vocabularies and strategies that enabled them to read as feminists, the process of repetition, imitation, and ghostwriting that transformed individual voice into collective utterance; and the deliberate marketing of individual novels, autobiographies, and histories as part of a collective body of work signed not only by author but by association.[108]

For suffrage drama, the Actresses' Franchise League was central to the network of associations that help us to understand the plays themselves and that gave plays significance beyond their formal meaning. The subjects discussed in its 1910–11 meetings demonstrate the AFL's conjoined interests in expanding women's roles within and beyond the theatre:

> 'The granting of Votes to Women'
> 'How Women will vote down the White Slave Traffic'
> 'Suffragette Tactics'
> 'That a knowledge of Politics is not injurious to Dramatic Art'
> 'That the Stage conception of Woman is conventional and inadequate'
> 'That in the interests of the country the Legal Profession should be open to Women.'[109]

The AFL defined its goals as being:

> 1. To convince members of the Theatrical profession of the necessity of extending the franchise to women.

2. To work for women's enfranchisement by educational methods, such as: –
   I. Propaganda Meetings.
   II. Sale of Literature.
   III. Propaganda Plays.
   IV. Lectures.
3. To assist all other Leagues whenever possible.[110]

Here, the actresses' work within their profession is clearly defined as a means to the broader political end of the vote.

The inclusion of 'Propaganda Plays' in the AFL's mission statement reveals how the League viewed the theatre as an 'educational' tool, indicating a confidence, as Dickens and Eliot had suggested, that the performer can exercise power over an audience. Bensusan, who served as the Honorary Organising Secretary of the Play Department, explained that the Women's Theatre's 'series of performances', which was first held 8–13 December 1913, was 'intended to assist financially all other Suffrage Societies that support it, as well as to spread accurate knowledge through the educational medium of the theatre'.[111] Thus, unlike J. T. Grein's Independent Theatre Society, and unlike Moore's 'realm of "high art", presided over . . . by the male artistic genius', the AFL defined itself as a commercial venture that sought to appeal to a broad, rather than select, audience.[112] In programme notes for the Women's Theatre the novelist Flora Annie Steel apostrophises actresses for their ability to communicate with both the unsophisticated and the cultured: 'you can hammer hard facts into dull brains; you can open still duller eyes that will not trouble to read a page of print! And to cultured minds you can present in concrete form many problems which must harass the thoughtful.'[113] In the same programme, Cicely Hamilton emphasises that the theatre can capitalise on its role as a mode of popular entertainment:

> We hope to appeal to a wide and varied public. I feel the right thing to say here would be that we hope to appeal to a thinking public; but if we only appeal to that we shall infallibly get into debt. . . . [I]t is an unfortunate fact that an appeal to the thinking public is apt to be construed as a warning-off to the public that does not think. Invite the superior person in, and the inferior person – who is a modest soul – will take it for granted you want to keep him out. The wreck of many a repertory theatre bears witness to the strength of this ingrained modesty in the average man and woman . . . what we hope for is a rush of inferior persons, all anxious to see how a pack of women are going to make fools of themselves.[114]

The suffragettes' didactic purpose and desire to influence many, rather than few, shaped the form of their entertainments and reverses the antitheatrical prejudice against such appeals to heterogeneous audiences as the *Pall Mall Gazette* series 'Why I Don't Write Plays', which we explored in the introduction of this book, evinced. Hamilton accordingly describes the conservatism of the Women's Theatre with regard to dramatic tastes:

> we have no unusual views on the presentment or production of plays. We have been influenced neither by the Russian Ballet nor by Reinhardt; we make our exits into the wings instead of into the stalls; and I have not heard of any particular struggles to attain that ideal of nobody acting better than anybody else which is frequently admired as 'ensemble'.[115]

Although the AFL may, '[l]ater on, perhaps, . . . put out the footlights and tinker with the building and go in for Really High Art', Hamilton states, '[m]eanwhile we take the theatre as we find it'.[116] Rather than pursuing avant-garde theatrical productions as the Independent Theatre Society did, the AFL employed well-worn theatrical conventions in order to fulfil its educational purpose. Its use of the theatre for propaganda, however, was predicated on an acute awareness of the interrelatedness of artistic forms and social attitudes, and superficial aesthetic conservatism served as a vehicle for the circulation of aesthetic and political innovation among broad audiences. In this way the AFL's feminist theatre is more closely linked to the Victorian, audience-responsive communalism that Garrett Stewart describes than to the protomodernistic avant-garde of which Moore was a part.[117]

In addition to noting the Women's Theatre's financial success ('the net profit was £442, and Shareholders received 11s. 6d. [57 1/2 per cent] in the £'), the AFL annual report for June 1913–June 1914 focused on the importance of a theatre run by women:

> The work of that inaugural week has proved invaluable; firstly, in the matter of proving the power of women to organise and run a theatre – since women were employed in every department as Producers – Stage Managers – Assistant Stage Managers – in the Box Office – as Stewards, etc., and the experience was valuable in the amount of confidence such enterprise inspired; secondly in demonstrating the appreciation of the public, seeing that the box office receipts were £522 during the week – which, of course, does not include the guaranteed money. Thirdly, and most important of all, is the proof that women can work together for a common purpose in perfect harmony and disinterestedness. It is perhaps a fitting moment to thank heartily all Members of the League, and

those who assisted us from other Leagues, in the various branches of the work, and it was this unity and co-operation that accounted for the final remarkable result.[118]

Theatrical efforts were significant displays of women's ability to function in the public world and to work as members of a community. This was a noteworthy accomplishment because in the domestic sphere women had long been viewed as competitors in the marriage market, and, as Corbett notes, in the professional theatre, actresses such as Irene Vanbrugh characterised 'the [theatrical] marketplace as a sphere ruled by natural laws of competition, a world in which there can be no possibility of trust or mutuality between workers, a battlefield on which one has no allies, only enemies'.[119] Corbett further points out that the actress-led initiatives of the 1890s, including those of Robins to stage Ibsen, 'attempted to circumvent just this kind of problem' as they rebelled 'against the power of actor-managers and playwrights' – against the sort of male-playwright-centred vision that we saw in 'Nona Vincent'.[120] Corbett notes that militant suffragette organisations employed an 'ethic of personal renunciation' in the service of 'the common cause', which some criticised as failing to alter women's traditional social position.[121] In contrast, the Actresses' Franchise League established that women could use and develop their individual creative talents to work co-operatively, productively and competently in a shared battle. Katherine Cockin emphasises that 'the women working collectively in producing drama for the women's suffrage movement challenged dominant beliefs about the possible roles for women in society by acting out those roles on and off stage'.[122] The League offers as a model for feminist collectivity the collaborative and coordinated work required to mount a theatrical production.

The success of the Women's Theatre in attracting the support and efforts of other organisations confirms that the suffrage movement as a whole believed that the theatre was a potent mode of changing perceptions about women. While the 1913–14 Annual Report thanks other Leagues for their support, a Secretary's report for 1913–14 details 'Instruction in elocution and practice classes ... held by members for other societies'.[123] The Secretary's Report for 1910–11 characterised the heavy demand for AFL entertainments:

> So much of the Organizing Secretary's time was found to be taken up supplying Singers and Reciters at Meetings held by other Suffrage Societies that it was decided to ask a small fee ... in consideration of our Members' services. We find this scheme has answered very profitably.[124]

Other societies also served as 'guarantors', or investors, in plays.[125] The AFL thus participated in an economic network of suffrage societies. Although the AFL committed itself to serving both the constitutional suffrage organisations that had been lobbying for women's enfranchisement since the nineteenth century and the newer, more militant organisations spearheaded by the Pankhursts and the Women's Social and Political Union, Holledge's detailed history of the AFL argues that this neutrality policy caused rifts within the League and suggests that most actresses were more sympathetic to the spectacular theatricality of the militant suffragettes.

Accounts of the activities of the Actresses' Franchise League reveal that actresses in the suffragette movement had cultural purchase on a politics of seduction through the performance of stock, audience-pleasing feminine roles, and that *Votes for Women* was an on-stage embodiment of strategies that suffragettes enacted in their political demonstrations – strategies that placed actresses at the centre of the suffragette movement. In the programme for the AFL's Women's Theatre, Steel explains that actresses are excellent vehicles for propaganda because they are 'bound over by every tradition of their art to be women indeed, to amuse, to charm, to be kindly and sympathetic to men at large'.[126] She describes how actresses occupied a key role in the suffrage movement because

> it is impossible for men to use such blessed words as 'wild woman', 'manads', [sic] or even 'old maid' when you have to deal with those whose whole lives are spent in the effort to make man himself more happier [sic], more cheerful, more contented; whose whole strength is devoted to stimulating the mind of humanity.[127]

Gail Marshall has pointed out that 'the English actress could advertise the persistence of desirable femininity in the midst of fears about women's masculinisation through professionalisation, and could thus be enrolled as a conservative social force'.[128] The Actresses' Franchise League, however, mobilised this conservative image in the service of a radical mission that subverted the traditional separation of spheres.

The AFL members who marched in the Coronation Procession on 17 June 1911, a week before the coronation of King George V, combine the seductive femininity that Steel describes with militantism, or even militarism (Figs. 5.2 and 5.3). Steel describes the actresses of the League by saying, 'how well dressed! How attractive! Not to say how seductive! Then – how full of smiles and tears, jests, retorts, kindnesses! The whole battery of femenine [sic] charms to be seen

From Playing Parts to Rewriting Roles 199

Figure 5.2 'Coronation Procession, 17 June 1911, the Actresses' Franchise League', A. Barratt, gelatin silver chloride print on postcard, 17 June 1911, TWL.1999.225, The Women's Library collection, LSE Library (Alpha Photo Press)

Figure 5.3 'Coronation Procession, 17 June 1911, Actresses' Franchise League Banner', Mrs Albert Broom, gelatin silver chloride print on postcard, 17 June 1911, TWL.1999.226, The Women's Library collection, LSE Library

in this naughty rebellious sisterhood.'[129] Decked out in flowers, their banner employs the iconography of the theatre rather than one of the militant images of the suffrage movement, but their other signs are shaped as battle shields.

In a photo of the Coronation Procession, the actresses, who are visible in the foreground, do not stand out (Fig. 5.4). Suffragettes were urged to wear, at formal occasions, white dresses accompanied with the colours of the movement: purple, white and green. The newspaper *Votes for Women* ran a regular fashion column titled 'Concerning Dress'.[130] Although such performances of femininity belie the earnest political work of the suffragettes, they were a key political strategy. The self-conscious performance of femininity in the public world dismantled the concept of the separation of spheres, and this emphasis on performance put actresses at the centre of the movement. 'Mrs Pankhurst was attracted to the idea of Elizabeth Robins as a suffragette precisely because she had been an actress.'[131] Both the actresses and the broader suffrage movement sought to create a spectacle that not only drew attention but appealed to the audience – the general public. This was also the mission of suffrage theatre: to entertain in order to gain supporters for the cause. To do so, suffrage theatre seduces its audiences with familiar theatrical conventions and then typically dismantles those very conventions.

The Coronation Procession itself provides an example of the centrality of theatrical performance to the suffragettes. Tickner's characterisation of the public demonstration reveals a melodramatic logic of '"seeing is believing"', and she also suggests that by putting themselves on public display the marchers, like the female performers that we have seen in plays and novels, had to negotiate with the expectations and strictures about women's proper sphere and behaviour – expectations with which they had been inculcated.[132] Like Cicely Hamilton's 'A Pageant of Great Women' (1909), the Coronation Procession relied on visual display to enact a spectacle of mass politics that visibly crossed class and cultural lines, including such visible constituencies as nurses in uniform and Irish women with emerald green 'colleen bawn' cloaks and gilded harps. It also included a series of costumed 'Voteless Women after the Reform Bill', depicting women such as Charlotte Brontë, Florence Nightingale and Harriet Martineau.[133] Such suffragette processions were shaped through costumes, props, banners and music. The fact that there is such a wealth of visual documentation of the suffragettes itself is the result of their spectacular, theatrical tactics.[134]

Figure 5.4 'Coronation Procession, 17 June 1911', gelatin silver chloride print on postcard, 17 June 1911 (© The March of the Women Collection/Mary Evans Picture Library)

An image of Elizabeth Robins that appears on the cover of the issue of *Sketch* in which *Votes for Women* was reviewed similarly displays the feminist playwright in feminine garb (Fig. 5.5). Robins had a self-described penchant for beautiful clothes but was not without ambivalence about her own femininity and propriety. Echoing an association of actresses and hair that harks back to William Makepeace Thackeray's 'The Ravenswing', she describes her long hair as both a 'crown of glory' and an 'incubus', as well as 'a doubtful glory – a crown that has to be eternally washed, brushed, combed, clipped, twisted, and attached to the poor head by the often painful use of those wires, hair pins'.[135] She relates how Henry Irving told her 'women have an easy road to travel on the stage. They have but to *appear* and their sweet feminine charm wins the battle.' Robins observed: 'What was wanted of the women of the stage was, first and mainly, what was wanted of women outside – a knack of pleasing.'[136] Like Klesmer and Armgart, Robins viewed the emphasis on appearances as a form of enslavement, but unlike Klesmer and Armgart, Robins did not see exceptional talent as a source of liberation. To her, the commercialism of the theatre, which Moore and other Victorian writers had deplored, particularly affected actresses, and her interest in an 'Endowed Theatre' focused on the freedom it would provide from 'the unworthy bondage of the *successful* as well as the unsuccessful women of the stage'.[137] Nevertheless, Robins and the Actresses' Franchise League sought to turn actresses' problematic relationship to femininity to political purpose.

In addition to employing feminine appearances, the AFL emphasised domesticity. An annual report describes their offices as 'the pride of the League' and itemises twenty-six objects donated or loaned by particular individuals, including such feminine accessories as 'a handsome afternoon Tea Service . . . in the colours of the League, namely pink and green', 'Blinds from Mrs Ryley. (These were beautifully embroidered by Miss Madeline Roberts, and the badge cleverly sewn on by her)', and a couple of tablecloths.[138] In addition to maintaining an office that is both equipped to meet the standards of domestic space, the League, like other suffrage groups, used domestic parlance for their public meetings, holding six 'At Homes' in the Grand Hall of the Criterion Restaurant, which included speakers and at least one debate.[139] These superficially feminine pursuits contrast with the more obviously 'political' activities of the AFL. They also engaged in 'peaceful picketing at the House of Commons during the sitting on the Reform Bill', passed 'Strong Resolutions' to send 'to the Government

Figure 5.5 Elizabeth Robins on the cover of *Sketch*, 17 April 1907

condemning the imprisonment of Mr Lansbury and others on account of their exercising their freedom of speech, and also protesting against the forcible feeding of Suffrage prisoners', and participated in 'a deputation that waited on the British Minister to the Argentine *re* means to be used to prevent the traffic in young girls to the State carried on by advertisement for theatrical companies and other means'.[140] With other organisations, they attempted to gain admittance to 'plead their Cause at the Bar of the House of Commons'.[141]

This combination of activities, evoking the domestic sphere in the context of public work, was echoed by the movement as a whole. A brochure of the Pankhursts' militant Women's Social and Political Union, for example, includes several suggestions for 'How You Can Help': 'join the Tea Table Committee: We shall be deeply grateful for your help in this purely housekeeping and domestic side of the work – of which there is a great deal to be done'; 'arrange Drawing-room Meetings and invite your friends to meet the Speakers and Leaders of the Union'; and, with regard to more public activities, 'go to Debates and Meetings where the subject of Votes for Women can be introduced and . . . watch every opportunity for bringing the question to the front'.[142]

The actress remained a preeminent figure for women who participate in public life by addressing an audience. In Hamilton's 'A Pageant of Great Women', a female narrator pleading for freedom chronicles the accomplishments of numerous women in history. The only historical figure who speaks for herself is the actress Nance Oldfield:

> By your leave,
> Nance Oldfield does her talking for herself!
> If you, Sir Prejudice, had your way,
> There would be never an actress on the boards.
> Some lanky, squeaky boy would play my parts:
> And, though I say it, there'd have been a loss!
> The stage would be as dull as now 'tis merry –
> No Oldfield, Woffington, or – Ellen Terry![143]

The actress speaks for herself doubly, both as Oldfield and as Ellen Terry, who originally played the role in Hamilton's pageant, and whose participation served to call attention to women's professional success. Aside from being a historical figure, Oldfield, like Peg Woffington, was also a character in a play by Charles Reade, and Terry appeared in the title role of the play at the Lyceum in 1893.[144] In fact, Gail Marshall describes how Terry bought the play after it was turned down by her manager at the Lyceum, Henry Irving, and in so doing 'challenge[d] the parameters of her role as the Lyceum's leading-lady, for in many of her activities, and especially as adaptor and owner of the play, she was usurping Irving's more usual responsibilities'.[145] Hamilton constructs this dizzying mis-en-abyme of actresses depicting actresses, including an allusion to two plays that Reade wrote about Victorian actresses, in order to underscore not only the popularity of the theatrical woman but also the fact that she had been subject to representation by others and that theatrical women such as Terry could help to shape the representation of women on stage. The actress in the pageant employs the point of Eliot's *Armgart* (1871) that women make a unique contribution to the stage, in order to argue for their enfranchisement.[146] Given this possible echo of Eliot, it is surprising that Hamilton does not include her among the novelists in the pageant, and this speaks to the vexed relationship between Eliot and later female writers. Nevertheless, the argument that women's voices, based on women's experiences, make a unique and necessary contribution to politics was key for suffragettes.

Suffrage theatre, therefore, does not limit the role of public speaker to actresses but depicts women of different classes and experiences addressing audiences, whether a crowd in Trafalgar Square or another woman in a domestic setting. While Elizabeth Robins's *Votes for Women* (1907) includes a 'Working Woman' among more educated speakers in a suffrage demonstration, monologues such as 'Jim's Leg' (1911) by L. S. Phibbs and 'The Mother's Meeting' (n. d.) by Mrs Harlow Phibbs show a working-class character speaking directly to the theatrical audience. These plays dramatise the transformation of working-class women into public speakers by virtue of their experiences. They provide a new twist on George Moore's realism since, like Moore, these depictions of working women locate the speaker's authenticity in domestic and work experience. This authenticity, however, gives her the authority to play a public and politically active role. Many of the plays, including Evelyn Glover's 'A Chat with Mrs Chicky' (1912) and 'Miss Appleyard's Awakening' (1911), incorporate a climactic speech made by a woman who finally has her say. The plays recognise, however, that self-articulation does not automatically grant power but is only valuable if used to communicate with an audience that in turn represents public opinion. Suffrage plays often dramatise the interaction between a speaker and an on-stage audience. In suffrage monologues, the speaker looks out at and directly addresses the audience. In this sense, they echo Eliot's emphasis on the importance of performing for an audience. In 'The Mother's Meeting', Mrs Puckle speaks to the theatre audience 'as if greeting friends'.[147] She proceeds to explain how, on accidentally attending an Anti-Suffrage meeting, she was moved to contradict the speaker by narrating her own experience of working to support a 'conic rhumyattic . . . 'usband' and 'eight kiddies', without being paid the equivalent of male factory workers.[148] Although critics often note how suffrage playwrights condescendingly turn the speech patterns of working-class women into comic relief, the use of dialect serves as a class marker that underscores how the suffragettes support all women's voices in the public sphere. Mrs Puckle describes how she takes on the 'anti' (a term used to designate those against women's suffrage), who turns out to be the genteel and titled Lady Clementine Pettigrew, and how a crowd of suffragettes cheers her on and encourages her.[149] George Eliot had sought to establish a sense of community among exceptional and ordinary women, giving voice to the ordinary woman as well as to the diva. The suffragettes extend Eliot's strategy a step further, making stars of charwomen and housewives. In fact, according to Holledge, the Actresses' Franchise League broke down distinctions between professionals and amateurs – distinctions that, as we have seen, Eliot and James asserted even as the plays of Robertson opened doors for middle-class women to enter the theatrical profession – by drawing on '[t]he tradition of drawing-room amateur theatre . . . to persuade women to produce their own suffrage plays'.[150]

In contrast to the silence of *Alan's Wife*, *Votes for Women* is about women expressing themselves in the theatre and in the political sphere. The play draws both a connection and a distinction between its heroine Vida's abortion and Jean's infanticide. When Vida gives her first public suffragette speech, her audience includes Member of Parliament Geoffrey Stonor, the father of the child that she aborted in order to protect his future political career. After seeing him, she describes the infanticide trial of a Manchester girl in terms of unspeakability – 'Even if we'd noticed it, we wouldn't speak of it in my world' – that echo *Alan's Wife*.[151] Her articulation of this incident to an audience, however, suggests that her own abortion is a revision of the figure of infanticide. In *Votes for Women*, the performer–audience dynamic dramatised on stage, as Vida commands the attention of a hostile crowd, is a figure not only for the negotiation between actress and theatrical audience, but also for the negotiation between playwright and theatrical audience. *Votes for Women* employs social and theatrical conventions to engage audiences depicted on the stage and viewing the play, but ultimately it accomplishes its political mission by criticising those conventions and effecting aesthetic innovations.[152]

Robins's novel *The Convert*, which she wrote because she was afraid that *Votes for Women* might never be staged, appeared in

October 1907, between the production and subsequent publication of the play.[153] In both the play and the novel, the dynamic and stylish suffragette Vida Levering gains the sympathy of a younger woman, Jean Dunbarton. Jean is engaged to marry Geoffrey Stonor, a prominent, conservative Member of Parliament who suddenly finds his re-election threatened by the liberal candidate. Geoffrey is also Vida's former lover, whom she left because she was unable to forgive him after concealing and aborting her pregnancy at his urging. Jean feels that Geoffrey must make amends by offering to marry Vida; Vida sees in Jean an opportunity to gain Geoffrey's support for women's suffrage. Although the action of the play depicts the same events as the novel's last few chapters, the novel, unlike the play, presents Vida's gradual conversion to the cause. Vida, moreover, is not the novel's only convert: it also narrates the moment of Jean's conversion. Jean's aunt, Mrs Heriot, who hopes to keep the naïve and sheltered Jean away from Vida, retells Vida's history so elliptically that Jean is uncertain whether she understands her aunt's references. As Mrs Heriot describes how she found Vida alone and dying, Jean becomes intrigued, and her curiosity about Vida mirrors the interest that Londoners in the novel show for suffragette rallies. Jean scrutinises Vida and, 'as the young girl studied the quiet figure, looked into the tender eyes that gazed so steadily into some grey country far away, the effect of Mrs Heriot's revelation was either weakened or transmuted subtly to something stronger than the thing that it replaced'.[154] Jean's curiosity is transformed into sympathy because she feels for the individual seated before her. This is the imaginative sympathy that Rae Greiner derives from Adam Smith's *Theory of Moral Sentiments*: 'When other people's situations rouse our interest, when we contemplate how the conditions of experience shape the attitudes that can be expressed within them, fellow-feeling forges imaginative, but no less powerfully affective, bonds.'[155] As such, it contrasts with the sensational communication of feeling through melodramatic display that we saw in *Masks and Faces*, *No Name* and *Caste*. It rather echoes the imaginative demand that Walpurga, in Eliot's *Armgart*, makes of her diva cousin when she points out that Armgart has failed to feel Walpurga's suffering that has been visible to her for five years, and urges Armgart to mobilise her own recent experience of becoming an unexceptional woman in order to imagine Walpurga's experience. Greiner claims that 'Changes of mind may be among the commonest crises represented in [Victorian] fiction, but they are also at the core of the realist novel's more routine ways of enabling sympathy, by changing one mind with, and for, another.'[156]

Such changes of mind, however, are also the subject, and purpose, of suffrage plays. Although the play *Votes for Women* does not narrate Jean's conversion with the omniscience of the novel, the process of conversion is its crux: the play focuses on how a woman can convert an on-stage audience through her public speaking performance and, by analogy, how drama itself can function as effective propaganda to convert its own audience. While suffrage dramas do employ some melodramatic conventions, particularly those that establish a character's authenticity through their emotional experiences or through domesticity, and while the suffragettes employ visual performance for a political purpose, suffrage dramas also consistently work to move beyond these conventional signs by revealing them as conventions.

Steel's praise of actresses identifies a specific convention that Robins and her heroine Vida employ and challenge in *Votes for Women*: 'And herein lies the great power which this League has, and which, doubtless, it will wield more and more effectively as time goes on. For argument never won a battle in this world, while emotion has won its thousands.'[157] Finding power in what Romney, in *Aurora Leigh*, condemned as women's interest in the particular rather than the abstract, in *Votes for Women* Robins engages and criticises the audience's tendency to care more about individuals' emotional stories than about abstract causes. Most of *The Convert* functions as a fictionalised depiction of the suffrage movement's demonstrations in public spaces such as London's Embankment, Hyde Park and Trafalgar Square. By contrast, the play devotes itself to the personal story of Vida. While the second act's political rally, in which Vida speaks, is overtly theatrical, she also performs a role when she allows Jean to believe that she was crushed by Geoffrey. Vida actively performs a personal drama for political ends because, as she says, voicing the strategy of the play itself: 'Jean isn't old enough to be able to care as much about a principle as about a person.'[158] Vida is not interested in personal vindication, but in political clout. She tells Jean: 'Bring [Geoffrey] to the point where he recognizes that he's in our debt. ... In debt to women. ... There are the thousands with hope still in their hearts and youth in their blood. Let him help *them*. Let him be a Friend to Women.'[159] Vida's ultimate goal in gaining Jean's loyalty is to use her as a bargaining chip in order to gain Geoffrey's parliamentary vote. Although she refuses Geoffrey's offer of marriage, which he makes at Jean's insistence, she blackmails him with the possibility that she can keep Jean from marrying by persuading Jean to devote her entire life to the suffrage movement.

Vida's emotional, personal experience, however, functions as more than a performance. As she consciously performs it for the benefit of her audience, channelling remembered emotional experience into an aesthetic representation, as George Henry Lewes had argued was the basis of outstanding acting, it also constitutes the basis of her own political involvement. While Moore uses a child's death to underscore the incompatibility of the artifice of an actress – a public woman – with domesticity and motherhood, Robins uses Vida's experience of helplessness and loss to advocate for women's entry into the public sphere. Vida's political involvement is both a replacement for and extension of her motherhood. In turn, Vida's political use of her experience reveals conventional femininity as trivial and a sham. Vida explains that the material conditions of present-day women are of greater concern to her than her past with Geoffrey, declaring:

> Geoffrey Stonor! For me he's simply one of the far back links in a chain of evidence. It's certain I think a hundred times of other women's present unhappiness, to once that I remember that old unhappiness of mine that's past. I think of the nail and chain makers of Cradley Heath. The sweated girls of the slums. I think of the army of ill-used women whose very existence I mustn't mention.[160]

Ridiculing the belief that women are preoccupied with personal concerns, Vida confides: 'You don't seriously believe a woman with anything else to think about, comes to the end of ten years still *absorbed* in a memory of that sort?'[161] In speaking about how women possess a 'self-control' to which they must not admit, Vida reveals that traditional femininity is performed. She explains that women perform regularly out of necessity, saying: 'Oh, we know what they want us to have. So we make shift to have it. If we don't, we go without hope – sometimes without bread.'[162] Reading this in the context of the theatrical representation of women and sex, Sos Eltis points out that Vida describes her relationship to Stonor as a 'form of prostitution' and that this is one way in which Robins 'use[s] Vida as a bridging figure, breaking down dichotomies between passive victimhood and active protest'.[163] In using her personal sufferings against Geoffrey, Vida consciously performs roles that her social audience demands. She does so to gain power over them in order to change women's social and political situation. Vida uses what Erving Goffman calls a 'pure' performance – one that is performed for the view of an audience – in order to dramatise the daily performances of self that women enact.[164] In this way, the play anticipates Judith Butler's idea that performance can be used to denaturalise gender roles by revealing them as performance.[165] But the play is also self-consciously aware of the power possessed by the audience viewing such performances, and it thematises that power in the act 2 rally scene. By writing an audience into the stage action, it suggests its own struggle to control the theatre audience.

Votes for Women was produced by the Court Theatre, a 'mecca for new playwrights' that, for the production of *Votes for Women*, attracted reviewers from nearly eighty publications in London, Birmingham, Liverpool and Manchester.[166] Desmond MacCarthy's chronicle of John E. Vedrenne and Harley Granville Barker's management of the Court from 1904 to 1907 emphasises that the complaints of Victorian critics about the condition of British drama 'had prepared the public to see the significance of the new management'.[167] Indeed, many of the innovative features that MacCarthy notes about the Court had their roots in the aims and accomplishments of Victorian novelists and playwrights. For example, as if in response to Moore's essays calling for a Théâtre Libre in England and to James's characterisation of the state of the English stage, MacCarthy compares the Court to the Théâtre Libre in Paris, noting that they both advanced 'a more natural style of acting', 'were practical protests against the tyranny of the "well-constructed play"', broke from the nineteenth-century theatre's tradition of the long run with its need to cater to large audiences, and 'very quickly collected round them a new school of young playwrights'.[168] According to MacCarthy, 'the same principle lay at the back of their successes and their influence; namely, a determination to get away from what was artificial and theatrical in methods and traditions, and to get back to actuality in gesture, diction, and sentiment'.[169] MacCarthy's 'actuality' is another manifestation of the Victorian drive to establish authenticity in the theatre. Just as Moore relied on the domestic setting to establish the authentic human behaviour that he claimed as his subject matter, MacCarthy notes that both the Court and the Théâtre Libre used the box set that we saw in Robertson's *Caste*, although he neglects to recognise it as a staple of British nineteenth-century realist drama prior to Grein's Independent Theatre Society and two subscription theatres that followed it – the New Century Theatre and the Stage Society – and prior to 'Ibsen's theory of the stage as a room with a wall knocked in to allow the spectators a view of the interior'.[170] MacCarthy argues, however, in accord with Moore's belief in the imagination and against Robertsonian realism ('the practice of crowding the stage with every conceivable property of the most realistic and costly description'), on the whole praising the Court for its lack of extravagant scenery: 'Elaborate scenery, however splendid, is, and must remain, a portentous matter of fact; while a scene which is suggested takes significance from all that happens, for it is formed itself out of the spectator's imagination'.[171] Like Moore, MacCarthy separates authenticity from showy material display. But *Votes for Women* moved beyond the box set in a way that MacCarthy did not recognise.

Votes for Women argues both for women's entry into public life and for a politically engaged drama, moving beyond the domestic box set of Robertson's realistic theatre to emphasise the importance of public and political involvement over merely private and personal concerns. The first of Robins's three acts is a box set (Fig. 5.6), self-enclosed and complete with the invisible fourth wall that separates the stage set from the audience. The inhabitants of the country house are preoccupied with the engagement of the heiress Jean to Geoffrey, and with observing social proprieties. The society drama enacted in this setting – the discovery of a character's past – had become a theatrical trend with the plays of Pinero and Wilde in the last decades of the nineteenth century. After employing them, *Votes for Women* proceeds to reject such conventions of society drama by representing the world outside the home. Vida's ultimate rejection of Geoffrey's offer

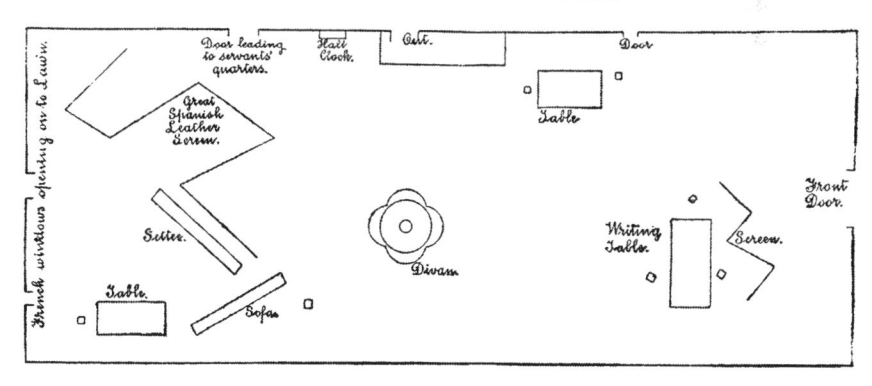

Figure 5.6 Diagram of the box set for act 1 of *Votes for Women* (Elizabeth Robins, *Votes for Women*, London: Mills and Boon, 1909)

of marriage in act 3 echoes and rewrites the climactic scene of Oscar Wilde's *A Woman of No Importance* (1893).[172] Wilde, a subscriber to the Independent Theatre Society, himself provided an alternative to the commercial theatre's typical depiction of the sexually fallen woman while employing conventions of the late-Victorian stage. At the same time that Arthur Wing Pinero's Paula Tanqueray, played on stage at the St James's Theatre, was consigned to suicide because she could not escape her sexual past, at another West End theatre just blocks away Wilde signalled Rachel Arbuthnot's redemption through the sympathy of a younger female character, Hester, who agrees with Rachel's decision that to accept the long-belated marriage offer of her seducer would be 'real dishonour . . . real disgrace'.[173] While Pinero's Paula was childless and had notable problems in her role as a stepmother, Wilde drew on the melodramatic convention of using motherhood in order to establish respectability, which we saw in Robertson's *Caste*, in order to vindicate Rachel, paradoxically, through her commitment to the illegitimate child who is the living evidence of her sexual transgression. Robins's play echoes Wilde's in the gradual build-up to the dramatic recognition scene between a politically powerful man from a wealthy family and the passionate woman whom he abandoned while she was pregnant, and the long-belated offer of marriage extorted by a well-meaning character as a form of amends. But while Wilde's Rachel rejects Lord Illingworth's proposal and refuses the 'Church-hallowed' and 'State-made' institution of marriage with an impassioned speech that asserts her dignity as a mother, Robins's Vida rejects Geoffrey's proposal by asserting that she has moved beyond her loss and committed herself to a political cause.

In contrast to the spatially confined and etiquette-bound domestic box set of act 1, the act 2 suffrage rally in Trafalgar Square (Fig. 5.7), a set opening into the wings of the stage, is an event in which classes and sexes mingle with no concern for the dictates of polite society. The speakers on the plinth of Nelson's Column include men and women who range across classes. Strikingly evocative of actual suffrage demonstrations (Fig. 5.8), the scene brings contemporary politics onto the theatrical stage. Like many reviews, MacCarthy's chronicle of the Court Theatre praised the 'brilliant piece of realism in the second act' of *Votes for Women* and observed that the scene foregrounded the interaction of performer and audience: 'this stage-audience represented the Chorus in a Greek play . . . in as much as they gave vent to the gnomic and critical remarks of the ordinary spectator'.[174] By putting

From Playing Parts to Rewriting Roles   213

Figure 5.7 Act 2 of *Votes for Women, Sketch,* 17 April 1907

Figure 5.8 'Mrs. Pankhurst at NWSPU [National Women's Social and Political Union] meeting, Trafalgar Square', 11 October 1908, World's Graphic Press, gelatin silver chloride print on postcard, 7EWD/J/06, The Women's Library collection, LSE Library

the suffragettes' audience on stage, Robins dramatised a reversal of the audience's gaze. The reviewer for the *Academy* observed how the staging of the scene elided the distinction between the theatre audience and the on-stage suffrage rally:

> The speakers on the stage faced the footlights. The crowd on the stage itself was merely a thin line of super[numeraries] facing the speakers and with their backs to the house. Behind the supers was We. WE were the real crowd and it was to US that the speeches from the plinth were addressed. We, it was, who, sometimes following the stage crowd and sometimes leading it, laughed or cheered or dissented, as orator after orator harangued us on Women's Rights and Women's Wrongs.[175]

Positioned at the chronological centre of *Votes for Women*, this scene is also central to the play's meaning.

MacCarthy's reviewer failed to recognise the relationship between the crowd scene and the structure of the play: 'The story of the play, which was almost entirely confined to the first and third acts, was dramatic indeed – even melodramatic.'[176] The reviewer for the *Academy* was equally blind, juxtaposing 'the familiar stage characters and the familiar stage situations' with the 'great scene at the Women's Suffrage meeting in Trafalgar Square'.[177] Later in the twentieth century, George Rowell, in his survey of Victorian theatre, described the play as 'a commonplace collection of the clichés of Society drama'.[178] These responses underscore how *Votes for Women* employs the traditional structures of Victorian drama. It does so, however, in order to reject them. Newey has argued that

> the cultural capital of five-act verse tragedy and poetic drama allowed women to interrogate fundamental questions of national importance, such as national principles of freedom and democracy, but for the discussion of immediately topical issues women playwrights resort to the popular genres of comedy and melodrama. The equation of cultural capital with authority and legitimacy . . . seems in this case to be balanced against the opportunity for insouciant and direct topical commentary, its impact deliberately disguised by the use of less authoritative forms and genres.[179]

Indeed, Robins's use of melodrama is part of a larger strategy of popular appeal, another element of which is 'the dialectical relationship between domesticity and the nation'.[180] Robins, however, also links the 'melodramatic', 'familiar' and 'cliché' with her innovative depiction of the suffrage rally to emphasise that the stage's realistic depiction of women's lives must not be bound by the box set. Sheila Stowell notes that for Edwardian playwrights, 'realism (in the form of naturalism) was championed as a means of challenging the ideological assumptions imbedded in melodrama and the well-made play'.[181] Robins's third act in *Votes for Women* returns to an interior but presents political action in that setting – this time in London rather than a distant aristocratic country environment – as the play points out that drama focused on individuals must not be disassociated from a broader social context.

Even as it exposes femininity as performance, *Votes for Women* draws on the melodramatic convention of the tear that signals authenticity (as explored in Chapter 1 of this book), in order to establish the authenticity of Vida's experience on which her public performance is based. In her last exchange with Geoffrey, her tears are evident as she makes the transition from her personal experience to the political world:

> You will have other children, Geoffrey – for me there was to be only one. Well, well – (*She brushes her tears away.*) – since men alone have tried and failed to make a decent world for the little children to live in – it's as well some of us are childless.[182]

Vida's suggestion that women who are not mothers will serve a motherly role in the public sphere echoes *Armgart*'s symbolic argument for the uniqueness of women's voices. The accompanying stage direction, in which Vida takes up her hat and cloak as she says, 'Yes, *we* are the ones who have no excuse for standing aloof from the fight', physically marks the transition from private to public.[183]

Moving beyond the box set also meant moving beyond the upper-middle-class denizens of the drawing-room box sets of Pinero and Wilde. Vida enters into and understands the experiences of women outside of her social class, thereby mediating and facilitating for the theatre audience a sympathetic identification between upper-middle-class women and working-class women that moves beyond the visual iconography of 'the image of the milliner or shopgirl shoulder to shoulder with the duchess' explored by Tickner.[184] Like actresses, Vida is able to cross class lines, and she brings the experience of homeless women and prostitutes into the drawing room when she describes how she 'put on an old gown and a tawdry hat' in order to experience first-hand 'the Underworld'.[185] Corbett points to suffragette hunger strikes and the genteel Constance Lytton's 1910 arrest disguised as a working woman as examples of how the suffragettes placed emphasis on understanding 'injustice and oppression' through personal experiences.[186] Although this cross-class sympathy is indeed based in part on personal, physical experience, it enables not only an emotional connection through the felt physical experience, but also the actively engaged sympathy of 'thinking along with' that Rae Greiner finds in the realist novel. Vida derives an intellectual understanding of historical oppression from the individual's physically felt experience: 'You'll never know how many things are hidden from a woman in good clothes. The bold, free look of a man at a woman he believes to be destitute – you must *feel* that look on you before you can understand – a good half of history.'[187] Echoing the point that Collins makes with his depiction of cross-class female friendship in *No Name*, Vida notes that the external, performable indices of class determine a woman's position in society. Corbett suggests that Lytton's need to disguise herself 'represents in miniature the problem of difference within the suffragette movement as a whole', a problem that the play explicitly addresses.[188] Green points out that the moment of Vida's disguise moves beyond 'a model of patronage' based on privileged women looking at women of other classes: 'Vida must abandon that (passive) position of spectatorship and embrace the (active) position of female spectacularity.'[189] Moving beyond the moment of melodramatic recognition and beyond felt sympathy through a visual connection, Vida not only imaginatively but physically enters into a sympathetic relationship with women of the street. When a house guest attempts to discriminate between women on the basis of class by stating, 'You needn't suppose ... that those wretched creatures feel it as we would', Vida responds by pointing out that '[t]he girls who need shelter and work aren't all serving-maids', referring to her own experience as a sexually fallen woman and thereby emphasising, as Collins's Magdalen Vanstone also does, the precarious social position of all women. The actions that led to Vida's fallenness reveal both her commitment to justice across class lines and the baselessness of social distinctions. She left her father's home because she took 'offence at an ugly thing that was going on under my father's roof'.[190] In *No Name*, Magdalen's authenticity was based on her family, and being separated from family freed her to act and to cross class lines. Although Vida, similarly, only begins to experience different class identities and to perform in the public sphere after she has detached herself from her family, her self-identity lies not in her family but in the ethical stance that she takes in leaving her family and in the experiences that she has after leaving the shelter of her home. Unable to find employment because of a useless lady's education that, like Gwendolen Harleth's, taught her to 'play several instruments, and sing little songs in four different tongues', Vida met 'a friend of [her] family' and became pregnant with his child.[191] Vida specifically argues that the shared plight of woman is 'why *every* woman ought to take an interest in this – every girl too'.[192] In Vida, the fallenness of Magdalen Harleth becomes a plea for cross-class feminist solidarity.

Echoing this central theme of suffrage drama and capitalising on the actress's cultural significance as a class-transgressor, the Actresses' Franchise League bridged genteel drawing rooms and the streets of London. On the one hand, the AFL had numerous titled financial patrons, and on the other, it organised 'East End Meetings . . . for the poor districts of London'.[193] At the same time, actresses in the suffrage movement enjoyed greater social acceptance within the movement than numerous works of fiction and criticism have revealed them to have in Victorian society. In the Coronation Procession, only the Women's Freedom League separated the AFL musicians from the Church League for Women's Suffrage, the Church Socialist League, the Free Church League for Women's Suffrage and the Catholic Women's Suffrage Society.[194] Indeed, the larger suffrage movement exhibited gestures towards erasing class in both rhetoric and spectacle, although whether these attitudes went beyond mere show is arguable. A souvenir programme for the Coronation Procession proclaims:

> to-day all barriers as between women will be swept away. Differences of party will be forgotten, differences of creed, differences of rank, differences of fortune, differences of age will be as though they were not; so intense will be the realisation of solidarity of womanhood and the bond of union in which women are held by their common destiny, their common service to humanity, their common burden, their common vision, and their common hope, faith, and high endeavour.[195]

Participants in the procession included the National Industrial and Professional Women's Suffrage Society, the Lancashire and Cheshire Women Workers Representation Committee and the Manchester and Salford and District Women's Trade Council.[196]

In her commitment to feminist solidarity with masses of people, Vida echoes Eliot's emphasis on 'collective need' and argues for collective action.[197] Vida challenges customary feminine theatrical roles as an actress on the stage at the same time that she challenges traditional feminine social roles as a character in the play. She rejects the conventions of drawing-room drama by stressing how the personal crises dramatised in the theatre are less important than political issues, a point underscored by the fact that Geoffrey, convinced that supporting women's suffrage would aid his political career, had written a telegram announcing his support immediately after witnessing the public spectacle of the suffrage rally and before Vida's 'attempt at coercion' in threatening to claim Jean for the cause.[198] Vida's speech about what her story can accomplish reflects both her demand that the personal be subordinated to the political and the play's demand that personal drama give way to political drama:

> One woman's mishap? – what is that? A thing as trivial to the great world as it's sordid in most eyes. But the time has come when a woman may look about her, and say, 'What general significance has my secret pain? Does it 'join on' to anything?' And I find it does. I'm no longer merely a woman who has stumbled on the way. I'm one . . . who has got up bruised and bleeding, wiped the dust from her hands and the tears from her face, and said to herself not merely, 'Here's one luckless woman!' but – 'here is a stone of stumbling to many. Let's see if it can't be moved out of other women's way.' And she calls people to come and help. No moral man, let alone a woman, *by herself*, can move that rock of offence. But . . . if many help, Geoffrey, the thing can be done.[199]

Her speech illuminates how *Votes for Women* self-consciously uses the experience of an individual to represent a broader social issue and convert large numbers of people to a cause. Vida's speech also reveals the power of the play. In using a personal story to attract sympathy for a social cause, both Vida and Robins embody the assertion that women can participate in and understand the public world. Unlike Armgart, whose behaviour Eliot criticises, they maintain an ability to sympathise with individuals: in the end Vida feels for even Geoffrey's suffering. Holledge points out that actresses

> had been trained to create three-dimensional characters for a naturalistic theatre and in the short propaganda plays – when a character was given a political as opposed to an emotional justification – they had been dissatisfied with the two-dimensional result. The dilemma they faced was whether to pursue the tradition of social drama which, by depicting victims, shamed the audience into political action, or develop a new form of theatre which could successfully represent an alternative.[200]

Although *Votes for Women* employs social drama and depicts a victim, Vida moves beyond victimisation. She does so by realising the political context of her personal experience and mobilising that experience for political change, just as the play operates in the realms of both personal emotions and politics, attempting to make its political and aesthetic innovations accessible to a mass audience. In telling a still emotionally moving story about Vida's political awakening as a result of her personal experience, and in showing how that story does 'join on' to something, *Votes for Women* stands out among other suffrage plays, interacts richly with Victorian cultural history, and boldly steps beyond its theatrical predecessors, claiming a broader political scope for the theatre and for women.

The actress, in becoming a playwright, had become a political woman and political activist. In so doing, she had turned what the Victorians had perceived as the drama's shortcomings into potent political tactics.

Notes

1. James, 'Nona Vincent', p. 5.
2. Ibid. p. 6.
3. Ibid. p. 6.
4. On James's 'theatrical failure' see Kurnick, *Empty Houses*.
5. James, *The Tragic Muse*, p. 945.
6. Ibid. p. 741.
7. Ibid. p. 783.
8. Ibid. pp. 747–8.
9. Ibid. p. 990.
10. Ibid. p. 1041.
11. Ibid. pp. 1042, 1038.
12. James, *The Scenic Art*, pp. 119–20.
13. Ibid. p. 121.
14. James, *The Tragic Muse*, pp. 957, 1041.
15. Ibid. p. 792.
16. Ibid. p. 836.
17. Ibid. p. 810.
18. Ibid. p. 844.
19. Ibid. p. 792; Lewes, *On Actors and the Art of Acting*, pp. 167–8.
20. James, *The Tragic Muse*, pp. 831–2.
21. Stokes, 'Memories of Plessy', p. 94.
22. James, *The Scenic Art*, p. 89.
23. James, *The Tragic Muse*, p. 933.
24. Archer, *Masks or Faces?*, p. 150.
25. James, *The Tragic Muse*, p. 935.
26. Ibid. p. 989.
27. Charles Reade, *Peg Woffington*, p. 241.

28. James, *The Tragic Muse*, p. 1128.
29. Ibid. p. 1129.
30. Ibid. p. 1038. Gail Marshall describes how the actress in Henry James, whether a professional on stage or a woman in the domestic sphere who is figured as an actress, has no 'inner life' or 'moral privacy' precisely because she is so adept at playing scripts ('Henry James's Houses', p. 709).
31. James, *The Tragic Muse*, p. 1129.
32. Ibid. p. 1133.
33. Ibid. p. 1180.
34. J. Hillis Miller, 'Oscar in *The Tragic Muse*', p. 31.
35. James, *The Tragic Muse*, p. 848; Wilde, *The Picture of Dorian Gray*, p. 197.
36. Wilde, 'The Decay of Lying', pp. 63–4, 77.
37. Wilde, *The Picture of Dorian Gray*, p. 249.
38. Scoffern, 'Cosmetics', p. 216.
39. Rappaport, *Beautiful for Ever*.
40. For an extended analysis of theatricality and authenticity in *The Picture of Dorian Gray*, see Voskuil, *Acting Naturally*, pp. 1–2.
41. Beerbohm, 'The Pervasion of Rouge', pp. 122, 100.
42. Ibid. pp. 112, 106.
43. Litvak, *Caught in the Act*, p. 272.
44. James, *The Tragic Muse*, p. 985.
45. Ibid. p. 985.
46. Litvak, *Caught in the Act*, p. 245.
47. James, *The Tragic Muse*, p. 1195.
48. James, 'Preface', pp. xv, xiv–xv.
49. James, *The Tragic Muse*, p. 986.
50. James, *The Scenic Art*, p. 135.
51. Ibid. p. 148.
52. Ibid. p. 124.
53. James, *The Tragic Muse*, p. 841.
54. Ibid. p. 842.
55. Ibid. p. 842.
56. Ibid. p. 843.
57. Ibid. p. 784.
58. Miller, 'Oscar in *The Tragic Muse*', p. 33.
59. James, *The Tragic Muse*, p. 909.
60. Ibid. p. 774.
61. Ibid. p. 769.
62. Ibid. p. 1238.
63. Ibid. p. 803.
64. Ibid. p. 774.
65. Ibid. p. 981.
66. Ibid. pp. 1081, 964.

67. Ibid. p. 871.
68. Ibid. pp. 869–70.
69. Ibid. p. 887.
70. Otten, 'Slashing Henry James', p. 293.
71. Ibid. p. 307.
72. Ibid. p. 317.
73. John, *Elizabeth Robins*, p. 64. For views on the friendship between Robins and James, see John, pp. 82–3, and Elizabeth Robins (commentary), *Theatre and Friendship: Letters from Henry James to Elizabeth Robins*.
74. John, *Elizabeth Robins*, p. 96.
75. Robins, *Theatre and Friendship*, p. 19.
76. James, *The Tragic Muse*, p. 1048.
77. James, *The Scenic Art*, p. 245.
78. Ibid. pp. 253–4.
79. Robins, *Ibsen and the Actress*, p. 33.
80. Ibid. pp. 7–8.
81. Ibid. pp. 10, 15.
82. Ibid. p. 15.
83. Ibid. p. 31.
84. Robins, *Both Sides of the Curtain*, pp. 83, 85, 87, 113, 139.
85. Robins, *Ibsen and the Actress*, p. 55.
86. Newey, *Women's Theatre Writing*, p. 171; George Bernard Shaw, *Saturday Review*, 26 January 1895, quoted in Nicoll, *Late Nineteenth Century Drama*, vol. 5 of *A History of English Drama*, p. 61.
87. Archer, 'The Free Stage and the New Drama', pp. 667, 665.
88. Ibid. pp. 667, 665.
89. Ibid. pp. 668, 663–4.
90. Gates, *Elizabeth Robins*, p. 67.
91. Corbett, *Representing Femininity*, p. 143.
92. Holledge, *Innocent Flowers*, p. 44.
93. John, *Elizabeth Robins*, p. 88.
94. Ibid. p. 89.
95. Showalter, *The Female Malady*, p. 59. For a nineteenth-century view of the social function of puerperal insanity see Scott, 'Dr. Scott's Case of Infanticide, with Remarks', *Edinburgh Medical and Surgical Journal* 26 (1826): 67–70, 73. For histories of infanticide see Higginbotham, '"Sin of the Age"' and Rose, *The Massacre of the Innocents: Infanticide in Britain, 1800–1939*. See also Krueger, 'Literary Defenses and Medical Prosecutions'.
96. Lyotard, *The Differend*, p. 9.
97. John, *Elizabeth Robins*, p. 88.
98. Williams, 'Melodrama', pp. 202–3.
99. Bell and Robins, *Alan's Wife*, p. 25.

100. 'Terry's Theatre', review of *Alan's Wife*, *Illustrated Sporting and Dramatic News*, 6 May 1893, p. 301.
101. Holledge, *Innocent Flowers*, p. 22. For an examination of the wages of actresses relative to actors, see Tracy C. Davis, *Actresses as Working Women*.
102. Holledge, *Innocent Flowers*, p. 15.
103. Ibid. p. 16.
104. Newey, *Women's Theatre Writing*, p. 155.
105. Ibid. p. 156.
106. Tickner, *The Spectacle of Women*, p. xii. Corbett complicates the relationship between art and politics in examining how Sylvia Pankhurst viewed her work in the visual arts and her political commitments as incompatible (*Representing Femininity*, p. 176). Another theatre organisation closely related to the AFL was the Pioneer Players, founded by AFL member Edith Craig. See Cockin, *Women and Theatre in the Age of Suffrage*.
107. Tickner, *The Spectacle of Women*, p. 10. For thorough explorations of the division between the militants and the constitutionalists, and the role of social class in these divisions, see Tickner, and Corbett, *Representing Femininity*.
108. Green, *Spectacular Confessions*, p. 17.
109. Actresses' Franchise League Secretary's Annual Report: 1910–11, ts., 2/AFL/A1/2, pp. 3–4.
110. Actresses' Franchise League printed list of officers and objects of league, n.d. [1912?], 2/AFL/C1/2. An earlier brochure, Actresses' Franchise League list of officers and objects of league, n.d. [1909?], 2/AFL/C1/1, does not mention 'Propaganda Plays'.
111. Actresses' Franchise League Annual Report June 1912–June 1913, 2/AFL/A3/1, p. 13.
112. Allen, *Theater Figures*, p. 172.
113. *Souvenir: Women's Theatre Inaugural Week*, 8–13 December 1913, 26099/4, p. 21. Also published in The Suffragette Fellowship Collection from the Museum of London.
114. *Souvenir: Women's Theatre Inaugural Week*, p. 17. The second ellipsis is original.
115. Ibid. p. 17.
116. Ibid. p. 17.
117. Stewart, *Dear Reader*, p. 150. The suffragettes' purpose is also consistent with Teresa Mangum's view of how New Woman novelist Sarah Grand appeals to 'middlebrow' tastes through her use of novelistic conventions (*Married, Middlebrow, and Militant*, passim).
118. Actresses' Franchise League Annual Report June 1913–June 1914, 2/AFL/A3/2, pp. 14–15.
119. Corbett, *Representing Femininity*, p. 148.
120. Ibid. p. 149.

121. Ibid. p. 158.
122. Cockin, 'Women's Suffrage Drama', p. 128.
123. Actresses' Franchise League Secretary's Annual Report: June 1913–June 1914, ts., 2/AFL/A1/5, p. 8.
124. Actresses' Franchise League Secretary's Annual Report: 1910–11, ts., 2/FL/A1/3, p. 6.
125. Bourne, Letter to the Secretary of the London Society for Women's Suffrage/Service, 10 January 1913, ts., 2/LSW/153/6.
126. *Souvenir: Women's Theatre Inaugural Week*, p. 20.
127. Ibid. p. 21.
128. Gail Marshall, *Actresses on the Victorian Stage*, p. 96.
129. *Souvenir: Women's Theatre Inaugural Week*, p. 20.
130. Atkinson, *Suffragettes in the Purple White & Green*, p. 19.
131. John, *Elizabeth Robins*, p. 9.
132. Tickner, *The Spectacle of Women*, pp. 55–6, 75.
133. Images of these constituent organisations can be found in Atkinson, *Mrs Broom's Suffragette Photographs*, pp. 29, 27, 30. Souvenir Programme and Order of March of the Women's Coronation Procession quoted in ibid. p. 30.
134. Many images were taken by Christina Broom, who worked under her married name Mrs Albert Broom, and who became a self-taught photographer at the age of 40, after her husband's death (Atkinson, *Mrs Broom's Suffragette Photographs*, p. 2). See also Sparham, *Soldiers and Suffragettes*.
135. Robins, *Both Sides of the Curtain*, pp. 190–1.
136. Ibid. p. 242.
137. Ibid. pp. 241, 254, 252.
138. Actresses' Franchise League Secretary's Annual Report: June 1909–June 1910, ts., 2/AFL/A1/1, pp. 3–4.
139. Ibid. p. 9.
140. Bourne, Letter to the Secretary of the London Society for Women's Suffrage/Service, 10 January 1913, ts., 2/LSW/153/6; Actresses' Franchise League Annual Report June 1913–June 1914, 2/AFL/A3/2, pp. 9, 10.
141. Bourne, Letter to the Secretary of the London Society for Women's Suffrage/Service, 10 January 1913, ts., 2/LSW/153/6.
142. Women's Social and Political Union brochure, 50.82/618.
143. Hamilton, 'A Pageant of Great Women', p. 44.
144. Auerbach, *Ellen Terry*, p. 277.
145. Marshall, *Actresses on the Victorian Stage*, p. 181.
146. For an exploration of how Eliot's *Armgart* and Elizabeth Barrett Browning's *Aurora Leigh* (1856) differ in their view of whether women's talents are uniquely female or undifferentiated from men's talents, see Chapter 3 of this book.
147. Mrs Harlow Phibbs, *The Mother's Meeting*, p. 81.
148. Ibid. p. 82.

149. Ibid. p. 82.
150. Holledge, *Innocent Flowers*, p. 72.
151. Robins, *Votes for Women*, p. 71.
152. Stowell calls *Votes for Women* 'a grab-bag of conventions recycled for feminist ends . . . that asked audiences to think not only about the subjects of feminist debate but about the very aesthetic structures to which they had grown habituated' (*A Stage of Their Own*, p. 2).
153. John, *Elizabeth Robins*, p. 149.
154. Robins, *The Convert*, p. 238.
155. Greiner, *Sympathetic Realism*, p. 21.
156. Ibid. p. 31.
157. Steel, in *Souvenir: Women's Theatre Inaugural Week*, p. 21.
158. Robins, *Votes for Women*, p. 80.
159. Ibid. p. 79.
160. Ibid. p. 80.
161. Ibid. p. 80.
162. Ibid. p. 80.
163. Eltis, *Acts of Desire*, pp. 169–70.
164. Goffman, *The Presentation of Self in Everyday Life*, p. 125.
165. See Butler, *Bodies That Matter*.
166. Whitelaw, *The Life and Rebellious Times of Cicely Hamilton*, p. 37. The Court Theatre staged matinees by new playwrights and featured plays by well-known writers in the evening to cover costs. Women were a majority in matinee audiences and a hostile review described the audience at the matinee of *Votes for Women* as consisting almost entirely of 'the propagoose (if that be the correct feminine of propagander)' ('Drama: Realism at the Court', pp. 367–8). Eltis traces the Court's inspiration to Grein's Independent Theatre Society and the Stage Society that followed it, as the Court relied 'on subscriptions and cross-subsidies between plays in order to present a repertoire of plays appealing primarily to a middle-class, educated, and largely socialist audience' (*Acts of Desire*, p. 164). The Court, however, attracted much more media attention than did the typical productions at the Independent Theatre Society. *Votes for Women*, performed at the Court between 9 April and 3 May 1907, was successful enough to gain acceptance as an evening feature. See Stowell, *A Stage of Their Own*, p. 36; Thomas, *Elizabeth Robins*, pp. 78–9; and Beerbohm, 'Miss Robins' "Tract"', pp. 459–63.
167. MacCarthy, *The Court Theatre*, p. xiv.
168. Ibid. p. 2.
169. Ibid. p. 2.
170. Ibid. p. 2.
171. Ibid. p. 8.
172. For a reading of how *Votes for Women* rewrites another play, Constance Fletcher's *Mrs Lessingham*, see Eltis, 'The Fallen Woman in Edwardian Feminist Drama'.

173. *A Woman of No Importance* opened at the Haymarket on 19 April 1893; *The Second Mrs Tanqueray* opened at the St James on 27 May 1893. Wilde, *A Woman of No Importance*, p. 454.
174. MacCarthy, *The Court Theatre*, p. 35.
175. 'Drama: Realism at the Court', p. 368.
176. MacCarthy, *The Court Theatre*, p. 34.
177. 'Drama: Realism at the Court', p. 368.
178. Rowell, *The Victorian Theater*, p. 135.
179. Newey, *Women's Theatre Writing in Victorian Britain*, p. 167.
180. Ibid. p. 167.
181. Stowell, *A Stage of Their Own*, p. 101.
182. Robins, *Votes for Women*, p. 87.
183. Ibid. p. 87.
184. Tickner, *The Spectacle of Women*, p. 66.
185. Robins, *Votes for Women*, p. 50.
186. Corbett, *Representing Femininity*, p. 166.
187. Robins, *Votes for Women*, p. 50.
188. Corbett, *Representing Femininity*, p. 165.
189. Green, *Spectacular Confessions*, pp. 64–5.
190. Robins, *Votes for Women*, p. 50.
191. Ibid. p. 51.
192. Ibid. p. 150.
193. Actresses' Franchise League Secretary's Annual Report: June 1911– June 1912, ts., 2/AFL/A1/3, p. 2.
194. 'Procession, Saturday, June 17 [1911]: Map of the Sections', 50.82/726.
195. 'Memento of [the] Women's Coronation Procession to Demand Votes for Women', 17 June 1911, 55–36/3, p. 2.
196. 'Procession, Saturday, June 17 [1911]: Map of the Sections', 50.82/726.
197. Hudd, 'The Politics of a Feminist Poetics', p. 79. See Chapter 3 of this book for a more detailed examination of Eliot's interest in collectivity.
198. Robins, *Votes for Women*, p. 86.
199. Ibid. p. 87.
200. Holledge, *Innocent Flowers*, p. 96.

Epilogue

The first English women received the vote in 1918, although it was not until 1928 that all English women enjoyed the right to vote. Women's entry into the voting rolls did not reflect the cross-class solidarity of the suffragettes. In 1918, the Representation of the People Bill, which provided 'universal manhood suffrage', extended the franchise to 'those women who were householders or the wives of householders, and had attained the age of thirty, enfranchising some six million out of eleven million adult women'.[1] The suffrage movement, however, had halted agitation for the vote with the advent of World War I four years earlier. In comparison to earlier reports of the Actresses' Franchise League that boasted high attendance rates and burgeoning activities, the Annual Report of the Play Department of the League for 20 October 1916, written by Inez Bensusan, is sombre: 'Since the last annual report . . . no regular work of the Play Dept. has been called into requisition, for the simple and natural reason that there has been no demand either for plays on the Suffrage questions, nor propaganda entertainments on the subject.'[2] Even its brighter note suggests the lean times that the war imposed on entertainers:

> The War Work, however, of this Branch of the Actresses' Franchise League which was started in November 1914 under the title of the Woman's Theatre Camps Entertainments has made good headway, and at the present moment an average of from 6 to 8 concerts per week are being given, which means employment for some 8 to 10 artists.
> Altogether something over 634 entertainments have been given and many hundreds of artists employed.[3]

In addition to such performances at camps, the League staged free concerts at hospitals.

Julie Holledge argues that, in entertaining men on the front, 'After their years of struggle before the war to represent the reality of women's lives, the actresses were back in their time-worn roles – an image of beauty like a china tea-cup with sexual overtones.'[4] Bensusan's report, however, provides a more sanguine point of view on the continuing impact of the AFL on the professional lives of actresses. Focusing on two accomplishments of the war work, she notes first that the AFL has formed 'the nucleus of an agency that may be exceedingly valuable, not only in a commercial sense at the conclusion of the war, but also extremely helpful to the artists themselves', because the Women's Theatre 'has been able to introduce an element that needs to be introduced, and that is the selection of artists on the basis of merit' rather than 'the accident of having found grace in the managerial eye'.[5] The second accomplishment she notes is

> the remarkable change in the standard of the entertainment submitted. Originally the programmes, in order to be popular had to include items that meant a distinct playing down to the audience. . . . To-day the good music, the really classical pieces, are not only listened to with rapt attention but are vociferously encored.[6]

The success of the AFL's seductive strategies is demonstrated by the fact that those strategies were no longer needed. While pursuing a political agenda, suffrage playwrights had made progress on the Victorian call to move beyond the male actor-manager's control and to elevate the quality of theatrical productions, thereby gaining greater independence for the performer and greater satisfaction for the audience.

Holledge reclaims the AFL and other 'Women in the Edwardian Theatre' as 'a lost tradition that must inform and influence the women's theatre of today'.[7] *The Victorian Actress* has shown how the innovations of suffrage playwrights, motivated by politics, developed out of the qualms that Victorian writers such as Dickens, Barrett Browning, Collins, Eliot and Moore had about the commercial theatre. While suffrage theatre has been neglected, as Sheila Stowell emphasises, because it was propaganda, its political mission pushed it to accomplish new artistic structures and modes of production, not only for women's theatre but for the stage in general.[8] Suffrage playwrights, however, were also indebted to their Victorian predecessors: not only playwrights such as Boucicault, Taylor, Reade and Robertson, but to the cultural imagination that invested the theatre and the actress with resonant power.

Notes

1. Kent, *Sex and Suffrage in Britain*, p. 221.
2. Bensusan, Annual Report of the Play Department of the Actresses' Franchise League, 20 October 1916, 2/AFL/A2/2, p. 1.
3. Ibid. p. 1.
4. Holledge, *Innocent Flowers*, p. 100.
5. Bensusan, Annual Report of the Play Department of the Actresses' Franchise League, 20 October 1916, 2/AFL/A2/2, p. 2.
6. Ibid. p. 2.
7. Holledge, *Innocent Flowers*, p. 165.
8. Stowell, *A Stage of Their Own*.

Bibliography

Actresses' Franchise League Annual Report June 1912–June 1913, 2/AFL/A3/1, Fawcett Library Archives, London.
Actresses' Franchise League Annual Report June 1913–June 1914, 2/AFL/A3/2, Fawcett Library Archives, London.
Actresses' Franchise League list of officers and objects of league, n.d. [1909?], 2/AFL/C1/1, Fawcett Library Archives, London.
Actresses' Franchise League printed list of officers and objects of league, n.d. [1912?], 2/AFL/C1/2, Fawcett Library Archives, London.
Actresses' Franchise League Secretary's Annual Report: June 1909–June 1910, ts., 2/AFL/A1/1, Fawcett Library Archives, London.
Actresses' Franchise League Secretary's Annual Report: 1910–11, ts., 2/AFL/A1/2, Fawcett Library Archives, London.
Actresses' Franchise League Secretary's Annual Report: June 1911–June 1912, ts., 2/AFL/A1/3, Fawcett Library Archives, London.
Actresses' Franchise League Secretary's Annual Report: June 1913–June 1914, ts., 2/AFL/A1/5, Fawcett Library Archives, London.
'Adelphi', review of *Peg Woffington* by Dion Boucicault, *Illustrated London News*, 28 June 1845, p. 403.
Allen, Emily, *Theater Figures: The Production of the Nineteenth-Century British Novel* (Columbus: The Ohio State University Press, 2003).
Altick, Richard D., *The English Common Reader: A Social History of the Mass Reading Public 1800–1900* (Chicago: University of Chicago Press, 1957).
Archer, William, 'The Free Stage and the New Drama', *Fortnightly Review* n.s. 50 (1891): 663–72.
Archer, William, *Masks or Faces? A Study in the Psychology of Acting* (London: Longmans, Green, and Co., 1888). Accessed via Google Books, 1 December 2013.
Archer, William, 'The Stage and Literature', *Fortnightly Review* n.s. 51 (1892): 219–32.
Archer, William, 'Why I Don't Write Plays', *Pall Mall Gazette*, 31 August 1892.
Ashley, Robert P., 'Wilkie Collins and the American Theater', *Nineteenth-Century Fiction* 8 (1954): 241–55.

Atkinson, Diane, *Mrs Broom's Suffragette Photographs: Photography by Christina Broom, 1908 to 1913* (London: Nishen Photography, [1989]).
Atkinson, Diane, *Suffragettes in the Purple White & Green: London 1906–14* (London: Museum of London, 1992).
Auerbach, Nina, *Ellen Terry: Player in Her Time* (New York: W. W. Norton and Company, 1987).
Auerbach, Nina, *Private Theatricals: The Lives of the Victorians* (Cambridge, MA: Harvard University Press, 1990).
Auerbach, Nina, *Romantic Imprisonment: Women and Other Glorified Outcasts* (New York: Columbia University Press, 1986).
Baker, Michael, *The Rise of the Victorian Actor* (Totowa, NJ: Rowman and Littlefield, 1978).
Barish, Jonas, *The Antitheatrical Prejudice* (Berkeley: University of California Press, 1981).
Barrett Browning, Elizabeth, *Aurora Leigh* [1856], introduction and notes by Kerry McSweeney (Oxford: Oxford University Press, 1993).
Baudelaire, Charles, 'In Praise of Make-Up' [1863], in *Selected Writings on Art and Literature*, trans. and intro. P. E. Charvet (London: Penguin Books, 1992).
Beer, Gillian, *George Eliot*, ed. Sue Roe (Bloomington: Indiana University Press, 1986).
Beerbohm, Max, 'Miss Robins' "Tract."' Review of *Votes for Women* by Elizabeth Robins, *Saturday Review*, 13 April 1907, pp. 456–7. Rpt. in *Around Theatres* (London: Rupert Hart-Davis, 1953), pp. 459–63.
Beerbohm, Max, 'The Pervasion of Rouge' [1894], *The Works of Max Beerbohm* (London: John Lane, The Bodley Head, 1921), pp. 99–124.
Bell, Florence, and Elizabeth Robins, *Alan's Wife* [1893], in *New Woman Plays*, ed. and intro. Linda Fitzsimmons and Viv Gardner (London: Methuen Drama, 1991), pp. 6–25.
Bensusan, Inez, 'Annual Report of the Play Department of the Actresses' Franchise League', 20 October 1916, 2/AFL/A2/2, Fawcett Library Archives, London.
[Bernard, William Bayle], *No Name: A Drama, in Five Acts; Founded on, and Adapted from, the Story So Entitled. By Wilkie Collins, Esq.* (London: G. Holsworth, at the Office of 'All the Year Round', 1863).
[Bernard, William Bayle], *No Name: A Drama, in Five Acts; Founded on, and Adapted from, the Story So Entitled. By Wilkie Collins, Esq. To Which is Added A Description of the Costume . . . and the Whole of the Stage Business* (Chicago: The Dramatic Publishing Company, [188–?]).
Bernstein, Susan David, *Roomscape: Women Writers in the British Museum from George Eliot to Virginia Woolf* (Edinburgh: Edinburgh University Press, 2013, 2014).
Betham-Edwards, Matilda, *Mid-Victorian Memories* (London: J. Murray, 1919).
Bodenheimer, Rosemarie, 'Ambition and Its Audiences: George Eliot's Performing Figures', *Victorian Studies* 34 (1990): 7–33.

Booth, Michael R. (ed.), *Prefaces to English Nineteenth-Century Theatre* (Manchester: Manchester University Press, 1976).

Boucicault, Dion, *The Life of an Actress, A Drama, In Five Acts* (London: Dick's Standard Plays, n.d.).

Boucicault, Dion, *Peg Woffington; Or, the State Secret. A Comedy, in Two Acts* (London: Dick's Standard Plays, n.d.).

Boucicault, Dion, *The Prima Donna; A Comedy in Two Acts* (London: T. H. Lacy, n.d.).

Boucicault, Dion, 'The Young Actress: An Interlude in One Act'. Licensing Copy. Adelphi Theatre. Plays Submitted to the Lord Chamberlain, British Library. *English and American Drama of the Nineteenth Century* (New York: Readex Microprint, 1965).

Bourne, Adeline, Letter to the Secretary of the London Society for Women's Suffrage/Service, 10 January 1913, ts, 2/LSW/153/6, Fawcett Library Archives, London.

Braddon, Mary Elizabeth, *Lady Audley's Secret* [1861–2], intro. David Skilton (Oxford: Oxford University Press, 1987).

Braddon, Mary Elizabeth, 'Why I Don't Write Plays', *Pall Mall Gazette*, 5 September 1892, p. 3.

Brantlinger, Patrick, *The Reading Lesson: The Threat of Mass Literacy in Nineteenth-Century British Fiction* (Bloomington: Indiana University Press, 1998).

Bratton, Jacky, *New Readings in Theatre History* (Cambridge: Cambridge University Press, 2003).

Brontë, Charlotte, *Jane Eyre* [1847], intro. Joyce Carol Oates (New York: Bantam Books, 1988).

Brooks, Peter, *The Melodramatic Imagination: Balzac, Henry James, Melodrama, and the Mode of Excess* (New Haven: Yale University Press, 1976).

Brown, Susan, 'Determined Heroines: George Eliot, Augusta Webster, and Closet Drama by Victorian Women', *Victorian Poetry* 33 (1995): 89–109.

Brownstein, Rachel M., *Tragic Muse: Rachel of the Comédie-Française* (New York: Alfred A. Knopf, 1993).

Buckley, Matthew, 'Introduction', *Modern Drama* 55 (2012): 429–30.

Burns, Wayne, *Charles Reade: A Study in Victorian Authorship* (New York: Bookman Associates, 1961).

Butler, Judith, *Bodies That Matter: On the Discursive Limits of 'Sex'* (New York: Routledge, 1993).

Carlisle, Janice, *The Sense of an Audience: Dickens, Thackeray, and George Eliot at Mid-Century* (Athens: University of Georgia Press, 1981).

Review of *Caste*, by T. W. Robertson, *Daily News* [London], 8 April 1867, p. 2.

Review of *Caste*, by T. W. Robertson, *Illustrated London News*, 13 April 1867, p. 370.

Clarence, Reginald, *'The Stage' Cyclopaedia: A Bibliography of Plays* (London: The Stage, 1909).

Clareson, Thomas D., 'Wilkie Collins to Charles Reade: Some Unpublished Letters', in Warren D. Anderson and Thomas D. Clareson (eds), *Victorian Essays: A Symposium* (Kent: Kent State University Press, 1967), pp. 107–24.

Cockin, Katherine, *Women and Theatre in the Age of Suffrage: The Pioneer Players 1911–1925* (Basingstoke: Palgrave, 2001).

Cockin, Katherine, 'Women's Suffrage Drama', in Maroula Joannou and June Purvis (eds), *The Women's Suffrage Movement: New Feminist Perspectives* (Manchester: Manchester University Press, 1998), pp. 127–39.

Colby, Robert A., '"Scenes of all Sorts": *Vanity Fair* on Stage and Screen', *Dickens Studies Annual: Essays on Victorian Fiction* 9 (1981): 163–94.

[Collins, Wilkie], 'Dramatic Grub Street: Explored in Two Letters', *Household Words* 17 (1858): 265–70.

Collins, Wilkie, Letter to W. H. Wills, 21 November 1862, Autographs Miscellaneous English, The Pierpont Morgan Library, New York.

Collins, Wilkie, *No Name* [1862–3], ed. and intro. Mark Ford (London: Penguin Books, 1994).

Collins, Wilkie, *No Name: A Drama, In Four Acts. (Altered from the Novel for Performance on the Stage)* (London: Published by the Author, 1870).

Collins, Wilkie, *No Name: A Drama, In Four Acts. (Altered from the Novel for Performance on the Stage)* (London: Published by the Author, 1870). With a typescript of a cast list for a performance at the Theatre Royal, Newcastle-on-Tyne. Lilly Library, Bloomington, IN. Also available on microfiche, New Canaan, CT: Readex [198–].

Corbett, Mary Jean, 'Performing Identities: Actresses and Autobiography', in Kerry Powell (ed.), *The Cambridge Companion to Victorian and Edwardian Theatre* (Cambridge: Cambridge University Press, 2004, pp. 109–26).

Corbett, Mary Jean, *Representing Femininity: Middle-Class Subjectivity in Victorian and Edwardian Women's Autobiographies* (Oxford: Oxford University Press, 1992).

Dames, Nicholas, 'Brushes with Fame: Thackeray and the Work of Celebrity', *Nineteenth Century Literature* 56 (2001): 23–51.

Davies, Emily, Letter to Annie Crow, 24 September 1876, *The Papers of Emily Davies and Barbara Bodichon*. Brighton: Harvester Microform, 1985. ED 5/16. Also published in *The George Eliot Letters*, ed. Gordon S. Haight, vol. 8 (New Haven: Yale University Press, 1978), p. 469.

Davis, Jim, and Victor Emeljanow, *Reflecting the Audience: London Theatregoing, 1840–1880* (Hatfield, Hertfordshire: University of Hertfordshire Press, 2001).

Davis, Tracy C., *Actresses as Working Women: Their Social Identity in Victorian Culture* (London: Routledge, 1991).

Davis, Tracy C., 'The Show Business Economy, and Its Discontents', in Kerry Powell (ed.), *The Cambridge Companion to Victorian and Edwardian Theatre* (Cambridge: Cambridge University Press, 2004), pp. 39–40.

De la Mare, Walter, 'The Early Novels of Wilkie Collins', in John Drinkwater (ed.), *The Eighteen-Sixties: Essays by Fellows of the Royal Society of Literature* (Cambridge: Cambridge University Press, 1932), pp. 51–101.

Dickens, Charles, 'The Amusements of the People', *Household Words* 1 (1850): 13–15, 57–60.

Dickens, Charles, *Great Expectations* [1860–1], ed. Angus Calder (Harmondsworth, Middlesex: Penguin Books, 1987).

Dickens, Charles, *The Life and Adventures of Nicholas Nickleby* [1838–9], ed., intro., and notes Michael Slater (Harmondsworth, Middlesex: Penguin Books, 1982).

Diderot, Denis, *The Paradox of Acting*, trans. Walter Herries Pollack, pref. Henry Irving (London: Chatto and Windus, 1883).

'Drama', *The London Daily News*, 3 March 1862, p. 2, <https://www.britishnewspaperarchive.co.uk/> (last accessed 6 December 2017).

'Drama: Realism at the Court', review of *Votes for Women* by Elizabeth Robins, *Academy*, 13 April 1907, pp. 367–8.

Du Maurier, George, *Trilby* [1894], intro. Leonee Ormond (London: J. M. Dent & Sons, 1992).

Du Plessis, Rachel Blau, *Writing Beyond the Ending: Narrative Strategies of Twentieth-Century Women Writers* (Bloomington: Indiana University Press, 1985).

Eliot, George, *Armgart*, British Library Add MS 34038, 1871.

Eliot, George, *Armgart*, *MacMillan's Magazine* 24 (1871): 161–87.

Eliot, George, *Armgart* [1871], in *The Legend of Jubal and Other Poems, Old and New*, *The Works of George Eliot*, Cabinet Edition (Edinburgh: William Blackwood and Sons, 24 vols, 1878–85), pp. 71–140.

Eliot, George, *Daniel Deronda* [1876], intro. Irving Howe (New York: Signet, 1979).

Eliot, George, *The George Eliot Letters*, ed. Gordon S. Haight, 9 vols (New Haven: Yale University Press, 1954–78).

Eliot, George, *Middlemarch* [1871–2], ed. W. J. Harvey (Harmondsworth: Penguin Books, 1988).

Eliot, George, review of *Aurora Leigh*, *Westminster Review* 67 (1857): 306–10.

Eltis, Sos, *Acts of Desire: Women and Sex on Stage 1800–1930* (Oxford: Oxford University Press, 2013).

Eltis, Sos, 'The Fallen Woman in Edwardian Feminist Drama: Suffrage, Sex and the Single Girl', *ELT* 50.1 (2007): 27–49.

Elwin, Malcolm, *Charles Reade: A Biography* (London: Jonathan Cape, 1931).

Farrow, Anthony, *George Moore*, Twayne's English Authors Series 244, ed. Kinley E. Roby (Boston: Twayne Publishers, 1978).

Fawkes, Richard, *Dion Boucicault: A Biography* (London: Quartet Books, 1979).

Franklin, J. Jeffrey, *Serious Play: The Cultural Form of the Nineteenth-Century Realist Novel* (Philadelphia: University of Pennsylvania Press, 1999).

Frederic, Harold, 'Why I Don't Write Plays', *Pall Mall Gazette*, 12 September 1892, p. 3.
Fried, Michael, *Absorption and Theatricality: Painting and Beholder in the Age of Diderot* (Berkeley: University of California Press, 1980).
Gasson, Andrew, *Wilkie Collins: An Illustrated Guide* (Oxford: Oxford University Press, 1998).
Gates, Joanne E., *Elizabeth Robins, 1862–1952: Actress, Novelist, Feminist* (Tuscaloosa: University of Alabama Press, 1994).
Gilbert, Sandra M., and Susan Gubar, *The Madwoman in the Attic: The Woman Writer and the Nineteenth-Century Literary Imagination* (New Haven: Yale University Press, 1979).
Gilbert, Sandra M., and Susan Gubar, *No Man's Land: The Place of the Woman Writer in the Twentieth Century, Volume 1: The War of the Words* (New Haven: Yale University Press, 1988).
Gilcher, Edwin, *A Bibliography of George Moore* (DeKalb: Northern Illinois Press, 1970).
Gissing, George, 'Why I Don't Write Plays', *Pall Mall Gazette*, 10 September 1892, p. 3.
Glover, Evelyn, 'A Chat with Mrs Chicky' [1912], in Dale Spender and Carole Hayman (eds), *How the Vote Was Won and Other Suffragette Plays* (London: Methuen Drama, 1985), pp. 104–13.
Glover, Evelyn, 'Miss Appleyard's Awakening' [1911], in Dale Spender and Carole Hayman (eds), *How the Vote Was Won and Other Suffragette Plays* (London: Methuen Drama, 1985), pp. 117–24.
Goffman, Erving, *The Presentation of Self in Everyday Life* (Garden City, New York: Anchor Books, 1959).
Green, Barbara, *Spectacular Confessions: Autobiography, Performative Activism, and the Sites of Suffrage 1905–1938* (New York: St Martin's Press, 1997).
Greiner, Rae, *Sympathetic Realism in Nineteenth-Century British Fiction* (Baltimore: Johns Hopkins University Press, 2012).
Hadley, Elaine, *Melodramatic Tactics: Theatricalized Dissent in the English Marketplace, 1800–1885* (Stanford: Stanford University Press, 1995).
Hamilton, Cicely, 'A Pageant of Great Women' [1909], in Viv Gardner (ed.), *Sketches from the Actresses' Franchise League* (Nottingham: Nottingham Drama Texts 20th Century, 1985), pp. 41–50.
Hardy, Thomas, 'Why I Don't Write Plays', *Pall Mall Gazette*, 31 August 1892, p. 1.
Henry, Nancy, *The Life of George Eliot* (Chichester: John Wiley and Sons, 2012).
Higginbotham, Ann R., '"Sin of the Age": Infanticide and Illegitimacy in Victorian London', *Victorian Studies* 32 (1989): 319–37.
Himmelfarb, Gertrude, 'Editor's Introduction', in John Stuart Mill, *On Liberty* [1859] (Harmondsworth: Penguin Books, 1986), pp. 1–49.
Hogan, Robert, *Dion Boucicault* (New York: Twayne Publishers, 1969).

Holledge, Julie, *Innocent Flowers: Women in the Edwardian Theatre* (London: Virago Press, 1981).
Hudd, Louise, 'The Politics of a Feminist Poetics: "Armgart" and George Eliot's Critical Response to *Aurora Leigh*', in Kate Flint (ed.), *Poetry and Politics (49): Essays and Studies* (Cambridge: D. S. Brewer, 1996), pp. 62–83.
Hughes, Kathryn, *George Eliot: The Last Victorian* (New York: Farrar Straus Giroux, 1998).
Hutcheon, Linda, *A Theory of Adaptation* (New York: Routledge, 2006).
James, Henry, 'Nona Vincent', in *Complete Stories 1892–1898* (New York: Library of America, 1996).
James, Henry, 'Preface', in *The Tragic Muse*, vol. 1 (New York: Charles Scribner's Sons, 1936).
James, Henry, *The Scenic Art: Notes on Acting and the Drama; 1872–1901*, ed. and intro. Allan Wade (New Brunswick: Rutgers University Press, 1948).
James, Henry, *The Tragic Muse*, in *Novels 1886–1890*, notes Daniel Mark Fogel (New York: Library of America, 1989).
John, Angela V., *Elizabeth Robins: Staging A Life, 1862–1952* (London and New York: Routledge, 1995).
Kent, Susan Kingsley, *Sex and Suffrage in Britain, 1860–1914* (Princeton: Princeton University Press, 1987).
Krueger, Christine, 'Literary Defenses and Medical Prosecutions: Representing Infanticide in Nineteenth-Century Britain', *Victorian Studies* 40 (1997): 271–94.
Kurnick, David, *Empty Houses: Theatrical Failure and the Novel* (Princeton: Princeton University Press, 2012).
Lancaster, Edward, 'The Manager's Daughter: An Interlude in One Act', Licensing Copy, Theatre Royal Haymarket 1837. Plays Submitted to the Lord Chamberlain, British Library. *English and American Drama of the Nineteenth Century*. New York: Readex Microprint, 1965.
Leonardi, Susan J., 'To Have a Voice: The Politics of the Diva', *Perspectives on Contemporary Literature* 13 (1987): 65–72.
Levine, George, *The Realistic Imagination: English Fiction from Frankenstein to Lady Chatterley* (Chicago and London: University of Chicago Press, 1981).
Lewes, George Henry, *On Actors and the Art of Acting* (London: Smith, Elder, & Co., 1875).
Litvak, Joseph, *Caught in the Act: Theatricality in the Nineteenth-Century English Novel* (Berkeley: University of California Press, 1992).
Lyotard, Jean-François, *The Differend: Phrases in Dispute*, trans. Georges Van Den Abbeele, Theory and History of Literature 46 (Minneapolis: University of Minnesota Press, 1988; trans. of *Le Différend*, 1983).
MacCarthy, Desmond, *The Court Theatre 1904–1907: A Commentary and Criticism* (London: A. H. Bullen, 1907).
McCormack, Kathleen, *George Eliot in Society: Travels Abroad and Sundays at the Priory* (Columbus: Ohio State University Press, 2013).

'Malet, Lucas' [Mary St Leger Kingsley], 'Why I Don't Write Plays', *Pall Mall Gazette*, 1 September 1892, p. 1.

Mangum, Teresa, *Married, Middlebrow, and Militant: Sarah Grand and the New Woman Novel* (Ann Arbor: University of Michigan Press, 1998).

Marshall, David, *The Figure of Theater: Shaftesbury, Defoe, Adam Smith, and George Eliot* (New York: Columbia University Press, 1986).

Marshall, Gail, *Actresses on the Victorian Stage: Feminine Performance and the Galatea Myth* (Cambridge: Cambridge University Press, 1998).

Marshall, Gail, 'Henry James's Houses: Domesticity and Performativity', in Juliet John (ed.), *The Oxford Handbook of Literary Culture* (Oxford: Oxford University Press, 2016), pp. 702–16.

Review of *Masks and Faces*, by Tom Taylor and Charles Reade, *The Times*, 22 November 1852, p. 8.

Masters, Joellen, '"A Great Part to Play": Gender, Genre, and Literary Fame in George Moore's *A Mummer's Wife*', *Victorian Literature and Culture* 29 (2001): 285–301.

'Memento of [the] Women's Coronation Procession to Demand Votes for Women', 17 June 1911, 55–36/3, Suffragette Fellowship Collection, Museum of London. Also published in *The Suffragette Fellowship Collection from the Museum of London* (Brighton: Harvester Microform, 1985).

Mill, John Stuart, *On Liberty* [1859], ed. and intro. Gertrude Himmelfarb (Harmondsworth: Penguin Books, 1986).

Mill, John Stuart, *The Subjection of Women* [1869], in John Stuart Mill and Harriet Taylor Mill, *Essays on Sex Equality*, ed. and intro. Alice S. Rossi (Chicago: University of Chicago Press, 1972).

Miller, Andrew H., '*Vanity Fair* through Plate Glass', *PMLA* 105 (1990): 1042–54.

Miller, J. Hillis, 'Oscar in *The Tragic Muse*', *Arizona Quarterly: A Journal of American Literature, Culture, and Theory* 62:3 (2006): 31–44.

Miller, Renata Kobetts, 'Imagined Audiences: The Victorian Novelist and the Stage', in Patrick Brantlinger and William B. Thesing (eds), *A Companion to the Victorian Novel* (Oxford: Blackwell Publishers, 2002), pp. 207–24.

Mitchell, Judith, 'A New Perspective: Naturalism in George Moore's *A Mummer's Wife*', *Victorian Newsletter* 71 (1987): 20–7.

Moore, George, Correspondence to Elizabeth Robins, The Elizabeth Robins Papers, Fales Library, New York University, New York.

Moore, George, *Impressions and Opinions* (New York: Charles Scribner's Sons, 1891).

Moore, George, *Modern Painting* (London: Scott Publishing Co., 1908).

Moore, George, *A Mummer's Wife* [1885], pref. Walter James Miller (New York: Liveright, 1966).

Moore, George, 'Why I Don't Write Plays', *Pall Mall Gazette*, 7 September 1892, p. 3.

'The New Adelphi Theatre', *The Morning Post*, 3 March 1862, p. 6, <https://www.britishnewspaperarchive.co.uk/> (last accessed 6 December 2017).

Newey, Katherine, *Women's Theatre Writing in Victorian Britain* (Houndmills, Basingstoke, Hampshire, and New York: Palgrave Macmillan, 2005).

Nicoll, Allardyce, *A History of Early Nineteenth Century Drama 1800–1850*, 2 vols (Cambridge: Cambridge University Press, 1930).

Nicoll, Allardyce, *Late Nineteenth Century Drama*, vol. 5 of *A History of English Drama 1660–1900*, 6 vols (Cambridge: Cambridge University Press, 1959).

Nightingale, Florence, *Cassandra* [1852], intro. Myra Stark, epilogue Cynthia Macdonald (Old Westbury, NY: The Feminist Press, 1979).

Nisbet, Ada, *Dickens and Ellen Ternan* (Berkeley: University of California Press, 1952).

[Noble, J. A.], 'An English Disciple of Zola', review of *A Mummer's Wife* by George Moore, *Spectator*, 17 January 1885, pp. 83–5.

Review of *No Name*, adapted for the stage by Wilkie Collins and Augustin Daly, Fifth Avenue Theatre, New York. *New York Times*, 8 June 1871, p. 4.

Review of *No Name*, adapted for the stage by Wilkie Collins and Augustin Daly, Fifth Avenue Theatre, New York. *New York Tribune*, 8 June 1871, p. 8.

Odell, George C. D., *Annals of the New York Stage*, vol. 9 (New York: Columbia University Press, 1937), 15 vols, 1927–49.

O'Farrell, Mary Ann, *Telling Complexions: The Nineteenth-Century English Novel and the Blush* (Durham: Duke University Press, 1997).

[Oliphant, Margaret], 'Novels', *Blackwood's Magazine* 94 (1863): 168–83.

Orel, Gwen, 'Reporting the Stage Irishman: Dion Boucicault in the Irish Press', in John P. Harrington (ed.), *Irish Theatre in America: Essays on Irish Theatrical Diaspora* (Syracuse: Syracuse University Press, 2009), pp. 66–77.

Otten, Thomas J., 'Slashing Henry James: On Painting and Political Economy, Circa 1900', *Yale Journal of Criticism* 2 (2000): 293–320.

Ouida, 'Why I Don't Write Plays', *Pall Mall Gazette*, 20 September 1892, p. 1.

Review of *Peg Woffington* by Charles Reade, *The Athenaeum*, 1 January 1853, pp. 15–16.

Review of *Peg Woffington* by Dion Boucicault, *Illustrated London News*, 28 June 1845, p. 403, <https://www.britishnewspaperarchive.co.uk/> (last accessed 6 December 2017).

Pearson, Richard, *Victorian Writers and the Stage: The Plays of Dickens, Browning, Collins, and Tennyson* (New York: Palgrave Macmillan, 2015).

Peterson, M. Jeanne, 'The Victorian Governess', in Martha Vicinus (ed.), *Suffer and Be Still: Women in the Victorian Age* (Bloomington: Indiana University Press, 1972), pp. 3–19.

Phibbs, L. S., 'Jim's Leg' [1911], rpt. in Julie Holledge, *Innocent Flowers: Women in the Edwardian Theatre* (London: Virago Press, 1981), pp. 169–71.

Phibbs, Mrs Harlow, 'The Mother's Meeting' [n.d.], in Viv Gardner (ed.), *Sketches from the Actresses' Franchise League* (Nottingham: Nottingham Drama Texts 20th Century, 1985), pp. 79–82.

Phillips, Henry Wyndham, 'Fanny Stirling [as Peg Woffington]', Garrick Club, London, <http://garrick.ssl.co.uk/object-g0778> (last accessed 23 May 2018).

Poovey, Mary, *Uneven Developments: The Ideological Work of Gender in Mid-Victorian England* (Chicago: University of Chicago Press, 1988).

Pope, Rebecca A., 'The Diva Doesn't Die: George Eliot's *Armgart*', in Leslie C. Dunn and Nancy A. Jones (eds), *Embodied Voices: Representing Female Vocality in Western Culture* (Cambridge: Cambridge University Press, 1994), pp. 139–51.

'Portraits: XXXI – Miss Heath', *The Theatre* 3, new series (London: Wyman and Sons, 1880), pp. 189–90.

Powell, Kerry, *Women and Victorian Theatre* (Cambridge: Cambridge University Press, 1997).

Price, Leah, *How to Do Things with Books in Victorian Britain* (Princeton: Princeton University Press, 2012).

'Procession, Saturday, June 17 [1911]. Map of the Sections', 50.82/726, Suffragette Fellowship Collection, Museum of London. Also published in *The Suffragette Fellowship Collection from the Museum of London* (Brighton: Harvester Microform, 1985).

Raimond, C. E. [Elizabeth Robins], *George Mandeville's Husband* (New York: D. Appleton and Company, 1894).

Rappaport, Helen, *Beautiful for Ever: Madame Rachel of Bond Street; Cosmetician, Con-Artist and Blackmailer* (London: Vintage, 2011).

Reade, Charles, *Hard Cash*, 2 vols (New York: P. F. Collier & Son, n.d. [1863]).

Reade, Charles, Letter, *Athenaeum*, 15 January 1853, p. 82.

Reade, Charles, *Peg Woffington* [1853], intro. Austin Dobson, illus. Hugh Thomson (London: George Allen, 1899).

Reade, Charles L., and the Rev. Compton Reade, *Charles Reade: Dramatist, Novelist, Journalist; A Memoir Compiled Chiefly from his Literary Remains*, 2 vols (London: Chapman and Hall, 1887).

'Reade's Niece a Pauper', *The New York Times*, 18 January 1914, p. 2, online archive <https://timesmachine.nytimes.com/browser> (last accessed 29 December 2017).

Rede, Leman Thomas, *The Guide to the Stage* [1827], ed. Francis C. Wemyss (New York: Samuel French, 1868).

Robertson, T. W., *Caste* [1867], in George Rowell (ed.), *Nineteenth Century Plays*, 2nd ed. (London: Oxford University Press, 1972), pp. 343–406.

Robertson, T. W., 'The Poor Rate Unfolds a Tale', in T[homas] Hood (ed.), *Rates and Taxes: and How They Were Collected* (London: Groombridge and Sons, 1866), Lilly Library, Bloomington, IN.
Robins, Elizabeth, *Both Sides of the Curtain* (London: William Heinemann, 1940).
Robins, Elizabeth, *The Convert* [1907], intro. Jane Marcus (London: The Feminist Press, 1980).
Robins, Elizabeth, *Ibsen and the Actress* (London: Hogarth Press, 1928).
Robins, Elizabeth, 'The Suffrage Camp Revisited', in *Way Stations* (New York: Dodd, Mead and Company, 1913), pp. 50–74.
Robins, Elizabeth, *Theatre and Friendship: Some Henry James Letters, with a Commentary by Elizabeth Robins* (New York: G. P. Putnam's Sons, 1932).
Robins, Elizabeth, *Votes for Women* [1907], in Dale Spender and Carole Hayman (eds), *How the Vote Was Won and Other Suffragette Plays* (London: Methuen Drama, 1985), pp. 35–87.
Robinson, Kenneth, *Wilkie Collins: A Biography* (London: Davis-Poynter, 1951).
Rose, Lionel, *The Massacre of the Innocents: Infanticide in Britain, 1800–1939* (London: Routledge and Kegan Paul, 1986).
Rowell, George (ed.), *Nineteenth Century Plays*, 2nd ed. (London: Oxford University Press, 1972).
Rowell, George, *The Victorian Theater 1792–1914*, 2nd ed. (Cambridge: Cambridge University Press, 1978).
Rutherford, Susan, *The Prima Donna and Opera, 1815–1930* (Cambridge: Cambridge University Press, 2006).
'Scene from *Caste* by T. W. Robertson, Prince of Wales Theatre, probably 1867', Neg. No. JA 736, Victoria and Albert Museum.
Schreiner, Olive, *The Story of an African Farm* [1883], intro. Dan Jacobson (Harmondsworth, Middlesex: Penguin Books, 1986).
Scoffern, John, M. B., '"Beautiful for Ever"', *Belgravia* 5 (1868): 227–36.
Scoffern, John, M. B., 'Cosmetics', *Belgravia* 4 (1867): 208–16.
Scott, David, 'Dr. Scott's Case of Infanticide, with Remarks', *Edinburgh Medical and Surgical Journal* 26 (1826): 62–73.
Shorthouse, J. Henry, 'Why I Don't Write Plays', *Pall Mall Gazette*, 1 September 1892, p. 2.
Showalter, Elaine, *The Female Malady: Women, Madness, and English Culture, 1830–1980* (New York: Pantheon, 1985).
Showalter, Elaine, *A Literature of Their Own: British Women Novelists from Brontë to Lessing* (Princeton: Princeton University Press, 1977).
[Smith, Alexander], 'Art. VI. – Novels and Novelists of the Day', *North British Review* 38 (1863): 168–90.
Souvenir: Women's Theatre Inaugural Week, 8–13 December 1913, 26099/4, Suffragette Fellowship Collection, Museum of London. Also published in *The Suffragette Fellowship Collection from the Museum of London* (Brighton: Harvester Microform, 1985).

Sparham, Anna, *Soldiers and Suffragettes: The Photographs of Christina Broom* (London: Philip Wilson Publishers, 2015).
Stewart, Garrett, *Dear Reader: The Conscripted Audience in Nineteenth-Century British Fiction* (Baltimore: Johns Hopkins University Press, 1996).
Stokes, John, 'Memories of Plessy: Henry James Re-Stages the Past', in Maggie Barbara Gale and Viv Gardner (eds), *Women, Theatre and Performance: New Histories, New Historiographies* (Manchester: Manchester University Press, 2000), pp. 81–101.
Stokes, John, 'Rachel's "Terrible Beauty": An Actress Among the Novelists', *ELH* 51 (1984): 771–93.
Stowell, Sheila, 'Actors as Dramatic Personae: Nell Gwynne, Peg Woffington and David Garrick on the Victorian Stage', *Theatre History Studies* 8 (1988): 117–36.
Stowell, Sheila, *A Stage of Their Own: Feminist Playwrights of the Suffrage Era* (Ann Arbor: University of Michigan Press, 1992).
Swift, Jonathan, 'A Beautiful Young Nymph Going to Bed' [1731], in *The Poems of Jonathan Swift* (New York: Collier Books, 1962), pp. 109–10.
Taylor, Jenny Bourne, *In the Secret Theatre of Home: Wilkie Collins, Sensation Narrative, and Nineteenth-Century Psychology* (London: Routledge, 1988).
Taylor, Tom, and Charles Reade, *Masks and Faces* [1852], in George Rowell (ed.), *Nineteenth Century Plays*, 2nd ed. (London: Oxford University Press, 1972), pp. 121–72.
'Terry's Theatre', review of *Alan's Wife* by Florence Bell and Elizabeth Robins, *Illustrated Sporting and Dramatic News*, 6 May 1893, p. 301.
Thackeray, William, *The History of Pendennis* [1848–50], ed. Donald Hawes, intro. J. I. M. Stewart (London: Penguin Books, 1986).
Thackeray, William, *Vanity Fair* [1847–8], ed. and intro. John Sutherland (Oxford: Oxford University Press, 1989).
'The Theatres', *The Era*, 29 June 1845, p. 5, <https://www.britishnewspaperarchive.co.uk/> (last accessed 6 December 2017).
'The Theatres', *The Era*, 9 March 1862, p. 10, <https://www.britishnewspaperarchive.co.uk/> (last accessed 6 December 2017).
'The Theatres', *The Illustrated London News*, 8 March 1862, p. 245, <https://www.britishnewspaperarchive.co.uk/> (last accessed 6 December 2017).
Thomas, Sue, *Elizabeth Robins*, Victorian Research Guides 22 (Queensland: University of Queensland Department of English, 1994).
Tickner, Lisa, *The Spectacle of Women: Imagery of the Suffrage Campaign 1904–14* (Chicago: University of Chicago Press, 1988).
Tomalin, Claire, *The Invisible Woman: The Story of Nelly Ternan and Charles Dickens* (New York: Alfred A. Knopf, 1991).
'Two Novels', review of *A Mummer's Wife* by George Moore, *Saturday Review* 59 (1885): 214–15.

Varty, Anne, *Children and Theatre in Victorian Britain: 'All Work, No Play'* (Houndmills, Basingstoke, Hampshire: Palgrave Macmillan, 2008).

Voskuil, Lynn M., *Acting Naturally: Victorian Theatricality and Authenticity* (Charlottesville and London: University of Virginia Press, 2004).

Watt, Ian, *The Rise of the Novel: Studies in Defoe, Richardson, and Fielding* [1957] (Berkeley: University of California Press, 1974).

Weltman, Sharon Aronofsky, 'Theater, Exhibition, and Spectacle in the Nineteenth Century', in Robert Demaria, Jr., Heesok Chang and Samantha Zacher (eds), *Victorian and Twentieth-Century Literature 1837–2000*, vol. 4 of *A Companion to British Literature* (Hoboken, NJ: Wiley Blackwell, 2014).

Whitelaw, Lis, *The Life and Rebellious Times of Cicely Hamilton: Actress, Writer, Suffragist* (Columbus: Ohio State University Press, 1991).

'Why I Don't Write Plays', *Pall Mall Gazette*, 3 August 1892, p. 1.

Wilde, Oscar, 'The Decay of Lying: An Observation' [1889], *De Profundis and Other Writings*, intro. Hesketh Pearson (London: Penguin Books, 1986), pp. 55–87.

Wilde, Oscar, *The Picture of Dorian Gray* [1890], in Richard Aldington and Stanley Weintraub (eds), *The Portable Oscar Wilde* (London: Penguin Books, 1981), pp. 138–391.

Wilde, Oscar, *Salomé*, illus. Aubrey Beardsley [1894], in Karl Beckson (ed.), *Aesthetes and Decadents of the 1890s: An Anthology of British Poetry and Prose* (New York: Vintage Books, 1966).

Wilde, Oscar, *A Woman of No Importance* [1893], in *The Complete Oscar Wilde* (New York: Crescent Books, 1995), pp. 410–60.

Williams, Carolyn, 'Melodrama', in Kate Flint (ed.), *Cambridge History of Victorian Literature* (Cambridge: Cambridge University Press, 2012), pp. 193–219.

Women's Social and Political Union brochure, 50.82/618, Suffragette Fellowship Collection, Museum of London. Also published in *The Suffragette Fellowship Collection from the Museum of London* (Brighton: Harvester Microform, 1985).

Wood, Mrs Henry, *East Lynne* [1860], intro. Stevie Davies (London: J. M. Dent & Sons, 1988).

Woods, Margaret L., 'Why I Don't Write Plays', *Pall Mall Gazette*, 2 September 1892, p. 2.

Zola, Émile, 'From *Naturalism in the Theatre*' [1878], trans. Albert Bermel, in W. B. Worthen (ed.), *The Harcourt Brace Anthology of Drama*, 3rd ed. (Fort Worth, TX: Harcourt Brace College Publishers, 2000), pp. 866–74.

Index

abortion, 206
The Actor (Hill), 59
actors: professionalism of, 10–11, 39, 44, 149, 176–7, 183; *see also The Paradox of Acting*
'An Actress of the Eighteenth Century' (Moore), 151
actresses
   authenticity, 15, 16, 17, 18, 72, 77, 158
   and class identity, 15, 17, 31, 40, 65, 72, 73, 217
   and domesticity, 15, 17, 18, 19, 21, 31, 86, 133, 146, 149, 150, 151
   middle class, 66, 148–9, 150, 167, 206
   in novels, 21, 29, 31
   as outsiders, 15, 16, 44, 46, 49, 50, 94
   power of, 53, 100
   relations with novelists, 31
   self-control, 37, 38–9, 109, 123, 124, 159, 160, 182, 183, 185, 209
   shaping of, 32
Actresses' Franchise League, 21, 174, 190, 192, 194–5, 197, 206, 207, 226–7
   and class bridging, 217
   in Coronation Procession (17 June 1911), 198–201 Figures 5.2–5.4, 217
   and domesticity, 202, 204
   and femininity, 198–202
   and political activity, 194, 202, 204, 222n
   and propaganda theatre, 20, 195–6, 198, 209, 218, 226, 227
adaptations, 41, 43, 78, 90, 95, 166
   of drama as novel: Reade, Peg *Woffington*, 16, 41, 51, 64, 78, 92
   of French plays, 3, 5, 73, 99, 176
   of novels as dramas: *The American* (James), 187; *Man and Wife* (Collins), 103n; *No Name* (Collins), 18, 72, 78, 88, 89, 90–3, 102–103nn, 207, 216–17; *Vanity Fair* (Thackeray), 34n; *The Woman in White* (Collins): request for adaptation refused, 103n
Adelphi Theatre, London, 43, 44, 68n
agency, 89, 90–1, 106, 191
Alan's Wife (Robins), 20, 190–2, 206
the Alcharisi (Eliot, *Daniel Deronda*), 18, 107, 115, 128, 132–3, 134, 135, 137, 144n
Allen, Emily, 12–13, 14, 147, 150, 153
Ameen, Elin, 'Befriad', 190

The American stage adaptation (James), 187
'The Amusements of the People' (Dickens), 118–19
'antinomy' of acting, 87
antitheatricality, 10, 19, 109, 111, 127, 146, 162, 166, 168, 182, 196
Arc, Joan of, 161
Archer, William, 5–6, 8, 11, 15, 16, 51, 52, 54, 58–9, 74, 176, 177, 178, 189–90
   Masks or Faces? (1888), 37, 38–9, 93
Armgart (Eliot, 1871), 18, 19, 106–8, 109, 112, 113, 115–22, 131, 141n, 175, 205, 207, 215, 223n
Armgart (Eliot, *Armgart*), 18, 112–13, 114, 115–17, 118–22, 130, 132, 133–5, 136–7, 138–9, 161, 185, 202, 207, 218
   and community between exceptional and ordinary women, 106, 131, 139, 206
   and consequences of loss of singing talent, 106–7, 108–9, 115, 122, 131, 137
   and participation in public sphere, 118, 121, 122, 129, 134
artifice, 19, 41, 55, 60, 61, 63, 74, 92, 98, 120, 123, 132, 136, 137, 146, 154, 156, 209
   and cosmetics, 45, 51, 53, 54, 64, 65, 182
audiences, 3–4, 10
   middle class, 12, 19, 21, 23, 93, 153, 224n
   power of, 107, 109–10, 119, 120, 125, 147, 148, 152–3, 167, 175
   power over, 9, 17, 19, 78, 100, 107, 108, 109, 112–13, 119, 122, 123, 126, 133, 210
   theatre compared with reading, 6–9, 22, 147, 161
   working class, 5, 8, 118–19
Auerbach, Nina, 64, 84, 162, 163
Aurora Leigh (Barrett Browning, 1856), 107, 108–12, 114, 117–19, 121, 129, 135–6, 144–5n, 208, 223n
   and review by Eliot, 19, 108–9, 111, 118
Aurora Leigh (Barrett Browning, *Aurora Leigh*), 19, 109–12, 117–18, 127, 129–30, 135–6
Austen, Jane, *Mansfield Park* (1813), 84
authenticity, 41, 43, 44, 179, 215
   of actresses, 15, 16, 17, 18, 60, 72, 77, 158
   and blush, 52, 64, 65

of children, 64
and class origins, 59, 92
and cosmetics, 52, 54
and emotions, 40, 60, 63, 66, 74–5, 98, 126, 176, 177
and mutability, 177–8, 180, 183, 220n
and Peg Woffington, 54–5, 58, 59, 63, 64–5, 66
see also artifice
avant-garde readership, 15, 19, 147, 153
avant-garde theatre, 196

backstage viewpoint, 73–4, 150, 156
Baker, Michael, 52, 60
Bancroft, Squire, 93
Barish, Jonas, 10, 26, 84, 162
Barker, Harley Granville, 210
Barrett, A., 199 Figure 5.2
Barrett Browning, Elizabeth, 162, 227
 'The Cry of the Children' (1844), 130
 'The Runaway Slave at Pilgrim's Point' (1850), 130
 see also Aurora Leigh
Baudelaire, Charles, 'In Praise of Make-Up' (1863), 53
Beardsley, Aubrey, 181
'A Beautiful Young Nymph Going to Bed' (Swift), 51–2
Becky Sharp (Thackeray, *Vanity Fair*), 21–9, 85, 110
Beer, Gillian, 107, 108, 124, 131, 132, 141n
Beerbohm, Max, 'The Pervasion of Rouge' (1896), 52–3, 55, 181–2
'Befriad' (Ameen), 190
Belgravia magazine, 54, 181
Bell, Florence, 187, 190, 191, 192
Bennett, Miss Rose, 60
Bensusan, Inez, 194, 195, 226, 227
Bernard, William Bayle, *No Name* stage adaptation (1863), 88, 89–90, 102n, 103n
Bernhardt, Sarah, 178
Bernstein, Susan David, 106, 120
Betham-Edwards, Matilda, 162
Blackwood, John, 134
blush: significance of, 24–5, 39, 51, 52, 64, 65, 85, 178, 179
Bodenheimer, Rosemarie, 112, 115
Bodichon, Barbara, 115
bodily expression: legibility of, 17, 39, 41, 64, 98
Booth, Michael, 59
Both Sides of the Curtain (Robins), 169n, 171n
Boucicault, Dion, 11, 31, 47, 67, 158, 227
 The Life of an Actress (1855, 1862), 17, 18, 41, 72, 73–8, 94, 100, 175
 Peg Woffington (1845), 16, 41, 44–6, 50, 68n, 80
 The Prima Donna (1852), 16, 41, 46–9, 73
 'The Young Actress' (1860), 16, 41, 43–4, 47, 73, 74

box set 18, 94, 98, 104n, 149, 189, 210–11, 211 Figure 5.6, 212, 215
Braddon, Mary Elizabeth, 9–10
 Belgravia magazine, 54, 181
 The Doctor's Wife (1864), 170n
 Lady Audley's Secret (1861–2), 52, 80, 181
Brantlinger, Patrick, 8–9
Bratton, Jacky, 2, 14
Brontë, Charlotte, 200
 Jane Eyre (1847), 4, 110–11, 111–12, 112–13, 123
 Villette (1853), 111
Brooks, Peter, 13, 14
Broom, Christina (Mrs Albert Broom), 199 Figure 5.3, 223n
Browne, Hablot K., illustration for Miss Snevellicci, 3, 4 Figure 0.1
Browning, Robert, 137
Brownstein, Rachel, 165
Buckingham, Duke of, *The Rehearsal* (1672), 31
Buckley, Matthew, 13
Butler, Judith, 209
Byron, Lord, 154

Campbell, Stella, 190
The Careless Husband (Cibber), 59
Carlisle, Janice, 22, 119
Carroll, Lewis, xiv
Caste (Robertson, 1867), 18, 19, 72, 94–100, 131, 148, 156, 183, 188, 207, 210, 212
changeability (theatrical), 17, 41, 78, 92
'A Chat with Mrs Chicky' (Glover), 205
Cibber, Colley, *The Careless Husband* (1704), 59
circulating libraries, 153
Clairon, Mlle, 151
class
 and authenticity, 59, 92
 and challenge to class hierarchies, 15, 16, 17, 40, 41, 62, 65, 66, 72, 77, 79, 85, 100
 and class fluidity, 15, 17, 21, 31, 41, 42, 43, 51, 60, 67, 80, 81, 82, 83, 85, 92, 193
 and cross-class sympathy, 215–16, 217, 228
 and performativity, 17–18, 72, 79, 88
 see also middle class; working class
closet drama, 1, 18, 106, 120, 131, 137
Cockin, Katherine, 197
collective; collective action, 141n, 145n, 171n, 194, 197, 217
Collins, Wilkie, 3–5, 6, 7, 95, 107, 133, 153, 193, 227
 'Dramatic Grub Street' (1858), 99
 friendship with Reade, 78
 Man and Wife stage adaptation, 103n
 The Woman in White, stage adaptation refused, 103n
 see also No Name

commercialisation
  of novel, 20, 147, 161, 170n
  of stage, 28, 67–8n, 93, 170n, 176, 189, 195, 202; *see also* Independent Theatre Society
Comte, Auguste, 113
control
  actresses' self-control, 37, 38–9, 109, 123, 124, 159, 160, 182, 183, 185, 209
  by actor-manager, 227
  by audiences, 107, 109–10, 119, 120, 125, 147, 148, 152–3, 167, 175
The Convert (Robins), 20, 206–7, 208
Corbett, Mary Jean, 97, 111, 163, 165, 190, 197, 215, 216
cosmetics, 45, 51–3, 54, 55 Figure 1.1, 64, 69n, 181–2
costume: gendered implications, 120
Court Theatre, 210–11, 212, 224n
Covent Garden theatre, 24, 52, 104n
Craig, Edith, xiv, 222n
'The Cry of the Children' (Browning), 130
cultural capital, 12, 147, 214

Daly, Augustin, 89, 103n
Dames, Nicholas, 29–30
Daniel Deronda (Eliot, 1876), 15, 18, 19, 65, 100, 107, 115, 120, 123, 132, 141n, 143n, 145n, 146, 166, 175, 177
  and domestic women *see* Gwendolen Harleth
  and talented women *see* The Alcharisi; Mirah Lapidoth
David Copperfield (Dickens), 4
Davies, Emily, 114–15
Davis, Jim, 24, 93
Davis, Tracy C., 62, 66, 94, 148–9
de Goncourt, Edmond, 151
death: Victorian associations with, 51, 65, 137
DeCamp, Marie-Thérèse see Kemble
'The Decay of Lying' (Wilde), 180
Dickens, Charles, 5, 11, 31, 95, 153, 162, 195
  'The Amusements of the People' (1850), 118–19
  David Copperfield (1849–50), 4
  Great Expectations (1860–1), 3
  Nicholas Nickelby (1838–9), 2–3, 78, 99
  The Pickwick Papers (1836–7), 7
Diderot, Denis, *The Paradox of Acting* (1773/1830), 10–11, 15, 36, 37, 38, 39–40, 58, 65, 79, 84–5, 86, 100, 126, 127, 143n
Dobson, Austin, 55
The Doctor's Wife (Braddon), 170n
A Doll's House (Ibsen), 189, 190
domesticity, 66, 72, 74, 85, 92, 116, 132, 148, 156, 189, 193, 202, 208, 209, 214
  and actresses, 15, 17, 18, 19, 21, 31, 86, 133, 146, 149, 150, 151

and female subjectivity, 13
and femininity, 11, 97, 117
of middle class, 150
and re-domestication, 18, 79
and respectability, 93, 95, 97–8, 100
drama
  closet drama, 1, 18, 106, 120, 131, 137
  drawing-room drama, 122, 150, 183, 215, 217
  intellectual drama, 93, 196
  and naturalism see realism: theatrical
  private theatricals, 81, 83–4, 90, 92, 126, 176
  and theatricality see antitheatricality; theatricality
  sensation drama, 12, 88
  sentimentalism in, 3, 16, 22, 39, 40, 64, 96, 150, 151, 154–5, 156, 158
  see also novels and plays: comparisons between
'Dramatic Grub Street' (Collins), 99
drawing-room drama, 122, 150, 183, 215, 217
Drury Lane theatre, 8, 24, 52
Du Maurier, George, *Trilby* (1894), 91, 109
DuPlessis, Rachel Blau, 158–9
Duse, Leonora, 52

Eliot, George, 15, 20, 53, 100, 153, 160–1, 164, 171n, 193, 195, 206, 217, 218, 227
  and anonymity, 163
  as exceptional woman, 139–40, 162, 163, 165
  and feminism, 108
  Middlemarch (1871–2), 108, 111, 120–1, 123, 134, 139, 153
  review of *Aurora Leigh*, 19, 108–9, 111, 118
  Romola (1862–3), 146
  The Spanish Gypsy (1868), 141nn, 145n
  see also *Armgart; Daniel Deronda*
Eltis, Sos, 209
Emeljanow, Victor, 24, 93
emotion
  and authenticity, 40, 60, 63, 66, 74–5, 98, 126, 177, 178
  and Esther Eccles (*Caste*), 98
  and Ibsen, 188
  and Jean Creyke (*Alan's Wife*), 191–2
  and Julia Dallow (*The Tragic Muse*), 185
  and Magdalen Vanstone (*No Name*), 88, 92
  and Miriam Rooth (*The Tragic Muse*), 178, 183
  and Peg (*Peg Woffington*), 61–6
  and self-identity, 65, 66, 72, 86–7, 88, 92
  and Vida Levering (*Votes for Women*), 208–9, 216, 219
  see also feeling
emotional connections, 46, 47, 48, 65, 76, 216

emotional detachment, 36, 178; *see also* actresses: self-control
emotional expression, 36–40, 46, 53, 58; *see also* blush; bodily expression; melodramatic conventions; tears
Escott, T. H. S., 169n
Esther Eccles (T. W. Robertson, *Caste*), 18, 94–5, 96–8, 131
exceptional women, 15, 19, 20, 97, 107, 112, 124, 134, 140, 141n, 160–1, 168, 171n, 193
  compared with the unexceptional, 106, 128, 131, 136, 137, 138, 139, 144n, 164, 165, 180, 206, 207

Farrow, Anthony, 153
Faucit, Helen, 51, 137
Fawkes, Richard, 46, 47, 73
feeling, 36–9
  distinct from sympathy, 13
  expression by melodramatic conventions, 14, 15, 16–17, 21, 40, 41–2, 72, 98, 177, 191, 208, 215
  genuine, 14, 16, 17, 18, 38, 39, 43, 48, 49, 51, 61, 63, 64, 65, 74
  see also emotion
Félix, Rachel (actress Rachel), 73, 128, 175
femininity, 11, 97, 115, 117, 118, 198, 200, 202, 209, 215
Fidelio (Beethoven), 122
Fifth Avenue Theatre, New York, 89, 92, 102–3n
'The First Night', 73
Fletcher, Constance, *Mrs Lessingham* (1894), 224n
flush *see* blush
foreignness, 110–11
The Forty Thieves (Sheridan), 24, 30
The Fotheringay (Thackeray, *The History of Pendennis*), 29–30
France and the English Victorian theatre
  adaptations of French plays, 3, 5, 73, 99, 176
  comparisons between French and English situations, 5–6, 27, 176, 177
  influence of Diderot, *The Paradox of Acting*, 10–11, 15, 36, 37, 38, 39–40, 58, 65, 79, 84–5, 86, 100, 126, 127, 143n
  influence of Théâtre Libre, 5, 184, 189, 210
Franklin, J. Jeffrey, 11–12
Frederick, Harold, 9

Gabriel Nash (James, *The Tragic Muse*), 175
Gasson, Andrew, 79, 102–3n
Gates, Joanne E., 163, 165
gender, 117, 118, 141n, 143n, 193
  and costume, 120
  cross-gender performances, 121

gender anxiety, 140
gender conflict, 13, 28
gender differences, 129
gender expectations, 94
gender hierarchies, 161
gender politics, 21
gender roles, 210
gender transgression, 17
George Mandeville (Robins, *George Mandeville's Husband*), 161–8
George Mandeville's Husband (Robins), 20, 148, 160–8
Ghosts (Ibsen), 190, 192
Gilbert, Sandra, 112, 115, 140, 165
Girton College, Cambridge, 114, 115
Gissing, George, 8, 9
Glover, Evelyn
  'A Chat with Mrs Chicky' (1912), 205
  'Miss Appleyard's Awakening' (1911), 205
Goffman, Erving, 209
governesses, 83, 85–6, 87, 111, 125, 175
Grand, Sarah, 222n
Great Expectations (Dickens), 3
greatness: ideas of, 19, 108, 114–15, 135; *see also* exceptional women
Green, Barbara, 194, 216
green room, 61, 62, 63, 73, 175
Grein, J. T., 5, 147, 189, 195, 210, 224
Greiner, Rae, 13, 14, 16, 26, 39, 131, 139, 207, 216
Grimaldi see The Life of an Actress (Boucicault)
Grisi, Carlotta, 124–5
Grisi, Giuditta, 124
Grisi, Giula, 124, 143n
Gubar, Susan, 112, 115, 140, 165
Gwendolen Harleth (Eliot, *Daniel Deronda*), 19, 65, 106, 107, 123, 124–6, 127, 128–9, 131–2, 137, 217

Hadley, Elaine, 13, 41
Hamilton, Cicely, 194, 195, 196
  'A Pageant of Great Women' (1909), 161, 200, 204
Hard Cash (Reade), 82
Hardy, Thomas, 6
Heath, Caroline, 46
Hedda Gabler (Ibsen), 188–9
Heinemann, William, 163
Hemans, Felicia, 140n
Hennell, Sara Sophie, 122
Henry, Nancy, 120, 138–9, 145n
Hill, John, *The Actor* (1755), 59
The History of Pendennis (Thackeray), 21, 29–31, 186
Hogarth, William, 57
Holledge, Julie, 192, 198, 206, 218, 227
Hudd, Louise, 107, 117, 121, 131, 144nn
Hughes, Kathryn, 139
humble work, value of, 115, 135–6
Hume, David, 13, 14

Ibsen and the Actress (Robins), 188
Ibsen, Henrik, 11, 20, 197, 210
  London productions of plays, 188–90, 192
identity fluidity see class: and class fluidity
imagination, sympathetic, 16, 39, 207
'In Praise of Make-Up' (Baudelaire), 53
Independent Theatre Society (Grein), 5, 189–90, 195, 196, 210, 212, 224n
infanticide, 19, 158, 206, 221n
intellectual novels, 148
intellectual theatre, 93, 196
internalised subjectivity, 18, 79
Irving, Henry, xiv, 15, 202, 204
  1883 preface to Diderot, *The Paradox of Acting*, 11, 39–40, 149, 169n

James, Henry, 187, 192, 206, 210, 220n
  The American stage adaptation, 187
  'Nona Vincent' (1892), 20, 173–4, 187, 197
  The Scenic Art (1948), 20, 175, 176, 183
  The Tragic Muse (1890), 20, 174–86, 187
Jane Eyre (Brontë), 4, 110–11, 111–12, 112–13, 123
Jean Creyke (Robins, *Alan's Wife*), 190–2, 206
Jean Dunbarton (Robins, *Votes for Women*), 207, 208, 211, 218
'Jeanne la Folle; or the Return of the Soldier', 96
Jennings, Gertrude, 193
Jerrold, Douglas, 'Mrs Caudle's Curtain Lectures' (1845), 23
'Jim's Leg' (Phibbs), 205
John, Angela V., 165, 187
Jones, Henry Arthur, 11
Julia (Boucicault, *The Life of an Actress*), 17, 74–7
Julia Dallow (James, *The Tragic Muse*), 20, 184, 185–6

Kate Ede (Moore, *A Mummer's Wife*), 150–2, 154–8, 159–60, 167, 190
Kean, Charles, 46
Kemble, Fanny, 24, 125
Kemble, John Philip, 23
Kemble, Marie-Thérèse, 4
Kendal, Madge, 98, 167
Kurnick, David, 2, 6, 28, 34nn, 120, 137, 140–1nn, 145n

Lady Audley's Secret (Braddon), 52, 80, 181
Lancaster, Edward, 'The Manager's Daughter' (1837), 16, 41–3
Lansbury, George, 204
Laura (Moore, *A Mummer's Wife*), 159–60
Lea, Marion, 188
Levine, George, 13, 14, 23, 34n, 53, 64, 66
Levison, Mrs Rachel, 52

Lewes, George Henry, 3, 15, 49, 75, 120, 143n, 153, 171n, 177, 209
  On Actors and the Art of Acting (1875), 37–8, 67nn, 87, 120, 126
The Life of an Actress (Boucicault), 17, 18, 41, 72, 73–8, 94, 100, 175
Litvak, Joseph, 108, 109, 111, 112, 120, 127, 132, 143n, 182
Loftus, Miss Cissie, 53
'A Lucky Sixpence' (Robins), 161
Lyotard, Jean-François, 191
Lytton, Constance, 215

MacCarthy, Desmond, 210–11, 212, 214
McCormack, Kathleen, 106, 120, 137, 138, 153
Macready, W. C., 2
Magdalen Vanstone (Collins, *No Name*), 18, 78–80, 100, 125, 131, 175, 177, 178, 179, 216
  mimicry by, 18, 41, 43, 79, 85, 86, 87
  stage adaptation removes agency and theatricality, 88–93
Malet, Lucas (Mary St Leger Kingsley), 6–7
Man and Wife (Collins) stage adaptation, 103n
Mangum, Teresa, 13
Mansfield Park (Austen), 84
Margaret (Lancaster, 'The Manager's Daughter'), 41–4
Maria (Boucicault, 'The Young Actress'), 44
Marshall, David, 120, 123, 145n, 198
Marshall, Gail, 2, 53, 58, 100, 120, 139, 204–5
Martineau, Harriet, 200
Masks and Faces (Taylor and Reade, 1852), 16, 41, 50, 54, 62, 63, 91–2, 93, 131, 175, 189, 207
Masks or Faces? (Archer), 37, 38–9, 93
The Master Builder (Ibsen), 190
Matthews, Charles, 104n
melodrama, 13, 18, 19, 39, 48, 93, 126, 140, 152, 214
melodramatic conventions, 14, 15, 16–17, 21, 40, 41–2, 72, 98, 177, 191, 208, 215
middle class
  actresses, 66, 148–9, 150, 167, 206
  audiences, 12, 19, 21, 23, 93, 153, 224n
  characters, 148–9, 167
  domesticity, 150
  plays, 9, 55, 66, 215
  women, 167, 193, 215
middlebrow taste, 222n
Middlemarch (Eliot), 108, 111, 120–1, 123, 134, 139, 153
Mill, John Stuart, 113–14, 119, 142n
  On Liberty (1859), 113
  The Subjection of Women (1869), 114, 117, 129
Miller, Andrew H., 25

Miller, J. Hillis, 180, 184
mimicry, 16, 36, 38, 39, 40, 52, 59
  Becky Sharp (*Vanity Fair*), 85
  Magdalen Vanstone (*No Name*), 18, 41, 43, 79, 85, 86, 87
  Margaret ('The Manager's Daughter'), 41, 42
  Maria ('The Young Actress'), 44
  Miriam Rooth (*The Tragic Muse*), 177
  Peg (*Masks and Faces; Peg Woffington*), 41, 50, 59–60, 63, 65, 66
Mirah Lapidoth (Eliot, *Daniel Deronda*), 106, 107, 127, 128, 132, 144n
Miriam Rooth (James, *The Tragic Muse*), 20, 174–5, 176, 177–80, 182–3, 184, 185, 188
  compared with Julia Dallow, 20, 184, 185–6
'Miss Appleyard's Awakening' (Glover), 205
Mitford, Mary Russell, 140n
A Modern Lover (Moore), 153
Moore, George, 20, 167, 176, 177, 188, 189, 195, 196, 205, 209, 210, 211, 227
  'An Actress of the Eighteenth Century', 151
  A Modern Lover (1883), 153
  'Mummer Worship' (1888), 148, 149, 150, 161
  A Mummer's Wife (1885), 19, 146, 150–8, 161, 192
  'Our Dramatists and Their Literature', 148
  'Sex in Art', 146
  The Strike at Arlingford (1893), 161
  'Why I Don't Write Plays', 146–7, 196
'The Mother's Meeting' (Phibbs), 205–6
'Mrs Caudle's Curtain Lectures' (Jerrold), 23
Mrs Lessingham (Fletcher), 224n
'Mummer Worship' (Moore), 148, 149, 150, 161
A Mummer's Wife (Moore), 19, 146, 150–8, 161, 192
music, 58, 75, 108, 109, 114, 117, 122, 124, 125, 126, 127, 133, 136, 149, 200, 227

naturalism, 19, 146, 151–2, 152, 159
  theatrical *see* realism, theatrical
New Century Theatre, 210
New Woman novelists, 140, 159, 182, 188, 222n
The Newcomes (1855), 4
Newey, Katherine, 12, 33n, 125, 193, 214
Nicholas Nickleby (Dickens), 2–3, 78, 99
Nicoll, Allardyce, 94, 99
Nightingale, Florence, 166, 200
No Name (Collins, 1862–3), 17–18, 72, 78–93, 100, 106, 107, 125, 131, 175, 207

  stage adaptation (Bernard), 88, 89–90, 102n, 103n
  stage adaptation (Collins), 88, 89, 90–3, 103n, 207, 216–17
  stage adaptation as *Great Temptation* (Melbourne, 1879), 102n
'Nona Vincent' (James), 20, 173–4, 187, 197
novels
  and authors' self-display, 162–3, 164–6
  and avant-garde readership, 15, 19, 147, 148, 153
  centrality of theatre and actresses to, 13, 29
  and naturalism, 19, 146, 152, 159
  and realism, 12, 13, 14, 23, 34n
  sensation novel, 17, 72, 80, 82, 88, 94, 108, 170n
  sentimentalism in, 22, 151, 154, 156, 157, 158
  and theatricality, 11, 29, 33n, 88, 108, 112, 123, 132
novels and plays: comparisons between, 6–10
  authenticity, 31, 78
  commercial success, 12, 21, 148
  communication with audience, 147
  narrative technique, 23–4
  representation of women, 13
  see also adaptations

O'Farrell, Mary Ann, 24, 64, 65
Oldfield, Nance, 204
Oliphant, Margaret, 92
Olympic Theatre, 88, 104n
On Actors and the Art of Acting (Lewes), 37–8, 67nn, 87, 120, 126
On Liberty (Mill), 113
O'Neill, Eliza, 52
Orpheus (Gluck), 119, 122
Otten, Thomas J., 187
'Our Dramatists and Their Literature' (Moore), 148
outsiders, actresses as, 15, 16, 44, 46, 49, 50, 78, 94

'A Pageant of Great Women' (Hamilton), 161, 200, 204
Pankhurst, Mrs, 200, 213 Figure 5.8
Pankhurst, Sylvia, 106n
Pankhursts, 198, 204
The Paradox of Acting (Diderot), 10–11, 36, 37, 38, 58, 65, 79, 84–5, 86, 126, 127, 143n
  Irving's 1883 preface to, 11, 39–40, 149, 169n
Parks, Gordon, 171n
Pearson, Richard, 2, 78, 89, 90, 93, 95
Peg Woffington (Boucicault), 16, 41, 44–6, 50, 68n, 80
Peg Woffington (Boucicault, *Peg Woffington*), 44–5

Peg Woffington (historical figure), 44–5, 57 Figure 1.3, 70n
Peg Woffington (Reade, 1853), 16, 41, 51, 64, 78, 92
Peg Woffington (Taylor and Reade, *Masks and Faces*; Reade, *Peg Woffington* novel), 16–17, 18, 31, 50–1, 62, 72, 77, 82, 92, 93, 106, 107, 149, 175, 196
  authenticity, 54–5, 58, 59, 63, 64–5, 66
  blush, 52, 64, 65
  mimicry, 41, 50, 59–60, 63, 65, 66
  portrait of, 55–6 Figure 1.2, 57
  tears, 59, 65
'The Pervasion of Rouge' (Beerbohm), 52–3, 55, 181–2
Peterson, M. Jeanne, 85
Phibbs, L. S., 'Jim's Leg' (1911), 205
Phibbs, Mrs Harlow, 'The Mother's Meeting' (n.d.), 205–6
Phillips, Henry Windham, 57
The Pickwick Papers (Dickens), 7
The Picture of Dorian Gray (Wilde), 58, 180, 182, 187, 220n
Pinero, Arthur Wing, 211, 212, 215
  The Second Mrs Tanqueray (1893), 190, 225n
Pioneer Players, 222n
Plessy, Madame Arnould, 178
poetry, 1, 2, 108, 109, 110, 111, 120, 127, 132, 143n, 154, 158, 162
political action, 12, 107, 168, 174, 185–6, 190, 192–3, 215, 218, 219
political theatre: twentieth-century, 12, 189, 192, 218; *see also* Actresses' Franchise League
'The Poor Rate Unfolds a Tale' (Robertson), 95
Poovey, Mary, 85
Pope, Alexander, 121
The Prima Donna (Boucicault), 16, 41, 46–9, 73
Prince of Wales's Theatre, 93, 94, 99 Figure 2.1, 183
private theatricals, 81, 83–4, 90, 92, 126, 176
productive exteriority, 106
professionalism
  and actors, 10–11, 39, 44, 149, 176–7, 183; *see also The Paradox of Acting*
  and actresses, 11, 95, 97, 124–5, 127, 133, 139, 167, 193, 197, 204, 206, 227: The Alcharisi (*Daniel Deronda*), 128; Magdalen Vanstone (*No Name*), 84, 85, 86, 89, 90; Miriam Rooth (*The Tragic Muse*), 175, 177, 183; Violet (*The Life of an Actress*), 100; Violet Grey ('Nona Vincent'), 174
  and authors, 30, 112, 163
  and musicians, 123, 126
  and singers, 125, 131
  and society, 176

propaganda theatre, 20, 195–6, 198, 209, 218, 226, 227
public opinion, power/influence of, 21, 106, 113–14, 119, 132, 193, 205
public sphere: women's participation in, 1, 19, 34n, 107, 115, 128, 132, 133–4, 139–40, 165, 168, 174, 185, 186, 188, 192, 193, 200, 209, 216, 218
  and actresses, 20, 134–5, 193, 204–5
  and Armgart, (*Armgart*), 118, 121, 122, 129, 134
  contrasted with private sphere, 13, 86, 94, 98, 106, 111, 112, 120, 147, 167, 211, 215
  criticised, 20, 117
  denied, 161, 166, 167
  and suffragettes, 206

Rachel (actress Rachel Félix), 73, 128, 175
Rachel, Madame, 181
Radziwill, Prince Léon, 125
Raimond, C. E. (pseudonym of Elizabeth Robins), 161, 163
'The Ravenswing' (Thackeray), 202
Ray, Gordon, 23
Reade, Charles, 31, 59, 78, 79, 96, 133, 204, 205, 227
  Hard Cash (1863), 82
  see also Masks and Faces; *Peg Woffington*
Reade, Charles L., 59
Reade, Rev. Compton, 59
realism, 21, 94
  novelistic, 12, 13, 14, 23, 34n
  'small', 183; *see also* drawing-room drama
  sympathetic, 13–14, 131, 140
  theatrical, 3, 12, 14, 15, 18, 19, 72, 96, 98, 146, 147, 148, 152
Rede, Leman Thomas, 54, 69n
Reeve, Wybert, 80, 102–3n
re-feminisation, 79
The Rehearsal (Buckingham), 31
'The Reigning Favourite', 73
respectability
  of actresses, 14, 15, 17, 18, 21, 23, 31, 39, 45, 60, 72, 75–8, 85, 126
  of domesticity, 93, 95, 97–8, 100
  of St John's Wood, 149, 169n
  of theatre, 12, 14, 15, 19, 23, 72, 146, 148
Roberts, Madeline, 202
Robertson, Agnes, 43, 46–7, 73
Robertson, T. W., 11, 31, 93, 107, 126, 132, 146, 148, 149, 152, 158, 206, 210, 211, 227
  'The Poor Rate Unfolds a Tale', 95
  see also Caste
Robins, Elizabeth, 140, 171n, 172n, 174, 187, 192, 197, 200, 202, 203 Figure 5.5, 221n
  Alan's Wife (1893), 20, 190–2, 206
  and anonymity of pseudonym C. E. Raimond, 161, 163

Both Sides of the Curtain (1940), 169n, 171n
The Convert (1907), 20, 206–7, 208
friendship with Henry James, 20, 187, 221n
George Mandeville's Husband (1894), 20, 148, 160–8
Ibsen and the Actress (1928), 188
'A Lucky Sixpence' (1894), 161
production of Ibsen's *Hedda Gabler* (1891), 188–9
'The Suffrage Camp Re-Visited' (1908), 160–1
Theatre and Friendship (letters from Henry James) (1932), 20, 187–8
see also Votes for Women
Robinson, Kenneth, 88
Robinson, Mary, 23
Romola (Eliot), 146
Rosmersholm (Ibsen), 190
Rougement, Mrs, 23
Rowell, George, 104n, 214
Royal Coburg Theatre, 3, 8n
Royal Princess's Theatre, 46
'The Runaway Slave at Pilgrim's Point' (Browning), 130
Ruskin, John, 11
Rutherford, Susan, 112, 119, 120, 121, 124, 125, 131, 143n
Ryley, Mrs, 202

St James's Theatre, 190, 212
St John's Wood: superficial respectability of, 149, 169n
Salomé (Wilde), 181
Salvini, 120, 143n
Sargent, John Singer, 187
The Scenic Art (James), 20, 175, 176, 183
The School for Scandal (Sheridan), 24
Schreiner, Olive, *The Story of an African Farm* (1883), 158–9
Scoffern, John, 54, 181
sculpture: significance of, 53
seating (theatre), 10
The Second Mrs Tanqueray (Pinero), 190, 225n
self-display
  in actresses, 167–8, 171n
  in novelists, 162–3, 164–6
  in women, 165–6
sensation drama, 12, 88
sensation novel, 17, 72, 80, 82, 88, 94, 108, 170n
sensibility, 29, 39, 40, 59, 79, 118
sentimentalism
  in drama, 3, 16, 22, 39, 40, 64, 96, 150, 151, 154–5, 156, 158
  in novels, 22, 151, 154, 156, 157, 158
'Sex in Art' (Moore), 146
Seymour, Katie, 31
Seymour, Laura, 31, 50
Shaw, George Bernard, 11, 69n, 162, 189

Shaw, Harry E., 26, 139
Shelley, Percy Bysshe, 154
Sheridan, Richard Brinsley
  The Forty Thieves (1806), 24, 30
  The School for Scandal (1777), 24
Shorthouse, J. Henry, 10
Showalter, Elaine, 140, 160
Siddons, Mrs, 23
singing, 53, 58, 106–7, 116–17, 118, 121, 121–2, 126, 127
Smith, Adam, *The Theory of Moral Sentiments* (1759), 13–14, 39, 207
Smith, Alexander, 79
The Spanish Gypsy (Eliot), 141nn, 145n
stage artifice *see* artifice
stage realism *see* realism: theatrical
Stage Society, 210, 224n
Steel, Flora Annie, 195, 198
Stella (Boucicault, *The Prima Donna*), 47–9
Stephen, Leslie, 139
Stewart, Garrett, 148, 196
Stirling, Mrs Fanny, 31, 57, 58 Figure 1.4, 60
Stokes, John, 178
The Story of an African Farm (Schreiner), 158–9
Stowe, Harriet Beecher, *Uncle Tom's Cabin* (1852), 7
Stowell, Sheila, 46, 63, 215
The Strike at Arlingford (Moore), 161
The Subjection of Women (Mill), 114, 117, 129
subscription theatres, 180, 210
'The Suffrage Camp Re-Visited' (Robins), 160–1
suffrage movement, women's, 1, 15, 19, 20, 108, 114, 140, 160–1, 182, 186, 208
suffrage theatre, 15, 20–1, 193, 194, 198, 205, 227; *see also* Actresses' Franchise League
Surrey Theatre, 24
Sutherland, John, 23
Swift, Jonathan, 'A Beautiful Young Nymph Going to Bed' (1731), 51–2
Sybil Vane (Wilde, *The Picture of Dorian Gray*), 58, 180–1, 182
sympathy
  cross-class, 215–16, 217, 228
  imaginative, 16, 39, 207
  with individuals, 130, 140, 218
  realistic, 13–14, 131, 140

talented performers, 15, 106, 122, 139
talented women *see* exceptional women
Taylor, Jenny Bourne, 79, 90
Taylor, Tom *see Masks and Faces*
tears: ability to produce, 40, 51, 59, 65, 85, 98, 158, 178, 179, 215
Tennyson, Alfred Lord, 11
Ternan, Ellen, 31
Terry, Ellen, xiv, 163, 204, 205

Thackeray, William Makepeace, 34–5nn
- *The History of Pendennis* (1848–50), 21, 29–31, 186
- 'The Ravenswing' (1843), 202
- *Vanity Fair* (1847–8), 21–9, 31, 34nn, 110, 111, 148, 182

Théâtre Libre, 5, 184, 189, 210
theatre
- blurring of line between theatre and society, 176–7
- complaints about, 2–6, 99
- materiality of, 6, 9, 32n
- *see also* audiences; box set; green room

Theatre and Friendship (letters from James to Robins), 20, 187–8
Theatre Royal, Haymarket, 41, 72
Theatre Royal, Newcastle, 103n
theatricality, 2, 12, 40, 49, 65, 67, 91, 92, 94, 108, 109, 111, 120–1, 123, 132, 133, 136, 137, 143n, 161, 162, 166, 182
- and business, 81–2
- and novels, 11, 29, 33n, 88, 108, 112, 123, 132
- and suffragettes, 21, 193, 198
- *see also* antitheatricality

The Theory of Moral Sentiments (Smith), 13–14, 39, 207
Thompson, Hugh, 55
Tickner, Lisa, 194, 200, 215
Tocqueville, Alexis de, 159
Tomalin, Claire, 31
The Tragic Muse (James), 20, 174–86, 187
Trilby (Du Maurier), 91, 109

Uncle Tom's Cabin (Stowe), 7

Vanbrugh, Irene, 197
Vanity Fair (Thackeray), 21–9, 31, 34nn, 110, 111, 148, 182
- dual-mode narrative in, 25–8

Vedrenne, John E., 210
Vestris, Madame, 104n
Viardot, Pauline, 120
Vida Levering (Robins, *Votes for Women*), 206, 207, 208–9, 211, 215–17, 217–19
Villette (Brontë), 111
Violet see The Life of an Actress (Boucicault)
Violet (Boucicault, *The Life of an Actress*), 17, 73, 74–8, 100
Violet Grey (James, 'Nona Vincent'), 173–4
Vizetelly, Henry, 151
Voskuil, Lynn M., 40

Votes for Women (Robins, 1907), 20, 193, 198, 202, 205, 206, 208, 210, 218–19, 224nn
- crowd scene, 212, 213 Figure 5.7, 214
- internal scenes, 211 Figure 5.6, 215

Wagner, Johanna Jachmann, 122
Wales, Prince of, 23
Ward, Genevieve, 169n
Watt, Ian, 94
Weltman, Sharon Aronofsky, 2
Wemyss, Francis C., 69n
'Why I Don't Write Plays', series in *Pall Mall Gazette*, 6–10
- Moore, 146–7, 196
The Wild Duck (Ibsen), 190
Wilde, Oscar, 11, 187, 211, 215
- 'The Decay of Lying' (1889), 180
- *The Picture of Dorian Gray* (1890), 58, 180, 182, 187, 220n
- *Salomé* (1894), 181
- *A Woman of No Importance* (1893), 212, 225n
Williams, Carolyn, 13, 39, 41, 191
Wills, W. H., 88, 102n
Wilton, Marie (Mrs Bancroft), 93, 97, 98, 167
Woffington, Peg
- historical figure, 44–5, 57 Figure 1.3, 70n
- in plays *see under* Peg Woffington
A Woman of No Importance (Wilde), 212, 225n
The Woman in White (Collins): stage adaptation refused, 103n
women
- performing women, 18–19, 59, 106, 107, 112, 133, 139, 146, 161
- power and influence of, 28, 31, 98, 124, 130, 136, 196; *see also* public sphere
- talents compared with men's, 223n
Women Writers' Suffrage League, 174
Women's Theatre series, 195–7
Wood, Mary, 187
Woods, Margaret L., 7, 8
working class
- audiences, 5, 8, 118–19
- characters, 17, 62, 98, 107, 205
- women, 205, 206, 215
world
- women's influence in *see* public sphere
- women's understanding of, 129, 130, 132, 135

'The Young Actress' (Boucicault), 16, 41, 43–4, 47, 73, 74

Zola, Émile, 151, 152, 190